PASS THE PICKLED PORCUPINE

& OTHER WILD FOOD STORIES

PASS THE PICKLED PORCUPINE

& OTHER WILD FOOD STORIES

GRAHAM CHALMERS

The Book Guild Ltd

First published in Great Britain in 2019 by
The Book Guild Ltd
9 Priory Business Park
Wistow Road, Kibworth
Leicestershire, LE8 0RX
Freephone: 0800 999 2982
www.bookguild.co.uk
Email: info@bookguild.co.uk
Twitter: @bookguild

Typeset in 11pt Minion Pro

Printed and bound in the UK by TJ International, Padstow, Cornwall

ISBN 978 1912881 215

British Library Cataloguing in Publication Data.
A catalogue record for this book is available from the British Library.

For Debra, Andrew and Matthew,
with love.

CONTENTS

PREFACE

I have been blessed with a life that allowed me to go out now and then and hunt, catch or collect various wild foods and then cook them for my family and friends as an enjoyable recreation rather than as a pressing and stressful matter of survival. I am a lawyer and a writer and not a professional hunter, gatherer or fisherman of any sort; I just like going out in the field or on the water and getting some wild things to eat. Nor am I a professional chef, although I am a good camp cook and I have over forty years' experience. There are many recipes in this book but it is not a cookbook. It is a collection of essays about fifty different types of wild food and about some of the adventures I have had getting my hands on it and then cooking and eating it.

These days the fact that food is wild does not mean it is free. There are very few places left where you can just wander out into the wilderness and hunt, catch or collect whatever you like. Normally, the wilderness is either owned outright by someone who requires a fee or is under the control of the State authorities, which also require a fee in the form of a permit or licence. Once you add the cost of transportation, accommodation and equipment to the fee for whatever it is you want to hunt, catch or collect, you are often talking about the exercise being a serious luxury, with some notable exceptions. Consequently, in today's world a wild food meal is an increasingly rare and sophisticated treat and certainly is no longer (if it ever was) the domain of the lowly peasant forced by circumstance into a subsistence on roots and the odd rabbit. For me the entire process is a legitimate recreation that is comparable to, say, golf or hiking or mountain climbing, and so I am quite happy that it has a cost attached like any other recreation. But it can be as complex and expensive or as simple and cheap as you would like it to be, from hunting Cape buffalo in the dusty dawn of some distant African thorn scrub to collecting blackberries in the hedgerows of Southern England in the late summer sunshine.

Naturally, the wild foods covered in this book are found in the places where I have lived or that I have visited frequently, in other words Britain, parts of Europe and Southern Africa. There is, however, plenty of overlap and many of the principles and recipes would suit the local equivalent of whatever species is being discussed, particularly in North America, Eastern Europe and East Africa. Although there are a few instructional sections on how to process certain wild foods, my primary aim is to entertain. I love reading about this sort of stuff myself and I simply hope that you enjoy my stories.

Surrey 2018

AARDVARK

I have a great book in my possession, a grand and weighty tome covering all foods and related topics in encyclopaedic fashion[1]. This book pushes its luck by starting with a short entry on aardvarks. It is a tentative entry, succinctly telling about the life and times of this 120-pound termite-eating African animal, but on the culinary side doing no more than advising that it has a good reputation as food and that it is 'commonly described as tasting like pork'. Now I must point out from personal experience that in normal times aardvarks are not actually considered food animals by anyone, but authors and publishers, being orderly, alphabetising-type folk see that double A and simply cannot help themselves. Of course, in hard times aardvarks are considered edible in the usual African way where absolutely every living thing is considered edible, but that is understandable.

The problem with eating an aardvark is getting your hands on one in the first place. This is difficult, not least because they are nocturnal. In the African bush one does not wander about at night hunting aardvarks – too dangerous, you see; bandits, lions, ancestral spirits and so on, not to mention that the activity would be considered weird and possibly unmanly. Certainly it would be illegal – aardvarks are a protected species in most

1   *The Penguin Companion to Food* by Alan Davidson – an excellent book.

places. You cannot effectively set traps or snares for them either (also illegal) because unlike many other nocturnal wanderers, aardvarks do not use the paths on their nightly search for food. So generally you only get to sample aardvark if you find one recently deceased by way of an accident. Now at first blush it might seem that happening upon an accidentally demised aardvark is an unlikely prospect, but it occurs surprisingly often and it is how I got to taste a chunk of flame-grilled aardvark steak. Let me explain:

The lowveld around the Limpopo River in Southern Africa is wild country. It is hot in summer, the mosquitoes carry malaria and the bush undulates in every direction with such uniformity that getting lost can be a problem. It was not uncommon to leave a bush camp in the late afternoon for a session of carousing at the main farmhouse only to find upon returning in the deep dark of the early morning that a large and ugly pothole had been dug in the middle of the road. The architect of the pothole would sometimes be seen at the last minute, scuttling off to the side just in time to save itself, but too late for the driver to do anything but thump into the hole, bursting tyres and bending rims. Of course, this was in the days when a road to a bush camp was made by simply getting hold of a Caterpillar grader, dropping the blade and then driving it from the farmhouse to the camp in a more or less straight line, avoiding big trees, ravines and other Caterpillar-wrecking natural features. While doing this the driver would pay no heed to the position of any termite mounds, which are generally no match for a Caterpillar, and this was the source of the trouble. Passing aardvarks, finding the topsoil conveniently removed, would tuck into the termite nests forthwith, excavating mightily with their tough digging claws. Great diggers, aardvarks; their abandoned tunnels provide spacious and extensive accommodation for all manner of creatures, including warthogs, hyenas and even leopards on occasion.

Late one evening a sad combination of dozy aardvark and a driver enthusiastically accelerating around a corner in a haze of after-dinner goodwill resulted in a horrible fleshy *thunk* from the front left side of the vehicle. Realising immediately that we had hit something of substance, we jolted to a creaking, dusty stop and got out to investigate. The aardvark was beyond help. The stocky body lay on its side, the long snout quivering slightly, but the eyes were open and blank. There was nothing to do but wrestle the dead creature onto the back of the truck and carry on. The next morning, not being entirely sure what to do with the body, I gave it away to the camp staff and they carried it off with little apparent enthusiasm. Later that evening we happened to pass by the staff housing set in its clearing in the thick thorn scrub. A fair crowd had gathered at this eclectic collection of abandoned farm outbuildings and corrugated iron shanty dwellings. A large fire had been set in the centre of the earthen square that served as a communal courtyard. The large fire signified a special occasion because rural African people are very careful about the reckless use of wood. Generally, they burn logs individually and progressively from one end to the other in a demonstration of considerable discipline and conservation of their primary source of energy. Here, though, a heap of logs burned merrily. Party time! We stopped the Landcruiser under a nearby acacia tree and strolled over to investigate. The people were in that happy early stage of one beer under the belt, a second one in the hand and a plenty-more-where-that-came-from kind of mood. We were greeted with smiles and a measure of bonhomie, the whiteness of our skins and the oppressions of our forefathers being kindly overlooked in the spirit of the moment. I accepted 'a beer' (in the African rural tradition being a 'quart' bottle containing a litre of lager – eat your heart out, Australians) and then moved over to inspect the fire. The air was acrid with the smell of burning flesh. On top of the fire rested the entire gutted and skinned carcass of the late lamented aardvark, busily crackling and fizzing in direct contact with the burning logs – no grid, no spit, nothing. The sight of this blackened corpse with its fissures of steaming pink flesh was profoundly shocking for some reason. Never before had I encountered such a brutally direct cooking method, although no doubt that is the way everything was once necessarily cooked. There was no necessity now though. The place operated as a game viewing and hunting lodge, and large barbecue grids and spits were available. I asked about the method, expecting to be told of a long tradition of cooking whole aardvarks directly on fires, but no, the reason was simply to do with spontaneity. No one had planned a party, but the existence of a large chunk of unexpected meat had lifted the mood. Soon crates of beer were dragged out of locked storerooms and extra logs were piled on the fire. Rather than making any elaborate plans for preparation of the meat, a couple of fellows had simply tossed the aardvark onto the fire. Now they simply dragged it off again, judging it to be cooked, and thumped it down onto a makeshift trestle table. From here the people helped themselves, tearing chunks from the bones as desired and eating directly from the fingers as a snack with drinks rather than a formal meal. I helped myself to a ragged section of rib and attached meat. The charred outer layer was inedible but caused little difficulty except for peppering the meat with flakes of ash that had to be brushed off. The cooked meat beneath was succulent and easily torn away. I ate it all.

It was good – somewhat stringy and with a sweetish flavour, but nothing at all like pork.

ABALONE

The streets of the West End of London are attractive on a wet December evening if you are fortunate enough to find yourself well dressed and well heeled. The light from the shop windows casts golden glitter across the pavement as you hop around the puddles and pull yourself deeper into your cashmere coat against the gusting northerly wind. You look in at the fabulous displays of burnished wood, pinstriped fabric and glowing leather and wonder if the time will ever come when you can stride confidently into these magical emporia as a player rather than slipping past as a spectator, vaguely fraudulent in being there at all. Amidst all this opulence in tribute to ancient Mammon there nestle equally opulent tributes to the gustatory gods of international cuisine in the form of numerous over-priced restaurants. Amongst these are some devoted to that deliciously entertaining but totally jumped-up Japanese fast food, sushi. In the really upmarket sushi bars, both the waiters and the patrons tend to wear black silk shirts – they are 'cool', in the same way that a bead of condensation running down the golden neck of a bottle of Cristal is 'cool', or at least that is the impression they seek to create.

In these sushi bars you can order a serving of *awabi*, as it is termed in Japanese, usually as one of a number of servings

5

of various types of sushi.[2] After a decent interval, during which you are expected to order and drink some *sake* or, if you prefer, some Japanese beer, you will be presented with, amongst other things, two walnut-sized servings of cooked sticky rice, served cold and flavoured with a sweet rice vinegar and a smear of grated green horseradish (*wasabi*), upon which rest two very thin slices of raw abalone about two centimetres square. You grasp these bite-sized sushi pieces using your fingers (I believe it is permissible to use chopsticks without being considered a completely uncivilised *gaijin*, but sushi originated as a finger food and is correctly eaten that way no matter how smart the establishment) and after dipping it briefly in soy sauce, you pop the whole thing in your mouth and chew. Now, what you are supposed to experience is a crisp and unique explosion of subtle ocean flavour, delicately enhanced by the touches of soy and *wasabi*. What I actually experience is an explosion of soy and *wasabi*, not so delicately enhanced by a sliver of what tastes and feels like chicken cartilage. Doubtless it is my fault as a crass and ill-educated barbarian because millions of Japanese people do not agree and have elevated fresh abalone into a really expensive luxury food. It is available in the West End of London because there are many very wealthy people there who hanker after the authentic in their ethnic dining experiences and some of them are even genuinely Japanese. How expensive is expensive? Well, the two pieces of sushi mentioned would cost something like the equivalent of one and a half hours of labour at the minimum wage. Given that a large fresh abalone would convert into

2   Abalone is also often served as *mizugai,* a sashimi-like preparation of very fresh, diced, raw abalone either floated in ice water or buried in crushed ice. The Japanese prefer to use abalone with blue-tinted flesh for this dish, as it is believed to be firmer and thus better suited. Abalone with yellow-tinted flesh is believed to be more tender and is reserved for grilling or steaming recipes. *Mizugai* is served with a dipping sauce – often soy – into which the diner can mix a little wasabi. My comments relating to abalone as sushi apply equally to *mizugai.*

about twenty pieces of sushi, a single abalone could realise the equivalent of two or three days' work for a box-packer in the vast warehouse of some online retailer.

So that is why commercial harvesting of abalone in the wild and trouble are more or less synonymous these days. Anywhere you get wild abalone in sufficient quantities for commercial harvesting you also get murky deals, shady officials, henchmen wearing black suits and gold chains, hugely powerful motorboats and pools of blood appearing on the quayside overnight. But it was not always like that and it still isn't in those places where abalone can be found in quantities of no commercial interest.

You get abalone for yourself by diving for it. This does not require much equipment, but along with the mask, snorkel and fins you need a weight belt, a decent diving knife and a net bag. The abalone are found attached to rocks in shallow inshore water up to about sixty-feet deep and take some practice to spot because the rough exterior of the ear-shaped shell is always camouflaged with seaweed and other bits of marine growth. Once you find one you have to sort of sneak up on it and then prise it from the rock in one fluid movement where you slip your knife blade under both the edge of the shell and the powerful, limpet-like foot muscle, breaking the suction used by the mollusc to stay attached to the rock. Get this wrong and you will not be removing that particular abalone. If an abalone gets any sort of idea that you are going to try and mess with it, it clamps down onto the rock with a ferocious power that is unbreakable by any ordinary means available to a human holding his or her breath in sixty feet of water. But given the correct level of surprise, it is not difficult to get the hang of detaching abalone and a few can usually be collected before hypothermia sets in.

Assuming you are not a sushi chef (incidentally, sushi does not taste right unless it is prepared by a sushi chef with at least four years' training and a special knife that costs about the same as a small luxury car – just one of those facts of life, so there is no point in trying to do it yourself), you now need to clean and prepare your abalone for one or other non-sushi method of cooking. This can be a bit daunting at first because an abalone is a tough customer and cleaning one involves lots of slime, plenty of unpleasant gore and a good measure of stickiness. It is quite simple, however:

CLEANING AN ABALONE

Slip a knife between the shell and the foot muscle, slide the tip of the knife along the shell until it meets some resistance (this is the ligament attaching the foot to the shell), push hard and work the knife from side to side and in and out until the ligament is cut and the foot muscle becomes loose in the shell. Put down the knife and lay the abalone back on its shell. While holding down the thick edge of the shell with one hand, pull and fold the foot muscle back toward the thin edge of the shell. The idea is to try and flip the foot over in the shell – if done correctly the mantle and internal organs are left behind in the shell while the foot comes free. Usually, though, that is not what happens and you are left cutting, pulling and scraping the guts and the mantle away from the edible white flesh of the foot. Ideally it is best if the whole cleaning process is done very quickly. The animal is alive and apart from moral considerations, the longer it takes the more tense the flesh becomes and the more tenderising it will require.

There are dozens of recipes for abalone, but they all constitute local variations on two themes. One theme is the very fresh, thinly sliced, tenderised with a mallet and cooked briefly approach. Get this right and it is truly delicious, with or without complex dunking in egg/milk/wine/vodka/sake and/or covering with breadcrumbs/batter/cornflakes/oatmeal/nori and whether or not the abalone is fried, grilled, steamed or poached. For my money, just thinly slice each abalone into steaks about five millimetres thick, whack them a bit with a piece of wood and then fry them in very hot clarified butter for less than one minute on each side. Serve instantly with a squeeze of lemon and a little salt. Garlic butter, a sprinkle of chopped parsley and maybe a serving of steamed rice are the only embellishments that should be allowed. The quick cooking totally transforms the flavour and texture of abalone and there is no similarity to the flavour of raw or marinated abalone as found in Japanese cuisine. As with Japanese cuisine though, absolutely fresh, in fact live, abalone is required.

The other theme is 'stewed-for-a-long-time' abalone. Abalone that is cooked for more than a few minutes goes very tough – much the same consistency as a sheet of rubber – and it stays tough unless it is subjected to either lengthy or intense cooking. In different parts of the world it is cooked with different mixtures of other ingredients, either for many hours or in a pressure cooker. The result is abalone that is cooked into tenderness, but which lacks any really noteworthy individual flavour. I suppose that is one of the purposes of a stew: to create a melange into which individuality is subsumed. Here is one recipe – a South African favourite:

PERLEMOEN BREDIE

'Perlemoen' is the South African name for a large indigenous abalone. 'Bredie' is an old Cape Colony name for a ragout-type stew invented by Malay slaves. The idea behind the character of a bredie is the long and slow simmering of meat and vegetables together to create a rich and full-bodied gravy. Bredies are considered national dishes in South Africa, particularly by Afrikaans people.

(Serves 4)
2–3 abalone cleaned and trimmed
6 large leeks

2–3 rashers streaky bacon
75 g butter
1 clove fresh garlic, crushed
A dried bouquet garni or a small bunch of seasonal fresh herbs,
preferably including parsley, bay leaves and thyme
Flour
Salt and ground white pepper

Cut the abalone into bite-sized chunks and dust with seasoned flour. Clean and slice the leeks and chop the bacon into small pieces. In a large saucepan, sauté the leeks in butter until soft, then remove and set aside. Add the bacon to the pan and sauté for a few minutes until the bacon fat is released and browning begins. Add garlic and sauté for a further minute. Add the reserved leeks, prepared abalone and herbs. Add enough hot water to barely cover the abalone, cover with a lid and simmer very, very gently for three to four hours. The abalone should be meltingly tender and the sauce thick. Serve with rice, a green salad and a chilled bottle of South African Chenin Blanc (a good one – costing about the same as a good New Zealand Sauvignon Blanc).

ANTELOPE

There are specific chapters on some of the antelope that are famously good to eat, but this section deals with the general principles applying to all antelope as food.

There are hundreds of species of antelope and they occur in many places in both the Northern and Southern Hemispheres, although the majority are African. Almost all antelope are eaten by humans and have been for some time, although not for as long or in such quantities as you might think. I am sure that for most of our history as a species the only time we got to eat antelope meat was when we came upon the remains of a kill made by a much bigger, faster and more ferocious predator. Of course, it goes without saying that the predator must have left the scene before we settled down to enjoy a little well-matured steak tartare, otherwise it would have been the predator that enjoyed fresh carpaccio of human, well run and slightly salty. That we would have had no difficulty with the pungent putrescence of the average piece of carrion can be confirmed by anyone who has ever walked downwind of a French *fromagerie.*

It is incredibly difficult for an animal as physically limited as a human to successfully subdue a creature as tough and fast as an antelope, even a small one. In fact, without an effective projectile weapon it is close to impossible using hunting methods involving any sort of 'fair chase' principle. Even throwing spears at antelope never really caught on as a stand-alone activity. Usually, they duck and dodge and run away long before a flung spear ponderously arrives. One method, still in use in a remote corner of Namibia amongst San people, is to run the animal to a standstill before flinging the spear. This is a lot of work and is only viable in relatively open terrain where both tracking and running are possible, but it does exploit the only physical advantage a human has over an antelope and that is stamina. They might not be fast and they might not be big, but humans can run for longer than almost anything else and in Namibia will pursue a large savannah antelope like a kudu bull for eleven or twelve hours until the creature is brought to a trembling stop. I have a feeling that this might once have been a widespread approach because to this day humans have a tendency to want to run after things when they are hunting them. It is a hard reflex to overcome even though there is no logic to it if you are armed with a good bow or a high-velocity rifle. Bows and rifles are very modern in the context of our existence as anatomically modern humans and they turn us into a predator even more effective than a big cat. Using them also requires cat-like techniques: a hidden stalk to within range, or an ambush, and then a sudden killing strike. Long-distance running after things is pointless if you are a cat. But you really want to if you are a human and this makes us anxious to get everything over with in a huge hurry. Of course, humans also kill antelope by the application of brainpower-driven trickery like digging dead-fall traps, forcing herds off cliff tops with fire and the use of the cruelly effective snare and other traps, but these are either relatively recent communal or technical innovations or are occasional and spontaneous activities determined by chance.

There are almost no domestic antelope. With few exceptions, attempts to domesticate antelope have failed. Antelope are thus almost always truly wild and like most truly wild things they have meat with a very, very low fat content. This business about fat content in meat can only be fully understood if you have gone without fat or oil in your life for a sustained period of at least several weeks. Good Lord, you miss it if you cannot have it! You spend all day dreaming about the sizzling drip of a plump lamb chop and even the pores of your skin cry out for the unctuous balm of a little slippery grease. It is truly terrible. You come to understand that in the primitive diet fat is the greatest of luxuries, not to mention its other useful attributes as a fuel for lighting, a base for soap and so on. You never look at a hippopotamus or a whale in quite the same way again. So, it is understandable that when it came to the selective breeding of domestic animals, bumping up the fat content was a high priority and the more fat the higher the perceived quality. Of course, as we usually do as a species, we have overdone it and domestic meat now contains more fat than is good for us, at least in the volumes we consume it in the developed world. When you eat antelope meat, however, you are transported back to a time before the domestication of animals and there is a kind of resonance to that thought that is very appealing. It does seem that the meat of antelope and other wild creatures rests more lightly on the digestion than the richer meats of modern domesticated fare.

All of the above applies to both antelope and deer, although antelope and deer are not the same thing. Antelope are of the taxonomic family *Bovidae*, which includes cattle, sheep, goats and their relatives. Deer are of the families *Cervidae* and *Muntiacinae*. Physiologically the main difference between antelope and deer relates to their horns. Antelope horns have a core of solid bone that grows out of the skull. The horns are thus strong, start growing when the animal is young and never fall off. In most antelope species both males and females have horns. Deer horns, on the other hand, do not have a bone core and consist of a protein matrix with some calcium. They are much weaker than antelope horns. Deer shed their horns every year in autumn and regrow them again in spring. In deer species, with the exception of reindeer, only the males have horns. There is a suggestion that the meat of deer is superior to that of antelope. As a totally sweeping generalisation there might be merit in this, but the variation in quality caused by individual factors relating to each particular animal can easily invalidate this conclusion – a good-quality antelope is far better to eat than a poor-quality deer.

Horns and meat quality are often related topics when discussing antelope and deer. From the most ancient of times it has been the practice of hunters to display the horns of large male antelope and deer as trophies of the hunt and as a decorative confirmation of the hunter's prowess and virility. Unfortunately, the big horns tend to be found on the mature males and the mature males are not renowned for the tenderness and sweetness of their flesh. This has led to a confusion of purpose on the part of some hunters. Is the hunter procuring the best-quality wild meat available or is he beating his chest and trying to equate the size of the horns he procures to the size of the most forward-projecting (hopefully) part of his own anatomy? It is this mixed motivation that has the unfortunate result that many people permanently reject venison at the first taste. Compared to domestic meat, slaughtered at less than two years old and often at less than one year, the acrid and sinewy flesh of an elderly behemoth is indeed something of a shock for both the taste buds and the teeth. Of course, not all trophy hunters have mixed motivations when hunting. Some have no illusions and concentrate only on the trophy. Although they are reviled in the 'civilised' world, such trophy hunters are at least honest in their purpose and, morality aside, probably do more good than harm for they pay much and shoot little. Many other hunters, though, are in truth trophy hunters, but in defending what remains of their shabby reputations amongst the intensely hypocritical members of so-called civilised society, pretend that they are 'hunters for the pot'. These are the dangerous guys because they must eat what they shoot and they might inflict it on you. Even genuine 'hunters for the pot' have a problem. The Victorian sporting ethic[3] is inculcated into most societies, particularly in Europe and America, and this can make it tricky to bump off some tender-fleshed juvenile or gentle-eyed female. Possibly it is best to say as little as possible and shelter behind the result of your combined hunting and culinary efforts. If it tastes really good, most people will forgo the asking of too many awkward questions or will even suspend rational thought entirely (*vide: foie gras*, baby chickens, suckling pig, fluffy little lambs, etc. etc. etc.).

All antelope are edible to some extent and I do not know of any species that is considered entirely inedible. Waterbuck in Africa are considered by some to be close, but this is for a very specific reason. Waterbuck have a layer of grease just under the skin, which is said to ooze a foul smelling and tasting insecticide out onto the animal's pelt. This layer is indeed very foul and if it gets smeared onto the meat during the process of skinning the animal then the culinary result is dreadful. I have also heard it said of waterbuck that the meat is stringy in the extreme and that the strings get caught between the teeth in twists and knots like tiny pigs' tails that are very difficult to remove. I do not know where this comes from because I have eaten carefully skinned waterbuck which tasted fine and did nothing terrifying to my dentition at all. Nevertheless, the fact that all antelope meat is edible does not mean that all antelope meat is palatable. Some species have very strongly flavoured meat and naturally the older and tougher the animal the stronger the flavour. It is best to eat strongly flavoured antelope meat as fresh as possible because maturing the meat for any length of time increases

---

3   The Victorian sporting ethic: a gentleman only shoots adult males under circumstances where the animal has a fair chance of escape. Only a cad or bounder would shoot at the women and children, what!

the pungency. The following is a recipe for pungent antelope meat that is loosely based (with profound apologies to Japanese cuisine) on the concept of teriyaki sauce, but very much more robust and Africanised. I usually use it for freshly shot impala, and my 'Impala Chops Teriyaki' have been a minor bushveld sensation for many years (author bows modestly to smattering of applause and rude comments from unreconstructed friends). It works well on any meat with a strong flavour:

IMPALA CHOPS TERIYAKI

(Serves 6–8)
2–3 kg fresh impala or any other strong antelope or deer meat,
cut into convenient loin chops or steaks of some sort
Large bunch green chives, chopped
A chunk of fresh ginger, say 3–4 inches long, peeled and finely grated
4 cloves of fresh garlic, finely chopped
2–3 bird's eye chillies, roughly chopped
500 ml strong, dark soy sauce
250 ml sweet cream sherry
250 ml light olive oil
4 tablespoons brown sugar
Freshly ground black pepper

Combine all the ingredients in a large bowl. Allow the meat to marinate for a few hours and then barbecue the steaks over hot coals in the outdoors, basting occasionally with the marinade. Serve immediately. It may be rough and robust, but it is outrageously popular with everyone who has ever tried it. Fresh bread is the best accompaniment and the only drink that can possibly work is cold beer.

BASS
(FRESHWATER)

The black bass (both largemouth and smallmouth varieties) is one of the most widespread freshwater angling fish. Originating on the east coast of North America, it has now been introduced all over the USA, most of continental Western Europe, the Philippines, Japan, New Zealand and the whole of Southern Africa.

I have done a little bass fishing, but I am not a serious bass fisherman in the quasi-religious way that some people become bass fishermen. I find it fun to cast some fuzzy nightmare of a lure that looks as though it was designed by Dr Seuss to a sulking gangster of a fish that actually has the audacity to take it, but I do not worship the process. I admire the skill involved in gently slithering a glutinous plastic worm up or down some underwater obstruction, but I do not revere the tense expectation of the subtle tap that signals a take. But many true believers do and have, to boot, their own arcane rituals handed down by gurus in the person of famous tournament professionals, much bedecked in sponsorship regalia and televised in action on Saturday afternoons in many parts of the USA.

One of the rituals invented by organised competitive bass fishing is the concept and practice of catch and release. This came about because in the past bass fishing tournaments would descend upon bass waters and strip them of all decent bass in a couple of days. This was understandably annoying to local anglers who would oppose the tournaments. The solution was to insist that all fish caught in the competition be handed in alive and in good condition before they scored any points for the angler. After the weigh-in they are released en mass by the organisers. Seeing their heroes practising compulsory catch and release in tournaments, using live-wells in their boats and special non-injurious keep nets off the bank, persuaded the masses that catch and release was 'cool' and was the mark of the professional, so much so that now catch and release has become a much vaunted philosophy in sport fishing circles generally and far beyond the remit of just bass fishing. Indeed, in many places it is now the law, particularly on heavily fished trout streams.

Catch and release is superficially a very attractive proposition. The angler gets to enjoy more of the 'sporting' element in angling through being able to catch limitless numbers of fish on the basis that everything caught is returned unharmed to the water to 'swim another day'. Were it not for this arrangement, fishing pressures in the modern era would soon strip the waters of all fish and that would be no good for anyone, or so the argument goes. But there is something philosophically disturbing about the concept, in the same way that building a vomitorium adjacent to your dining room would be philosophically disturbing, possibly even to a Roman. To my mind it may be fundamental to the satisfaction and pleasure obtained from hunting and gathering that the genuine purpose of the exercise is to cook and eat what gets hunted or gathered. If pressures are such that you should only be permitted to catch one fish per week or even one fish per year, then so be it. Possibly, to go through the exercise 'just for fun', and indeed even for a debauched and gluttonous surfeit of fun, is to entirely miss both the point and the true satisfaction

– somewhat like washing your feet with your socks on before kissing your sister.

But this is very much the minority view and catch and release is here to stay. An odd result is that many anglers will never taste the fish they catch. In the case of bass, that is a great pity because it can be a most delicious and succulent fish, although in common with many freshwater fish it tends to take on the flavour of its surroundings; bass from a high, clear mountain lake will be lean and clean tasting, while those from a rich lowland stew pond will be fat on the unctuous flesh of crayfish and minnows, but may have a touch of muddiness or dank vegetation about them. The very best are from water that is slightly saline – brackish in other words – but I have no idea why.

A clean-tasting bass should be cleaned, skinned, filleted, dusted in seasoned flour and gently fried in butter for a few minutes – nothing more.

Those with a more robust flavour are excellent in one of the following robust dishes:

TEXAN BLACK BASS

(Serves 4)
1 kg boneless black bass fillets, skinned
75 g butter
200 g new potatoes
1 large habanero chilli, chopped
30 g chopped ginger
125 g diced red pepper
125 g diced green pepper
1 small red onion, diced
1 large tomato, diced
250 ml sweetish white wine
50 g chopped chives
Salt and pepper

Heat half the butter in a non-stick frying pan. Fry the bass fillets briskly on a high heat for two to three minutes to achieve a crispy exterior. Lower the heat and continue to cook for a further few minutes until just undercooked. Remove from the pan and set aside.

Cut the potatoes in half lengthwise and blanch in boiling salted water for five minutes. Drain the potatoes, add half the remaining butter to the pan and then sauté until golden brown and cooked through. Remove from the pan and set aside.

In the same pan add the remaining butter and sauté the habanero, ginger, peppers and onion for two minutes to release the flavours. Add the tomato, wine and chives, and season with salt and pepper. Cook briefly until the liquid is reduced by twenty-five percent.

To serve, arrange the potatoes on the bottom of a large soup plate. Place the fish on top of the potatoes and spoon the hot broth from the pan around and over the fish. Serve immediately.

The basic concept of the next recipe was discovered on a trout fishing trip some forty years ago. As students with very little money, our catering was necessarily limited. For a ten-day camping trip we brought along a box of tomatoes, a sack of onions, some flour, a head of garlic, five pounds of butter, two tins of anchovy fillets (God knows why), salt, pepper and many, many bottles of beer. We relied on catching trout and eating them, which is exactly what we did for the first seven days. If you eat trout three meals a day for seven consecutive days, YOU ARE READY FOR A CHANGE! Change came in the form of a superb smallmouth bass caught by yours truly whilst fishing a deep sunk fly for big trout rumoured to frequent a small and mysterious water nearby. This beautiful fish was so much nicer to eat than trout and the dish we collectively created was so powerfully flavoursome, I have never forgotten it.

BASS WITH TOMATO AND ANCHOVY CRUST

(Serves 4)
800 g bass fillets, skinned
2 ripe tomatoes, sliced
2 cloves fresh garlic, roughly chopped
2 tablespoons flat-leaf parsley or watercress leaves, roughly chopped
50 g tinned anchovies in olive oil, finely chopped
2 medium slices of bread (any kind)
75 g butter or 3 tablespoons olive oil
Freshly ground black pepper

Put the garlic, parsley/watercress, anchovies and a little black pepper into a bowl. Break up the bread into little pieces and add to the mix. Add 25 g of butter (or one tablespoon of oil) and crush into a rough paste using a pestle (or the back of a spoon).

Spread the paste over the fillets.

Heat a cast iron frying pan (you can use a non-stick but it does not work as well in the creation of a crusty finish). Add 50 g of butter (two tablespoons of oil) and fry the tomato slices over a very high heat. When the tomatoes begin to soften and release juices into the pan, add the bass fillets. Fry the lot at a high temperature until the fish is cooked and a caramelised, crusty mixture of the tomato and the paste is created in the pan and on the fillets – wonderful with some salad leaves and a cold beer.

BLACKBERRIES (AND RASPBERRIES)

Brambles do not grow in Africa as far as I know and so the only taste of blackberry I enjoyed whilst growing up was a splash of Echte Kroatzbeere on vanilla ice cream. This was a very special treat dished out after Sunday lunch now and then. Echte Kroatzbeere is a startlingly good and very intense wild blackberry liqueur made in Germany and it is undoubtedly the finest use, amongst many uses, to which wild blackberries can be put.

In Britain there are brambles everywhere and also over much of Europe and North America. The term 'bramble' is used to denote the thorny, tangled creeper-type plants upon which blackberries and raspberries grow. Blackberries and raspberries are the collectable of choice for the completely novice hunter-gatherer. Blackberries, particularly, are abundant to say the least, and in late summer and early autumn the hedgerows and tangled banks are densely speckled with the small dark fruits. The berries start as small white buds and progress through various shades of red to the shiny, dark purple of full ripeness. The ripe fruit is sweet and abundantly juicy and is very good simply popped into the mouth then and there. The convention is one for the mouth and one for the basket until the collector is full, then all go into the basket. You can collect as many berries as you like, or at least you can in Britain, because there are so many that eating them all defeats even the birds.

Raspberries are less common than blackberries, but are nevertheless locally abundant where they occur. I think raspberries have a more subtle and sophisticated flavour than blackberries and that flavour particularly complements chocolate. The ordinary red raspberry is the one usually found growing wild in Britain, but there are in fact over 200 species of raspberry, including the spectacularly sweet and delicious golden variety.

Like most common fruits, both raspberries and blackberries have been domesticated and the domestic version is available in supermarkets for most of the year. As with many other fruits, the domestic version is bigger, juicier, glossier and more splendid looking. However, the flavour, whilst pleasant, is far less intense than the wild variety. I much prefer the wild ones and I am quite happy to limit my blackberry and raspberry consumption to the short wild seasons.

After many years of blackberry harvesting and subsequent experimentation, my family has settled upon only one cooked blackberry recipe: apple and blackberry crumble. This is such a ubiquitous and simple dish that you do not need a recipe from me, but served with warm custard or cream (or both) it is actually a seasonal delicacy that should get more culinary attention than it usually receives. Raspberries, on the other hand, have a very interesting tartness as a background flavour and are splendid just cooked down into a coulis with a good dollop of sugar. By varying the amount of sugar used, the coulis can be appropriate as an accompaniment to anything from chocolate mousse to medallions of venison loin.

BOAR

A big wild boar is a formidable customer. There is a stuffed one in the Natural History Museum in London that gives you an idea of what such a creature can be. In life it would have weighed about 400 pounds, with shoulders coming up to your waist and a large, sleek head that would thump into your solar plexus in a charge. This was a dense and bristling chunk of solid muscle, but streamlined in a very menacing way. If you messed with this animal it would have caught you and killed you, no doubt about that. Its five-inch fighting tusks, longer and sharper than a lion's fangs, would have sliced into your delicate flesh in that chattering, snapping bite that all angry pigs employ and you would most likely have expired forthwith. Those with you, shrieking from their perches in the branches of nearby trees, would have been forcefully reminded of the principle that it is never, ever a good idea to get casual around pigs.

The European wild boar is the precursor to, and ancestor of, the domestic pig. They are one and the same species, but the domestic pig fell under the sway of humans a very long time ago. As with dogs from wolves, selective breeding produced a widely varying selection of domestic pig types – from gigantic and immobile European farmyard varieties, pink skinned, almost hairless and layered in valuable fat, to pocket-sized, pot-bellied little fellows suitable for transport on small island boats and life amongst the pye-dogs of Asian villages. Feral domestic pigs that escape into the wild can and do therefore cross-breed with wild boar where the two occur together and the result can be, well, Hogzilla[4]. This is virtually unknown in Europe and Asia, but in the USA and in Argentina there are large populations of feral pigs that have cross-bred with introduced pure strain wild boar, resulting in 'wild hogs' that can allegedly top the 1000-pound mark, although such big ones are probably mythical. Usually in these places a 300-pound hog is considered big, but they can reliably grow to 600 pounds and if they feel like it, these really big ones eat sheep. Needless to say the intrepid backwoods hunter in the USA, stepping out after a little bacon for the smokehouse, arms himself with a weapon only slightly smaller than the Paris Railway Gun. Quite right too, for an animal potentially bigger, heavier and with sharper teeth than the average lion.

Of course, in Argentina things are done slightly differently on the pampas. It must be the hot Latin blood, but there hogs are traditionally hunted on horseback by crazy gauchos armed only with a large knife and two or three specially bred pig hunting dogs called *dogos Argentinos*. These powerful, mastiff-type dogs first track the hog using scent and then pursue it by sight until the animal is brought to bay in some inhospitable thicket. The gaucho rides up on his foam-lathered horse, leaps from the saddle, draws his knife and attacks the hog. This is the signal for the dogs also to attack. Just as well, otherwise this chapter would probably conclude with a few recipes for roasted gaucho. The dogs are trained to grab hold of some convenient appurtenance

---

4   'Hogzilla' is the name given to a male hybrid of wild boar and domestic pig shot and killed in Georgia, USA, in 2004. The animal allegedly weighed over 1000 pounds and was twelve feet long. Originally considered a hoax, exhumation of its remains and subsequent forensic investigation revealed that it in fact weighed about 800 pounds and was about eight feet long – a considerable specimen, regardless of the initial exaggeration.

projecting from the hog, like an ear or a tail or a leg and then hang on. This slows the hog down somewhat. The theory is that the gaucho then pirouettes gracefully into range and like a muscular matador, stabs the hog from above, sliding the blade between the vertebrae and severing the spinal cord. Ha! I am sure it has been done and it is indeed a most impressive and sporting manner of dispatching a furious, squealing, 600-pound pig, but I am reliably informed that most often the pig is done in by the backup team, being one of the gaucho's mates armed with a .44 magnum handgun. Casualties amongst the dogos are often severe.

The country with the greatest enthusiasm for wild boar as food is France. They also have enthusiasm for hunting them, but in a very French way. As in Argentina, dogs are heavily involved. One arrives at a French boar hunt on a winter's morning at about breakfast time, in an estate car in the back of which is at least one hunting dog. Every Frenchman present is an expert boar hunter and just so happens to own the finest boar dog[5] ever born. Nobody can tell anybody anything, but they all try to at the top of their voices. All are dressed most nattily, in the finest combinations of camouflage, oiled cotton, silk-lined goose down and Goretex. Dogs bark incessantly and the first order of business is to break out the coffee, the *marc*, the *saucisson*, the cheese and the baguettes. Every Frenchman present is an expert on coffee, *marc*, *saucisson*, cheese and baguettes. Nobody can tell anybody anything, but they all try to... etc. etc. Dogs continue to bark incessantly. Somehow in all this noisy chaos, a plan is made – of the we go here, you go there and they go somewhere else variety. The basic idea is that those who are going to do the shooting take up position alongside clearings or

---

5   Boar dogs for driven boar hunting in France can be any kind of dog and are not necessarily boar hounds. Boar hounds proper are used for hunting boar on horseback – an activity similar in principle to fox hunting that still takes place in the central region of France.

on raised platforms giving a good view. The shooters are armed with an extraordinary array of weaponry, ranging through elderly double-barrelled shotguns and strange carbines from the Second World War to the latest cutting-edge 7 mm, 8 mm and even 9 mm rifles. Everybody else and all the dogs function as beaters. They go off into the deep woods and then drive the boar out of the thick cover and towards the waiting guns. Now here is the trick: your boar dog is supposed to drive the pigs specifically towards you personally as you wait in the misty rides and not just generally towards all the guns. The worth of a boar dog is judged by how well it does this, which in turn is measured by how many boars you shoot. In fact, it is all pure luck. The cacophony of dogs, beaters and hangers-on does drive the boar towards the guns. Some slip silently and gently along, well in front of the dogs, heading in an orderly fashion for some alternative woodland. Others, having left departure a little late, come crashing flat-out through the undergrowth, sometimes with a dog or dogs close behind. It is incredibly difficult to hit one of these fast-moving pigs. They literally flash past. So it is usually the first type of passing pig that gets shot and that has little or nothing to do with individual dogs. Either way, any Frenchman who shoots a boar will effusively (and endearingly) attribute his success to the magnificence of his dog, even though his dog may in fact be missing. It is a remarkable feature of some French boar hunts that by the end at least half the dogs will be missing – sometimes for several days. They are not lost or anything, they are just having such a good time they cannot bring themselves to stop.

From a culinary point of view, the younger a boar is the better. Boars under a year old are fine eating. The French call them *marcassin* when they are less than six months old, *bête rousse* when they are between six months and a year, and strictly distinguish older animals which are called many different names as they grow older, the best known of which is *sanglier*. *Marcassin* are for grilled medallions or cutlets. *Bête rousse* are for roasting and for beautiful, rich stews. *Sanglier* and other older animals are for *saucisson* and maybe for a terrine if the flavour is not too strong. One would expect there to be more than a passing similarity between the flavour of boar meat and domestic pork as we know it, but there really is not. In a blind tasting, most would identify boar as venison of some sort, perhaps lightly larded. One area of similarity, though, is a compatibility with the same sorts of ingredients so that virtually any recipe for domestic pork will also be suitable for boar, although the flavour of the end result will be completely different.

The following recipes are all well worthwhile:

MEDALLIONS OF WILD BOAR WITH BANANA

This strange combination is from Ian McAndrew on Poultry and Game. *Weird, but absolutely delicious.*

(Serves 4)
8 x 65 g medallions of boar cut from the saddle of a marcassin
Salt and freshly ground white pepper
2 teaspoons oil
40 g unsalted butter
350 ml veal stock
1 teaspoon whole grain mustard
3 ripe bananas
2 teaspoons caster sugar
For the cooked marinade:
4 tablespoons oil
2 carrots, sliced
2 stalks celery, sliced
4 shallots, sliced
1 onion, sliced

2 cloves garlic, chopped

A few parsley stalks

2 sprigs fresh thyme

2 sprigs fresh rosemary

1 bay leaf

3 juniper berries, crushed

6 black peppercorns, crushed

1 tablespoon red wine

150 ml red wine vinegar

300 ml water

Salt

Make the cooked marinade by heating the oil in a saucepan, adding all the vegetables and sweating over a low heat until they start to soften but not colour. Add the rest of the ingredients and bring to the boil. Reduce the heat to low and simmer for thirty minutes.

Let the marinade go cold before using.

Place the medallions into the marinade and marinate overnight.

When ready to cook, drain the medallions from the marinade and strain off 150 ml of the liquid for use in the sauce. Lightly season the medallions with the salt and white pepper. Heat the oil and 15 g of the butter in a frying pan and quickly fry the medallions on both sides so that the meat is slightly pink in the centre. Remove the medallions from the pan and keep warm. Pour off the fat and add the reserved marinade. Reduce until it is almost gone. Add the veal stock and reduce until only about 200 ml remains. Pour the sauce through a fine strainer onto the mustard. Stir well and keep warm.

Cut the bananas into 1 cm slices. Melt the remaining butter in a clean frying pan, add the banana and sprinkle with the sugar. Fry until golden brown.

Serve by dividing the fried banana evenly and neatly arranging in the centre of warmed plates. Place two medallions on top of each pile of banana and pour the sauce around.

Only an off-dry Vouvray or a spicy dessert wine can handle this combination of powerful savoury and fragrant sweetness. If money is no object, try a good Hungarian Tokaji aszú 5 puttonyos, otherwise Australian liqueur Muscat. The result will be something your guests will never forget and you will henceforth be seen as a radically adventurous cook.

The classic rural approach to dealing with a haunch or shoulder of boar that is a touch more *sanglier* than *bête rousse* is a stew. The wild mushrooms referred to below can be anything edible you can find in the woods or fields, in any combination, although chanterelles and pied de mouton are very good (on edible mushrooms see page 138). The sausages and red wine in combination can give a regional flavour to the dish: for a Spanish flavour use chorizo and Rioja; for a South of France flavour use Toulouse sausage and Cahors etc.

WILD BOAR STEW

(Serves 6)
For the marinade:
2 bay leaves
6 sprigs thyme
6 sprigs rosemary
6 large sage leaves
6 cloves
2 sticks celery, chopped
1 large onion, chopped
8 black peppercorns, lightly crushed
8 juniper berries, lightly crushed
300 ml local red wine as below

For the stew:
1.5 kg boneless shoulder or deboned leg of wild boar
4 tablespoons oil

250 g local sausages
4 large tomatoes, skinned and chopped, or 1 x 400 g tin of
chopped tomatoes
50 g dried porcini mushrooms
250 g mixed wild mushrooms (if unavailable substitute commercial
chestnut, shitake and oyster mushrooms), sliced if large
2 teaspoons plain flour
200 g cooked and peeled chestnuts
15 g butter
200 ml local red wine
350 ml veal, beef or game stock
Salt and freshly ground black pepper
Chopped parsley

Cut the boar into bite-sized chunks and cover with marinade. Mix the meat and marinade ingredients together well and leave in the fridge for twenty-four hours. Stir now and then.

Remove the meat from the marinade and season. Strain the marinade and separately reserve both liquid and solid marinade ingredients.

Heat the oil in a large flameproof casserole and fry the meat until nicely browned. Add the sausages and fry until lightly golden. Add the solid marinade ingredients and fry until soft and browned. Stir in the flour followed by the wine, the liquid from the marinade, the stock, tomatoes, porcini mushrooms, salt and pepper. Bring to the boil, cover and then simmer gently for one and a half hours.

Add the chestnuts to the stew and simmer for a further thirty minutes.

When the meat is very tender and the stew is ready to serve, heat the butter in a frying pan and fry the fresh mushrooms quickly over a high heat for a few minutes, adding a little salt. Stir the mushrooms into the stew. Garnish the stew with parsley just before serving.

This is very good with loaves of fresh, crusty bread and a couple of bottles of whatever red wine you put into the stew.

BUFFALO,
BUSHBUCK
AND BUSHPIG

I have grouped these three somewhat dissimilar animals together for the admittedly unusual reason that all three are very good to eat, but are also dangerous to hunt. You are unlikely to get to taste one unless you hunt it yourself or have gone along for the ride on someone else's hunt.

I am a total sucker for this dangerous game thing. For me the risk adds huge quantities of spice to the process of procuring a couple of steaks for dinner. There is something appealingly elemental about the concept of taking on a creature that is both inclined to and capable of sticking you one if you make a mistake, with possibly fatal and definitely unpleasant consequences. This is infinitely refreshing if you live in a world where health and safety regulations subvert all normal aspirations to physically live a little on the edge from time to time. Dangerous-game hunting is very real and it forces you to pay full attention in a zero-replay environment. It is the antithesis of the modern computer game where you just press restart if the shot goes wide or you ducked when you should have jumped. It is now also very rare in most places, particularly in the developed world. In the

Northern Hemisphere there is only one truly dangerous animal left, the bear, which might conceivably be hunted for the pot, but killing such an animal for food seems unconvincing.

Traditionally, the 'big five' in African dangerous-game terms are elephant, buffalo, lion, leopard and rhino. The omission of hippos from this list was a result of them not being a popular quarry species and certainly not because they are less dangerous than the others. Hippos are extremely dangerous and kill many unarmed civilians every year. Naturally, bushbuck and bushpig are not on the traditional list because they are not big and because, honestly, they are not in the same league. However, as you will see, they are genuinely dangerous and kids growing up in the African bush are taught to treat them with great respect at all times. In view of its position on the traditional list we will start with buffalo.

BUFFALO

Some people rate the Cape buffalo (*Syncerus caffer*) as the *most* dangerous of all game animals. I suspect these people have not hunted either elephant or lion, both of which are more terrifying in my book. There is nothing that buffalo can come up with that compares to twenty or so really annoyed elephants seeking your imminent demise in a carefully executed co-operative plan. This will allow you to explore the concept of 'running really fast' in a most intimate way and, in fact, nobody would ever escape if elephant had better eyesight. The only way to extricate yourself from attack by a herd of elephants is to 'cut the wind' on them. The presence of mind necessary to even remember which way the wind is blowing, let alone run in such a direction that the elephants can no longer smell you, is considerable. A lion, on the other hand, although it has a well-developed sense of smell, is unlikely to need it to catch a human that has offended in some way. Conflict with lions tends to be at short range and bearing in mind that it can charge at over forty miles per hour, a lion will cover fifty metres in 2.8 seconds[6]. In 2.8 seconds most people, even very experienced hunters, can do little more than think a few words along the lines of 'oh golly', point the rifle roughly in the direction of the huge oncoming halo of tawny hair and teeth and pull the trigger. Also, the noise a lion makes when annoyed is primordially disturbing to a human. We are, after all, nothing but jumped-up apes and obviously were once eaten like popcorn by big cats. If an angry lion snarls at you, your genes remember and you suddenly discover that all those hackneyed expressions much disapproved of by editors and schoolteachers – 'my blood ran cold'; 'my hair stood on end'; 'I felt weak at the knees' – and so on are not only true, but are considerable understatements.

Buffalo, on the other hand, do not usually terrify you into immobility with horrifying snarls or hunt you down in herds, although being charged by an entire buffalo herd can and does happen. Buffalo are just very big, between 1000 and 2000 pounds, are unbelievably tough, particularly when struck by a misplaced bullet, and can be decidedly irate when wounded. Most buffalo hunts are straightforward affairs. A stalk to within short range is undertaken, a large-calibre rifle is deployed to propel a significant projectile at supersonic speed towards a target zone bigger than some entire antelope and if the target zone is struck, the buffalo usually either falls over on the spot or rushes off for a couple of hundred yards and then expires with a mournful bellow. Not difficult and pretty much like shooting a domestic cow. *However*, if you cock it up by missing the target zone (the heart/lung area) or use an insufficiently powerful rifle (or an insufficiently robust bullet) that cannot penetrate far enough through the thick hide and dense musculature to damage some rapidly fatal organ, you are potentially in considerable trouble.

---

6   By contrast, Usain Bolt, the world's fastest sprinter, covered the first fifty metres of a hundred-metre race in about 5.5 seconds. It follows that running away from lions is never an option.

Following up a wounded buffalo can be the most dangerous recreational pastime still actually permitted by law, with risk to life and limb far in excess of skydiving, motor racing, cave diving, paragliding or indeed, engaging in all four of these activities during a single afternoon after having a few drinks. We are talking about one of life's few totally uninsurable risks here and it is not a happy thing for amateurs to undertake on their own. Mind you, only about twenty percent of wounded buffalo are a problem. The vast majority run away and hide and then run away again once approached on the follow-up, eventually receiving sufficient bullet strikes[7] to succumb without any real drama, but the problematic twenty percent are pure hell to deal with. These become possessed by an understandably vengeful malice and set about trying to murder anyone who has the temerity to pursue them. They do this by running away downwind initially, then circling back on their own tracks to wait stealthily in ambush behind some thick bush or stand of tall grass. Buffalo have the ability to hide effectively behind a few sticks and leaves by dint of remaining absolutely motionless, which they will do until you are within thirty or forty yards. Then they burst forth in a blindingly quick charge, not much slower than a lion. At this point I would rather have a lion coming at me than a buffalo. A buffalo is huge and is, in these circumstances, unstoppable

---

7   An unusual thing about buffalo is their extraordinary ability, once wounded, to withstand repeated impacts from heavy-calibre bullets without falling over. No one has ever come up with a satisfactory explanation for this phenomenon. There are various theories relating to the thickness of their skins dissipating the shock potential of bullets or the effects of enormous quantities of adrenaline released into their systems when wounded, but all seem inadequate to explain why an animal with seventeen bullets through the chest, totally shredded lungs and a heart that looks like a colander should still be capable of running away or of putting together a potentially lethal charge. This is all the more remarkable if one realises that if only the first bullet had been correctly placed the animal would have succumbed forthwith, just like everything else.

by anything short of a bullet placed precisely through the brain or one that severs the spine. These are not big targets on an oncoming buffalo and the consequence of missing is probably death for at least one member of the follow-up team and sometimes for everyone. There can also be casualties resulting from wildly fired high-velocity rifles discharged in the panic of the moment.

After all this potential drama and accompanying nervous tension, one has earned a juicy buffalo steak even if nothing really dangerous actually happened. Although they are only a distant relative of domestic cattle, buffalo taste pretty much like very lean beef. Depending on the age of the animal and the circumstances of the hunt that brought it to the table, buffalo can be on the tough side. Steaks cut from the large interior fillet (tenderloin) are invariably excellent roasted or grilled, but much of the rest of the animal will probably have to be minced for use in lasagne, cottage pie, hamburgers and so on. The tough, long-fibred muscles also make one of the best versions of *biltong,* the universally popular wind-dried snack of Southern Africa (see page 127). Buffalo do, however, produce three real delicacies there and then in the field if you have a cook with the know-how required. These are:

BUFFALO TONGUE

(Serves 8–10)
1 buffalo tongue
2 large onions, peeled and roughly chopped
2 large carrots, scraped and roughly chopped
2 sticks celery, roughly chopped
20 peppercorns
4 bay leaves
Large pinch each of whatever dried herbs are available,
particularly thyme and/or oregano

Wash the tongue and then soak it in cold water for about two hours. Drain and then place in a large saucepan with enough water to cover. Bring slowly to the boil and remove the scum that will form on the surface.

Add all the remaining ingredients to the pot, cover and boil gently for three to four hours.

Remove the tongue from the saucepan and discard the stock. Carefully skin the tongue and remove any small bones that might be present.

The tongue is very good, hot or cold, sliced thinly and served with sweet mustard sauce, apricot chutney, curry sauce, or in fact any spicy condiment whatsoever. It is one of the finest bush lunches, with a cold beer or an ice-cold gin and tonic. You can also do this to the tongue of any large antelope or deer with very good results. Buffalo, however, is the best of them all.

BUFFALO-TAIL SOUP

(Serves 4–6)
1 buffalo tail, divided into joints
2 tablespoons red wine vinegar
2 tablespoons olive oil
25 g unsalted butter
2 onions, peeled and chopped
2 carrots, peeled and chopped
1 swede, peeled and chopped
2 rashers streaky bacon
2 litres stock (stock made with buffalo off-cuts if time is not of the essence, otherwise good-quality commercial beef stock cubes or stock-pots combined with 2 porcini mushroom stock cubes)
4 bay leaves
3 stalks of fresh thyme
Salt and freshly ground black pepper
2 tablespoons flour

1/4 teaspoon freshly ground nutmeg
1 teaspoon lemon juice
50 ml Marsala

Place the tail pieces in a saucepan and cover with cold water. Add the vinegar and soak for six to eight hours. Drain and wipe dry.

Heat one tablespoon of olive oil in a large, heavy-based saucepan and fry the buffalo tail pieces over a high heat, turning frequently until they are deeply browned on all sides. Remove the pieces from the saucepan.

Add the onion, carrot, swede and bacon rashers to the pan and cook over a medium-high heat until the onions are golden brown and the bacon is crisp. Return the buffalo tail to the pan, add the stock, herbs, salt and pepper and bring to the boil. Skim off any scum.

Simmer for about three hours until the meat is ready to fall off the bones. Strain the stock into a large bowl and discard vegetables, bacon and herbs. If at this stage there is a significant quantity of fat on the surface of the stock then either blot it off the surface using kitchen paper or leave the stock to cool and then place it in the refrigerator for several hours, after which the hardened fat can simply be lifted from the surface.

Remove the meat from the bones and chop finely. Heat the remaining olive oil together with the unsalted butter in the cleaned saucepan. Add the flour and stir over a medium heat until well browned (but not burnt). Gradually add in all the stock and boil until the soup thickens into a smooth, thick consistency. Add the meat, nutmeg and lemon juice. Check the seasoning and add the Marsala just before serving. Very good on a cold bushveld evening sitting round a big hardwood fire with a large glass of the Marsala.

BUFFALO MARROW BONES

As I write this in 2017, beef marrow bones have just made it back onto the shelf of my local supermarket in the UK after a twenty-year absence caused by the 'mad cow disease' scare of the 1990s. They were not often seen in other parts of the English-speaking world either during that period because the concept of Creutzfeldt-Jakob disease turning your brain into a liquefying sponge is terrifying. This is a pity because marrow is a rich and unctuous comfort food that really has no substitute and many people have never tried it or have simply forgotten about it. Buffalo thigh and shoulder bones make excellent marrow bones if you have a saw robust enough to cut them into manageable lengths. In a kitchen, marrow bones are prepared by sealing the cut ends of each bone with a paste of flour and water, tying each bone in a cheesecloth or muslin and then simmering gently in a court-bouillon for a couple of hours. The marrow is then extracted and is either spread on toast or added to a savoury red wine sauce and served with steak. Out in the bush the bones can simply be roasted on an open fire for as long as it takes to cook the marrow. Sucking buffalo marrow from the bone and listening to the hyenas cackle in the background is an especially primordial experience.

BUSHBUCK

A bushbuck ram is one of the few antelope that will actually charge a human if sufficiently annoyed. Bushbuck rams share an irate intolerance of being wounded with buffalo, but with this significant difference: whereas only twenty percent of buffalo become vindictively malicious when wounded, *all* wounded bushbuck rams will attempt to kill you at the very first opportunity, if they are still physically up to the job. They are by far the most dangerous antelope and have caused some fatalities and many serious injuries. The rams usually weigh between

150 and 180 pounds and have solid, sharp, single-twist horns between twelve and sixteen inches long, sometimes longer. This is long enough to dangerously penetrate the abdomen of the average human or, probably more significantly, place an irreparable hole in your femoral artery as you attempt to run away.

Bushbucks are common and are found throughout Sub-Saharan Africa. Both genders are essentially solitary and spend their days hanging about in a relatively small territory of very thick bush where they browse or graze on every conceivable edible plant. Males are very much larger than females and generally only the males are hunted. They are very difficult to spot buried away in the thick bush and so the most effective hunting technique is to take cover downwind near the edge of a clearing and wait for a bushbuck to come out for a bit of sunbathing. This is something bushbucks like to do early in the morning just after sunrise and again in the late afternoon, usually moving just a few feet out of the thick bush to do so. They will regularly appear in a favourite spot, so the method is not that haphazard.

Sitting and waiting for a bushbuck ram is one of the most nerve-wracking African hunting experiences because there is plenty of time to contemplate the consequences of a misplaced shot and you know there will inevitably be some level of drama once the shot has been taken. This is because it is quite common for antelope to rush off for some distance after being struck by a bullet, even if the shot is perfectly placed and the antelope is effectively dead on its feet. Bushbucks are no exception and often instantly disappear into the morass of vegetation once the shot is fired. The hunter then simply does not know whether the bushbuck is lying dead a few yards into the thick stuff or has been wounded and has retreated into the most inaccessible patch of thorn to await the follow-up. What the hunter can be sure of, though, is that if the bushbuck is wounded it will allow the hunter and anyone else with him to approach and will then charge from a distance of about thirty feet. Unless this charge is stopped by a well-placed shot, serious injury is extremely likely. For this reason, hunters often use a shotgun loaded with heavy buckshot for the follow-up. An experienced bird-shooting friend is a fine companion on a bushbuck follow-up. Experienced bird shooters have finely honed reflexes when it comes to swinging a shotgun and have little difficulty hitting a bushbuck at thirty feet. Others have every chance of missing entirely in the pressure of the moment and getting gored.

As a bushbuck is comparatively easy to stop with a blast from a shotgun, bushbuck hunting is the best possible introduction to dangerous-game hunting for a beginner, as long as the bush is not too thick or too thorny. In very thick and thorny conditions, following up a wounded bushbuck can verge on the suicidal. I have seen tough, vastly experienced professional hunters, capable of staring down the average lion without a twitch of tension, point-blank refuse to follow up a bushbuck in the thorn forests of the Eastern Cape region of South Africa. In those circumstances special dogs are used instead. But in normal bush, a follow-up on a wounded bushbuck with an experienced friend or a professional hunter will allow the novice to discover an extremely important fact without being placed in unconscionable danger and that is whether or not they suffer from 'jelly-legs'. It is not anyone's fault, but a significant portion of the human race suffers from this difficulty when faced with an urgently hazardous situation. They choke up completely in response to the adrenaline rush and are literally unable to move or take any appropriate action at all – their legs 'turn to jelly' and they are 'frozen to the spot'. This is not cowardice or anything like that, it is a completely involuntary reaction, but the time to find out that you suffer from this affliction is not when the buffalo is ten paces away and your professional hunter has just missed with both barrels.

Bushbucks are excellent to eat. Their meat has similar herbal notes to those often encountered in roe deer venison, which is not surprising bearing in mind that both live an extensively woodland existence. Bushbuck meat is somewhat darker and richer than roe deer, but it can be put to almost any use with success.

BUSHPIG

Young hunters with no money often have little choice. I hate hunting monkeys, but the deal was that in return for a couple of days' bird shooting we would spend an entire day pursuing a large troop of vervet monkeys with the remote hope of possibly shooting some, but the more realistic prospect of simply scaring them into leaving the farmhouse and vegetable garden alone for a few days. We were unsuitably armed for monkey hunting, having with us only twelve-bore shotguns and a 9 mm pistol. Still, having received a handful of buckshot cartridges from the farmer, we felt we might stand a chance if luck favoured us and we could get within range. This is not easy with monkeys who quickly realise you mean them harm and take to keeping at least 200 yards between them and you. The correct weapon is therefore a high-velocity rifle, but there was a critical shortage of ammunition in those days and the farmer was not offering.

The monkeys were not hard to find. The allure of ripe tomatoes beckoning from the vegetable garden was hard to resist. But one look at us and they were off – very intelligent creatures, monkeys. We followed them for miles across farm bush kept relatively thin by grazing cattle, now and then seeing them climb to the top of distant trees to keep an eye on our progress. Eventually we moved away from the cultivated section of the farm, the bush thickened and the ground became broken, with small hills here and there. The broken ground allowed us to close the gap on the monkeys. Monkeys have difficulty with the concept of a hill. They seem not to realise that if you keep going around a hill, you end up heading back in the direction you just came from. Time and again, as the monkeys went round one side of a hill we would go round the other and suddenly we would find ourselves heading towards one another, much to the urgent consternation of the monkeys. Just as we were thinking we might get somewhere, the monkeys found a very dense thicket on the side of a hill and simply vanished.

As my companion set off on a route around the hill that would intercept any monkeys who exited unseen from the other side of the thicket, I ambled quietly over to where the monkeys had disappeared. 'Very dense thicket' does not really adequately convey the fifteen-foot-high tangled mass of wind-woven grass and shrubbery extending for several acres beneath the over-arching branches of the big trees. Confronted by this seemingly impassable obstacle, I was about to give up when I noticed a low tunnel bored into the undergrowth and heading roughly in the direction the monkeys had taken. In an extraordinary lapse of common sense I simply thought, *Well, that's convenient*, got down on all fours and proceeded to crawl, pushing the shotgun along in front of me.

To fast-forward to the action, after crawling for about thirty yards there was a sudden piercing growl and a large bushpig appeared in the tunnel thundering towards me on churning legs, eyes ablaze and white mane fully expanded. That pig looked enormous, as big as any buffalo, and in a surreal moment of slow motion all I could do was lift the shotgun, push the safety catch forward and pull the trigger. Thankfully, idiots sometimes receive special protection – the pig received a chest full of buckshot at about five feet and that was enough to turn him slightly off-course so that he just brushed against me in passing rather than smashing into me and delivering a *coup de grace* with his razor-sharp fighting tusks. Upon reflection later, I was surprised that the buckshot did not kill him outright on the spot. I had that very week read an engaging account written by a famous American hunting writer about a lioness he had disturbed while bird shooting. The lioness charged and he allegedly dispatched her instantly at similarly close range with number 7½ birdshot. Well, maybe bushpigs are tougher than lionesses, but my bushpig didn't even slow down much and kept going right out of the thicket and on a hundred yards or so down the hill, there expiring in a blood-soaked and hoof-threshed circle of vegetation after colliding head-on with a tree.

The above tale epitomises the risks inherent in taking on bushpigs. They do not like to feel cornered or pressured in any way and so, almost uniquely amongst African animals, will attack a human even when they are not wounded. Of course, if you wound one then it is very likely to come at you and they are famously dangerous customers, particularly a big male, which can weigh over 200 pounds and takes a great deal of stopping. They have exceptionally sharp tusks and quickly deliver numerous flesh-slicing slashes that can entirely eviscerate a dog in moments or ensure a long rest in hospital for you while waiting for the 300 stitches to be removed from your legs. Perhaps fortunately, bushpigs are very shy and nocturnal in areas inhabited by humans and you have to go out of your way to come into contact with them. One goes to the considerable trouble of finding bushpigs because a young one (under a year old) turns into the very best pork you will ever have tasted.

Somewhat strangely, I was reminded of bushpiglet, and how good it is, on a trip to Barcelona of all places. For me, Barcelona is the most attractive of Spanish cities, particularly if you like food. The flight arrived from London around eight at night and after the taxi ride in to the hotel it was after nine before we began to look for somewhere to eat. This is no problem in Spain where no one eats dinner much before eleven and restaurant kitchens stay open well after midnight. What a marvellous culture it is that allows one to have a four-hour nap between, say, five and nine, before setting out, completely refreshed, for tapas and a few drinks and then a fine meal in one of literally hundreds of good, reasonably priced restaurants. We chose a place on the basis of a recommendation in an entertainment guide in the hotel room – a tiny little restaurant in the Gothic Quarter called *Re Pla*. What a tremendous place. I imagine restaurants in Paris used to make this sort of impression before the current more or less all-pervading commercial cynicism set in. These people really care about food and about wine and about you sharing this enthusiasm with them and it really did seem as if it was nothing to do with the money. They suggested an unusual roast piglet dish. The pork is slow cooked with various herbs and in various liquids until the meat falls off the bone. The meat is then pressed together into thick slices, is basted with a glaze and then roasted briefly in a wood oven at a very high temperature to achieve a smoky, caramelised finish. It is delicious. We ordered a bottle of rare white Priorat to accompany it and the match was perfect – the complex character of a wine wrested with difficulty from hot slate hillsides was beautifully offset by the sweet meat. For some reason this dish reminded me of bushpiglet and if I ever get my hands on another one, I will attempt a copy.

CROCODILE

Whilst in the mood to talk about dangerous things, let us consider the crocodile. Over the many millennia of our co-existence, far more people have been eaten by crocodiles than crocodiles have been eaten by people. In the rural parts of the world where crocodiles still occur in the wild, particularly in Africa, someone being taken by a crocodile is still almost a weekly occurrence. There are twenty-three species of crocodile extant in the world today, but the two that eat almost all the people are the Nile crocodile in Africa and the saltwater (or estuarine) crocodile in the Indo-Pacific. These two creatures are similar in appearance and habits, grow to between fifteen and twenty feet long and can weigh over 2000 pounds. The saltwater crocodile grows biggest, but the Nile crocodile kills more people, probably because it has more opportunity.

It is difficult to convey to an urban reader just how dangerous a crocodile is. It is an apex predator of formidable power that has survived all changes on the planet over a period of at least four and a half million years by the simple expedient of killing and eating anything it can catch, either in the water or up to a hundred yards from the water's edge. It is one of those creatures that has not changed much over all those years because it enjoys an almost perfect design for what it does – a true water-borne killing machine. Really big ones are capable of catching (and then usually drowning) even a small elephant, so a human presents very little difficulty. You cannot see them, you do not hear them and everything looks fine as you survey the untroubled surface of the water. Then as you bend down to fill your bucket there is a sudden surging rush of white foam, a quick, grabbing bite as long jaws close around legs or waist, a brief struggle and piercing scream as the croc turns back into the water and submerges with you between its jaws like a dog with a stick. Thirty seconds later all is as untroubled as before, with the sun shining, the birds singing and the last of the ripples fading to nothing against the muddy bank. Beneath the water you scream and struggle for a very short while and then drown. However, this will have been enough to attract any other crocodiles in the area. Two or three of these will shortly arrive and taking a grip on some part of your now limp body, will provide a useful counterpoint for the first croc and each other in your hasty dismemberment. This is achieved by means of the famous 'death roll', a rapid spinning of the crocodile's body, resulting in the detachment of a limb or a large chunk of flesh, which is then swallowed. In this way you completely disappear in bite-sized pieces into several crocodiles over a very short period and no trace of you is ever found again. This is profoundly upsetting for your relatives and friends who often have difficulty in accepting your death, particularly if the incident is unwitnessed. It also deeply troubles life-insurance companies.

Crocodile numbers plummeted during the twentieth century, largely as a consequence of the popularity of 'crocodile skin', as the very fine leather created from the belly skin of crocodiles is known. This resulted in large numbers of crocodiles, particularly big ones, being hunted for their skins, often illegally. Not to make light of this serious situation, I am reminded of the story of the Australian who desperately wanted a pair of crocodile-skin shoes in order to make a sartorial statement to his city friends and colleagues. With this in mind he took himself off to the outback and set about the pursuit of crocodiles with great vigour. After an absence of over a week, some locals came upon the fellow hiding in the bush on the bank of a billabong, looking ragged and exhausted. Just at that moment, a large crocodile heaved itself up onto a nearby sandbank. Immediately our city friend raced off across the sandbank, flung himself onto the crocodile and wrestled the thrashing creature onto its back. Then he just stood up and walked away, looking disconsolate and shaking his head. As he approached the incredulous locals he was heard to say, 'Damn it, man! Another one not wearing shoes.'

Sadly, in Africa they use rifles, and the proliferation of Kalashnikov AK47s during the 1970s and '80s meant that crocodile poaching became a realistic option for a destitute tribesman, along with elephant and rhino poaching, in many rural parts of Sub-Saharan Africa. The situation was saved by the introduction of crocodile farming in many parts of Africa and the Indo-Pacific in the later stages of the twentieth century. This very sustainable activity produced a steady flow of high-quality leather at much reduced prices and the commercial viability of poaching was destroyed. Wild populations have now recovered in many areas.

One of the side effects of farming crocodiles for their skins is that you end up with a lot of crocodile meat. This meat is now widely available almost anywhere in the world, including the UK, mainly via online exotic meat retailers. It would be correct to say that it has not really taken off in a big way, but it is nevertheless interesting. Crocodile is one of those foods that strongly divides people. Some, predictably, think it tastes like chicken ('looks like fish but tastes like chicken' is a common response). Others are reminded of crab or of lean pork. Yet others cannot stand the stuff and run screaming from the room. I must confess, the first time I tasted crocodile I was not impressed. It was served grilled, with a Pernod sauce. It was tough and the flavour was entirely swamped by the aniseed of the liquor. The chef must have misread the recipe and added a cup rather than a tablespoon, or maybe there were other sins to hide. Since then I have eaten crocodile several times and my reaction has varied from mildly disappointed to really quite enthusiastic. My guess is that, in common with most animals, young crocodiles are tenderer than older ones and certainly some parts of the crocodile are better to eat than others. In general, the tail is thought to be the best eating, but the description of a frozen packet of white meat as 'crocodile tail' could refer to about a third of the creature. What we need to know is what part of the tail and to learn what part eats best.

Notwithstanding the culinary risks, if you enjoy seeing your guests' eyes widen in surprise, serve crocodile at a dinner party. You will be looked upon as very exotic and really quite mad, but they will talk about it for a long time afterwards. The following very simple way of preparing crocodile is worth a shot:

FRIED CROCODILE STEAKS

Treat the crocodile much as you would treat fish. Slice a tail fillet into steaks about an inch thick. Squeeze some lemon or lime juice over the steaks. Fry in foaming unsalted butter on a griddle pan for two minutes on each side. Remove from the pan and sprinkle with a little salt and pepper. Allow the steaks to rest for five minutes and then serve with lemon butter or garlic butter (or both), chips and a fresh green salad.

CRUSTACEANS

The first time my friend Mishek set eyes upon a prawn he was extremely apprehensive. Living in a landlocked country and without access to even a medium-sized river, he had never seen any type of crustacean before. I chased him around the garden, brandishing a fine example of a Mozambique tiger queen and he fled, shrieking. Later, when he had calmed down, I explained to him that this was the greatest delicacy known to man[8] and that my extended family proposed to eat an entire five kilo box of them for lunch. He was horrified, absolutely horrified – as though I had proposed eating cockroaches with rat-dung sauce. This just goes to show that edibility is in the mind of the beholder, to mash up a metaphor, and crustaceans do look very alien and, well, disgusting, if you have never seen one before and have no idea what they taste like. For Mishek was not far wrong in his instincts. Crustaceans are somewhat cockroach-like in their habits and ecological niche. Many crustaceans, and in particular prawns, spend their lives scavenging amongst the detritus of the ocean floor, mopping up all manner of substances

---

8   This was absolutely true for a twelve-year-old living in Zimbabwe in the 1960s. There was nothing in our culinary experience that topped Mozambique prawns, deep-fried or grilled and served with chips and peri-peri sauce.

of worrying provenance. In fact, the Mozambique prawn with which I was terrorising Mishek came from the Indian Ocean just off the coastal town of Beira where the pumping of raw sewage into the sea had resulted in the off-shore prawn beds expanding considerably both in size and productivity.

The prawns we enjoyed as a rare treat growing up in Zimbabwe were all deep-frozen and were very good as long as you allowed them to defrost completely before cooking, particularly if they were to be deep-fried. Until going on holiday to Mozambique as a teenager, I had never enjoyed a fresh prawn. There is a considerable difference between the two and this is something of a recurring theme with crustaceans – they are much better when fresh, stunning in fact, but are still very much worth eating if frozen. On our first day in Beira, after pitching our tents in the beachside camping ground, the first order of business was to visit the fish market in search of fresh prawns which were both cheap and abundant. For this purpose we took along several zinc buckets in which to transport the still-kicking shellfish displayed in great profusion in wooden trays under scruffy canvass awnings. After paying a large number of *escudos* (which equated to a ridiculously small sum in hard currency), for about thirty dozen prawns, we returned to camp and commenced the preparation of a prawn feast of truly stupendous proportions. We boiled them, fried them, grilled them, added peri-peri sauce, added lemon butter sauce, added garlic butter sauce and stuffed our greasy faces until we could not stand another mouthful and still there were prawns left over. These we boiled and ate cold the next day with mayonnaise and halved avocado pears, a sort of robust version of the 'Avocado Ritz' then *de rigueur* in restaurants all over the world. We felt spoilt and we knew somehow that the whole experience was special and was unlikely to ever be repeated. Which it was not – shortly thereafter war broke out in Mozambique and continued unabated for twenty years of savagery and destabilisation.

Holidays became impossible and the prawn beds were suction-dredged by a Soviet fishing fleet. It took about thirty years for the prawn beds to recover. The country itself has still not fully recovered.

It is possible to catch your own prawns or shrimps, as long as you have a seine net and about twenty helpers. I was once involved in such an effort at a river mouth on the Indian Ocean coast. African rivers flowing into the Indian Ocean almost always have a population of what we call 'swimming prawns', a prawn about five inches long that is very delicious to eat and is the very best of all baits for estuarine fish, if you can bear to sacrifice one to such an uncertain and speculative purpose. The method employed on this occasion was of a most robust and casual nature and was presided over by a leader with highly developed 'Captain Bligh' proclivities. To the booming shout of many instructions, often contradictory, and a liberal plastering of deeply personal insults, the team stretched the fifty-metre-long net across the river and dragged it upstream against the flow for a short distance. Then the one flank was instructed to curl round towards the bank to entrap whatever unfortunate creatures were within the encircling net. This was much more difficult to achieve than you might think, the principal challenge being to keep the lower edge of the net on the bottom of the river, yet free of the many rocky and wooden snags. Eventually the task was completed and yielded a surprisingly meagre haul of three six-inch mullet and seven fat swimming prawns, the latter being immediately appropriated by the said Captain Bligh, who left in a hurry shouting instructions for the packing up of the net over his shoulder as he went.

As time passed and the strictures of little land-locked Zimbabwe became replaced for me by exposure to the variety and sophistication of a wider world, so prawns became eclipsed by other more glamorous crustaceans. I speak here of the incomparably delicious lobster. My eldest son Andrew and I had an annual ritual when he was at university in Scotland. At the end of each academic year I would drive up there to fetch him and all his stuff and we would return through Edinburgh, taking the opportunity to stop for the night at a nice hotel in Leith. Leith has some of the finest seafood restaurants in the world and one of them serves up the most delicious grilled lobster. At the time, grilled lobster was Andrew's favourite food[9] and he ate them with a rapt concentration that was delightful to watch. The whole process took well over an hour and was enjoyment of food at the highest level. I too delight in grilled lobster and particularly like to wash one down with a good white wine. Thus our little annual treat was ruinously expensive, but as it was the only time we behaved so outrageously we got away with it.

There are dozens of different lobster species commonly eaten throughout the world. The one we eat in Scotland is the European lobster that lives in the North Sea. The European lobster is also found in the north eastern Atlantic, the western and central Mediterranean and the western part of the Black Sea. It is very closely related to the American lobster of the east coast of the USA and from a culinary point of view can be regarded as identical. Any perceived differences in quality are down to marketing, some areas being better at this than others, and here I think particularly of Maine, whose lobsters are extra famous, but in reality no different to anyone else's. These days lobster is a serious luxury item everywhere, with a corresponding price tag. In past days it was not thought of very highly in some places and was fed to prisoners and lowly peasant types, who would often complain bitterly when served lobster more than twice a week and would seek to include limiting clauses in employment contracts. It was even used as pig food and fertiliser. I find this totally strange. How can something so utterly delicious have been held in such low regard? The only conclusion I can come

---

9   He is now a vegetarian for admirable moral and spiritual reasons and displays much strength of character in not eating lobsters.

to is that they must have been unable to preserve it and must not have known how to prepare it. Decomposing lobster stirred unshelled into a stew to bulk things up might have been very unpleasant, not to mention the considerable risk of salmonella poisoning.

Freshness is a crucial element in the lobster equation. A lobster will start to go off within a few hours of death unless cooked or frozen. If cooked, usually by boiling briefly, a lobster will last for a couple of days in a refrigerator. If frozen and kept at a temperature of -16°C, it can last for between three and six months. If cooked and then frozen, it can last for upwards of a year. But it is at its best when completely fresh, that is alive, immediately before cooking. Some cooks get into a moral pickle about how and when to kill a lobster and believe that the standard practice of submerging the living creature in boiling water is cruel. Personally, I have a feeling that submersion into boiling water is instantly fatal and that any thrashing about the lobster might do just after submersion is little more than reflexes and contraction of shell and membranes. Most certainly the chalk-on-blackboard screeching noise that sometimes emanates from the pot is not the lobster screaming but is the shell contracting in the heat. If you are particularly worried about this, an alternative is to put the lobster into the deep freeze for about forty-five minutes before cooking. This kills it quietly, although freezing to death might also be unpleasant if lobsters, who lack a cerebral cortex, can appreciate such things. Another method is to slice down through the carapace just behind the eyes shortly before cooking – violent, but with a decisive finality.

For me, charcoal-grilling a fresh lobster is the best way to enjoy it. This is very simple:

CHARCOAL-GRILLED LOBSTER

First, plunge the lobster into boiling water for a couple of minutes. Its shell will change from its natural blue-green colour to bright orange-red. Take it out of the boiling water and plunge it into a basin of iced water to arrest the cooking process. Once cooled, I prefer to detach the large claws at the joint closest to the body. Lobster limbs are easy to detach – just bend the limb backwards and snap the joint. Some prefer to keep the claws attached, but I find this makes the claws much more difficult to grill. Place the lobster belly-down on a chopping board and using positive movements with a large and very sharp knife, cut the lobster in half lengthways. The interior of the lobster will now be revealed. The head will contain a pale green-yellow mushy substance called 'tomally'. This is the creature's liver and is considered a delicacy by some and is discarded by others. It will also contain the dark green stomach and intestines which should be removed. There may also be dark green, almost black, roe in a female lobster. This turns a wonderful red colour when grilled and is a great addition. The white tail meat will also be revealed. There might be a visible alimentary canal running through the tail meat. If so, remove it. In my view, lobsters are best grilled on real charcoal rather than on a gas grill, but this is admittedly more difficult because of haphazard temperature control. What we are attempting to achieve at this point is to complete the cooking of the lobster whilst simultaneously imbuing the delicate flesh with both a subtle hint of charcoal smoke and a fine patina of caramelised flesh and shell. It is also nice to achieve visually appealing dark grill stripes on the white flesh of the tail. This is all a question of timing and temperature which is where the skill in grilling lobsters lies. For an ordinary-sized lobster grill flesh-side down for two to two and a half minutes and then turn the lobster halves over and cook shell-side down for one to two minutes. It is nice to baste the flesh with garlic butter whilst the lobster is shell-side down to keep it moist and unctuous. A subtle garlic flavour is an enhancement to the natural taste of lobster. As for grilling the claws, I like to crack the shell of the claw before placing the claw on the grill. This is to allow a little of the smoke to penetrate and flavour the very delicate flesh inside the claws. The claws will grill in the same time as the rest of the lobster.

Some enjoy a squeeze of lemon and a sprinkling of salt on their grilled lobster. I disagree. Both lemon juice and salt directly on lobster flesh mask some of the more subtle and gentle flavours. Don't get me wrong, it is still very good to eat, but the dish becomes rather one-dimensional and the complexity of the flavours is dumbed down. A better approach is to seek the lemon element in the flavours of an accompanying wine and no wine does that better in the context of a lobster than a good white Burgundy. And as for the salt, put it on the chips.

The big-clawed European/American lobster is the quintessential lobster. However, there are other very worthwhile lobsters. The Norway lobster (*Nephrops norvegicus*), otherwise more exotically known as a 'langoustine' or more prosaically as 'scampi', is an excellent, delicate shellfish that is very much better enjoyed fresh and after no more preparation than to be boiled for a minute or so in a very mild court-bouillon or even plain water. It has sweet flesh (an attribute lost if first frozen) that is enhanced by a simple melted butter sauce. How it ever came to be considered a suitable candidate for conversion into the common battered and deep-fried pub food known as scampi in Britain is remarkable. Mind you, 'scampi' in the average British pub is usually a reconstituted product that might contain some Norway lobster, but also contains prawn, shrimp and other fish. The term scampi has a different meaning in America and usually refers to an Italian-American dish of prawns cooked in garlic butter, often served with pasta. As the term 'chicken scampi' is quite common in the USA, it can be concluded that there 'scampi' refers to a style of cooking rather than as a reference to a specific crustacean.

The rock lobsters so popular in the Southern Hemisphere rival the European and American lobsters for flavour of the tail meat but, of course, lack big front claws. Another difference is that hunter-gatherer types can dive for them from the shore and thus do not need investment in lobster pots, long lengths of rope and expensive boats. Diving for rock lobsters is considered a sport amongst aficionados, ranking alongside spearfishing and often undertaken as an adjunct to that more familiar method of putting fish on the table. Indeed, there are many not-so-intrepid spear-fishermen who spear rock lobsters instead of adopting the generally recommended method of grabbing them from their rocky lairs in a surprise attack. Spearing them is a little easier because it can be done from a greater distance than an arms-length reach for the base of the creature's antennae. This latter technique is something that requires practice and considerable stealth, but that is not why they spear them. They do it because they are subconsciously nervous about touching the horny shell and wrestling with something that looks like it should pack a ferocious sting or venomous bite, even though they know it is completely harmless. In this I confess to a certain wimpishness and I too much prefer to spear a rock lobster than grab it. During those long holidays in the early 1970s on the remote and then almost untouched tropical coast of Mozambique we ate rock lobster often, particularly when away from the regular supply of prawns found in the coastal towns. Two inshore reefs run along much of that shore, the outer one of coral and the inner one of sandstone. The outer coral reef calms the water further inshore and allows for almost swimming-pool-like conditions for diving on the sandstone reef. Here we found many rock lobsters, seemingly of several species and occurring in abundance. Some of these rock lobsters were huge, such that when you held one by the base of the antennae with arm straight down beside you, its tail would touch the sand as you walked proudly up the beach. We killed and ate a few of these big ones and thought nothing of it at the time. It was only much later that I learned such rock lobsters achieve great age and ones the size we were so nonchalantly eating were probably well over a hundred years old. I like to think that if we had known that, we wouldn't have eaten them.

Another pastime that might be considered a sport is the genuinely hazardous activity of catching crabs. There are many different types of crabs in the world and some of the larger edible species weigh many kilograms and enjoy the protection of mighty claws capable of shearing off a finger in a spray of crimson, to everyone's shocked surprise. I only have experience of catching the 'swimming crab' (sometimes also called 'mud crab') in Southern Africa. This is a large customer, around three kilograms when full-size, and it looks similar to the brown or common crab of Britain and Northern Europe. It is found in estuaries all along the east coast of Africa and it has formidable nippers, similar in effectiveness to a pair of bolt-cutters. This crab also has the unsettling ability to arch its claws right back over its head to bury the sharp points into the back of the hand of anyone foolish enough to grab it from behind, but too high up. Thus treated, a hand naturally releases its hold and many a succulent swimming crab has made good its escape after being dropped by an incautious captor.

The first time I was involved in catching one of these crabs, we employed a very basic, brute-force method whereby a long-handled gaff was inserted into a series of large crab holes in an estuary mud bank until a very unwilling crab was hauled out, claws swinging, onto the shiny surface of the surrounding mudflat. Here a hessian sack was tossed onto it to neutralise the claws and it was bundled into a bucket without further ceremony. This is not the most effective way of capturing a crab and has the added disadvantage of covering you almost entirely in smelly estuarine mud. A far better way is to employ a crab net of the mesh basket type, with collapsible mesh sides so that the crab can easily access the rotting offal bait normally secured to the base. You toss several of these nets out into an estuary or tidal river known to hold crabs, each attached to a long rope and a high-visibility float. This is best achieved from a boat, as is the next part of the operation. After a couple of hours you return to the floats and one by one, haul the baskets to the surface. In doing this you must maintain a constant rate of retrieve so that water pressure presses the crab down and prevents it from swimming out of the net and away, something it will do with great alacrity if given a chance. Of course, once the net is lifted from the water and into the boat, the water pressure disappears and the crab is free to climb out if the sides of the net are shallow enough to allow this, which they often are. You have to tip the crab into a bucket in a smooth, unhurried movement or otherwise it gets loose into the bottom of the boat and the fun really starts. One of these crabs on the rampage in a small boat full of semi-naked holidaymakers is a real circus and I have seen a crab drive every single human off a boat and into the water, leaving the boat empty but for the crab – a ridiculous proposition.

I was taught how to catch crabs by a fifteen-year-old girl. Her family owned a magnificent house on the banks of the Nahoon River on the Eastern Cape coast of South Africa and I arrived there one day with some friends en route to a holiday on the Wild Coast of the Transkei. Our colourful and generous hosts, former owners of a famous Wild Coast hotel, made us most welcome and a long lunch ensued during which very many bottles of beer were consumed. At a point in the late afternoon when the baking sun had finally slipped down towards the horizon and the surface of the passing river had taken on a silvery gloss, it was suggested that someone ought to catch some crabs for supper as our hosts had a new crab curry recipe they wanted us to experience. The eldest daughter, a tanned and bouncy teenager in a speedo swimming costume, volunteered, but an assistant over the age of eighteen was required to drive the boat. Never having caught crabs with crab nets before and being nineteen years old, I agreed to go along. There followed one of the most memorably pleasant couple of hours I can recall. Sometimes a thing is just perfect. I slipped the boat out of its mooring alongside the house and into the main channel of the river and then gently followed it upstream as it twisted and narrowed between beds of reeds. Hundreds of weaver birds rustled amongst the arching stems and small fish dimpled and popped across the water surface as the boat pushed forward, heading for a series of bays where my young teacher assured me that many crabs lived. I watched with admiration as the lithe youngster tossed the nets overboard one by one with strong physical grace, all the while keeping up a bright chatter about the crabs, the river, her school and life generally in a small coastal city. This was an authentically warm person with a lovely smile and over the next while I found myself enveloped by a genuinely affectionate and completely unaffected personality, a rare privilege which I immediately appreciated in spite of the youthful arrogance I wore like a suit of armour in those days to disguise my basic insecurity. This girl became and remains one of my favourite people and we were briefly lovers some six or so years later, before circumstances once again swept us off in different directions. We also captured half a dozen swimming crabs on this first encounter, which were enjoyed that balmy evening during a dinner served on a table covered by a black velvet tablecloth, with silver cutlery, crystal glass and flickering candlelight on a balcony overhanging the river, at the time an incomparably glamorous circumstance for a young man from a comparatively remote African backwater.

Crabs can be intimidating to prepare for the uninitiated and so many people buy crab meat ready-prepared. This is usually nowhere near as good as the meat from a fresh crab you prepare yourself, so instructions for the preparation of a fresh crab follow:

PREPARING FRESH CRAB

Like lobsters, dead crabs go off very quickly, so get hold of a live crab. Unlike lobsters, crabs must be killed before being placed in boiling water otherwise they shed their claws and legs (a natural defence mechanism in reaction to attack). This allows ingress of water during cooking, which spoils the flavour of the meat by waterlogging it. You kill a crab by either stabbing it through the mouth with a thin blade and then twisting the blade to sever the central nervous system or, more simply, by turning it onto its back, lifting the flap of shell at the anterior of the underbody and stabbing down into the hole revealed with a thin, sharp instrument like a screwdriver or a deboning knife. This last method is best done by positioning the blade into the hole and then banging down on the handle with the palm of the other hand until the blade reaches the shell of the carapace on the other side of the crab. Death is instantaneous. The crab can then be boiled in plenty of heavily salted water in a big pot for fifteen to twenty minutes, depending on size (twenty minutes for a crab of around two kilos). Remove the crab from the pot and allow it to drain and cool.

Once the crab is cool enough to handle easily, open the crab. This is done by turning the crab on its back, placing your hands underneath it at the back and getting your thumbs right behind the body directly under the hindmost legs. Push upwards with your thumbs, and the body, with legs attached, should detach from the carapace. The next bit is what frightens people and keeps fishmongers in business. Inside the body and carapace will be a whole load of dark brown muck, together with pale, finger-like gills (known as 'dead man's fingers'). Remove all the gills, some of which might have detached and fallen off the body into the carapace. Then locate the mouth, which will be at the front of the carapace. With your thumb, press downwards on the mouth to detach the mouth parts and attached digestive material. Discard these.

You now need three pieces of equipment: a spoon; a heavy, sharp knife; and a small instrument with which to pick meat out of nooks and crannies. Scoop out the murky-looking brown crab meat using the spoon. This meat looks unappetising, but is in fact good tasting in a strongly flavoured way and is used in mousses, pâtés, bisques and such-like recipes. Mashed up by hand into a rough-textured paste (or into a smooth one using a food processor), it also makes excellent filling for sandwiches or topping for blinis. Using the heavy knife, crack open the claw shells, snap open the legs with your hands and then commence to pick out the white meat from everywhere. Once all the legs have been removed, the central body section can be cut into three or four pieces to give access to the sweet white meat concealed within. The white meat has a granular appearance much like grains of rice.

There is really only one way to properly enjoy the sweet, white flesh of a crab and that is boiled, cold and with a simple fresh mayonnaise on crusty slices of good bread, all washed down with a bottle of decent Muscadet. Eaten this way, crab is as good as (some think better than) lobster and certainly gives any prawn or shrimp a run for its money.

Another good way to enjoy crab is in the form of 'stuffed crabs', where the meat is removed from the shell, mixed with finely chopped spring onion, herbs, olive oil and breadcrumbs (or some similar combination) and then packed back into the boiled and cleaned carapace before being deep-fried. Different versions of this dish appear in various places in the world from Louisiana to Sichuan, but I most recently encountered it in a tiny shack restaurant in the marketplace of Tofo, a remote beach resort in the Inhambane Province of Mozambique. After an absence of over forty years, I visited Mozambique again in

2015 to find, understandably, that on some levels everything had changed and, surprisingly, that on others very little had changed. Of course, the colonial Portuguese are gone and the place is now very African, but a continental European influence can still be detected in the way food is prepared, in the flavour of the beer and the bread and in the fact that you can still order a bottle of Portuguese Vinho Verde with your stuffed crabs, even if the restaurant is little bigger than a garage lean-to and is made from woven palm-fronds and corrugated iron sheeting. Mired in extreme poverty, with corrupt state officials on the take in every area of life, Mozambique remains nevertheless impossibly romantic, attractive and slightly dangerous, with some of the best unspoilt beaches on the planet, excellent seafood and beautiful women.

DEER

There are at least ninety species of animal commonly referred to as 'deer', most of them occurring in the Northern Hemisphere. All of them are, or have been, eaten by someone at some time, but the species most commonly eaten today (and generally considered to be 'venison' by Anglo-American/European people) are red deer, fallow deer, roe deer, white-tailed deer, mule deer, reindeer, wapiti (USA elk) and moose (Eurasia elk). These eight species have very similar meat and can be grouped together from the culinary point of view, in the sense that any recipe for one will probably work just as well for the other. However, the roe deer is generally considered to be the best of the bunch, particularly by French people.

The taxonomic differences between deer and antelope have been discussed on page 13, but there is another significant practical difference. Deer are nowhere near as tough to kill as antelope, particularly African antelope, and this has consequences for both those trying to kill them and those trying to cook them. For those trying to kill deer, a less powerful rifle can be used relative to the size of the animal (thereby reducing meat damage) and the animal generally does not wander far if wounded. For those trying to cook deer, there is much less prospect of the meat being tainted by an overload of adrenaline and other chemicals following upon the wounding of the animal. It is interesting to speculate why this should be. One theory has it that the difference is analogous to the difference observed between freshwater fish and sea fish. Sea fish are very much stronger, faster and tougher than their freshwater counterparts. It is thought that this is because marine habitats are far harsher than freshwater ones and also abound in predators that instantly eliminate any creature with defects or injuries, leaving only the very fit and strong to nervously live life and perpetuate the species. In similar vein, there is a considerable difference between the moist, relatively predator-free woods of the Northern Hemisphere and the harsh, dry terrains of the Southern Hemisphere with their legions of powerful predators. This might account for the difference in 'toughness' between deer, predominantly an animal of the north, and antelope, predominantly an animal of the south. Another consequence of this difference finds reflection in the hunting methods popularly used for deer and antelope respectively. In Europe particularly, deer are often hunted (alongside boar) by means of a drive using beaters and dogs. Intrinsic to this type of hunting is the necessity of taking running shots at passing animals. Although hitting running animals with a rifle requires very advanced marksmanship skills, the effort is assisted by the fact that the animals die fairly easily and are fairly straightforward to find if wounded. By contrast, driven antelope hunts are a rarity in Africa and this is in no small measure down to the fact that antelope wounded under the circumstances of a drive, with all the attendant noise and commotion, usually take off for the far distant hills at a blistering pace and can take days of effort to retrieve. In fact, there is a strong ethic in African hunting that not only do you never shoot at a moving antelope (unless it is already wounded), you also always rest the rifle on a nearby tree or rock, or if these are not available, on 'shooting sticks'[10]. This is entirely because antelope are so incredibly tough that precision shot placement is an absolute necessity if days of expensive time are not to be wasted on follow-ups.

Venison is arguably the finest of all red meats. There is a distinction between venison from truly wild deer and that from semi-domestic animals. Although deer do not fully domesticate, it has been the practice (for over 1000 years) to enclose deer, particularly red deer and fallow deer, in a greater or lesser area in order to facilitate either hunting them or culling them for meat. In the modern era, these 'deer parks' have become quite small in places, sometimes no more than a few fields and trees, and the animals are artificially fed on commercially produced deer feed. Although this compromises the authenticity of the 'wild food' experience, these animals can be delicious to eat, being something of a compromise between ultra-lean wild meat on the one hand and fat-marbled domestic meat on the other. Along with my French friends, I hold the truly wild roe deer to be the greatest of all venison, but must confess that a haunch of semi-domestic red deer can produce a roast that is very difficult to beat, evoking in its succulence all the imagined bonhomie of Robin Hood and his Merry Men and the atmosphere of Sherwood Forest.

Haunch, shoulder or saddle of good venison cut from a young animal can be so good that it is a shame to do anything to it other than enjoy it as a roast or, if we are talking about loin or tenderloin, as steak. The rump of a young animal also makes excellent steak. Cook venison steak like beef steak – on a cast iron griddle pan at a very high temperature for a very short time. If medallions of venison are required, grill or fry the

---

10 A bipod or tripod made from two or three shoulder-high sticks bound together at the top with rubber strips, ideally from a tyre inner tube. This is usually carried for the hunter by a tracker and is positioned by the tracker when a suitable target is spotted.

loin or tenderloin in one piece before slicing it into medallions. If sliced first, it is very difficult to achieve a rare or medium-rare finish. Some comments on preparing roast venison follow. The rest of the bits and pieces of the animal make nice stews or can be reduced to mince, in which form they can successfully substitute for beef mince in any of the hundreds of recipes calling for beef mince.

There is no need to marinate venison that is to be roasted. If it needs to be marinated, you should not be roasting it. It belongs instead in a stew or pie. Venison should be aged in a cold room at 4.5°C for between five and seven days before consumption. In my view this is enough maturation to sufficiently tenderise the meat and to enhance the flavour to its maximum pleasantness before onset of the very 'gamey' flavour much enjoyed by a tiny minority of so-called aficionados. The rest of us really don't like it at all, so if you are buying venison ask the butcher how long it has been hanging for.

Venison is a very lean meat and so it can lend itself to 'larding', a process where strips of pork fat are laced into the meat by means of a larding needle. This is easy to do, but you must remember that you are unavoidably altering the flavour of the venison by mixing it with the flavour of pork fat. Depending upon the flavour of the two meats this need not be a bad thing, but it requires thought and a little pre-roasting experimentation to ensure that the end result will be an improvement on simply roasting the venison. The best pork fat to use for larding venison is often bacon fat. The flavour of bacon can complement venison and produces a harmony of flavour that is often an improvement, particularly with strongly flavoured meat.

In my opinion, a rare roast shows venison off to best advantage and certainly it should not be cooked to more than medium-rare. This is achieved as follows:

ROAST VENISON

Generously coat the venison joint with good olive oil, then cover with sea salt flakes and freshly ground black pepper, almost to the extent that a salt and pepper crust is formed.

Heat a roasting pan to a high temperature on the hob and then brown the joint briefly. If using a kettle barbecue, there is no need to brown the meat initially and this stage can be left out.

Place the joint in a very hot oven (230ºC) and cook for around ten minutes per 750 g of weight; alternatively place it in a hot kettle barbecue for ten minutes per 1.5 kg, approximately. No hard and fast cooking times can be given because different joints of different sizes and different cuts all vary. You just have to use your intuition and skill as a cook and err on the side of too little cooking time rather than too much. A thing can always be cooked a bit more. It cannot be uncooked. As a rule, kettle barbecues cook things in about half the time required in a conventional oven.

Allow the meat to stand for at least ten minutes before serving. Meat roasted in a kettle barbecue will be noticeably more succulent, but not everybody likes the charcoal-grilled flavour this method produces.

If your chunk of venison is too tough for roasting, then a stew or pie is the answer. Virtually any combination of common stew ingredients will work well with venison, but my favourite stew recipe follows. My favourite pie recipe is exactly the same as the stew recipe, apart from some procedural differences at the end of the cooking time involving the pastry. These are also set out below.

VENISON STEW

(Serves 4)
1 kg venison
2 large potatoes

1 butternut or coquina squash
1 large sweet potato
2 large or 3 medium onions, sliced
1 litre vegetable stock (from cubes or 'stockpots' is fine)
A handful of dried porcini mushrooms (put into the stock)
500 g mixed fresh mushrooms (wild are best, but a mixture of
commercial oyster, shitake and chestnut mushrooms also works
well), sliced into manageable-size pieces
1 x 400 g tin of chopped tomatoes
1 tablespoon red wine vinegar
250 ml red wine
1 tablespoon white flour
1 teaspoon dried oregano
2 teaspoons dried thyme
4 tablespoons olive oil
Salt and freshly ground black pepper

Dice the venison into pieces roughly 2 x 2 cm. Peel the potatoes, squash and sweet potato and similarly dice into 2 x 2 cm pieces.

Put the squash and sweet potato pieces onto a baking tray, toss with one tablespoon of olive oil and then roast in the oven at 200°C for thirty-five minutes.

Heat two tablespoons of olive oil in a large pot or casserole. Brown the venison pieces and then set aside.

Add the onions and fry until soft and just light golden.

Return the venison to the pot and add the red wine vinegar and the red wine. Reduce the liquid until it is almost all evaporated.

Add the potatoes and the flour. Stir well to ensure even distribution of the flour and to allow it to cook for a few minutes. Add the vegetable stock (with the porcini mushrooms still in it), the tinned tomatoes, the dried herbs and some salt and pepper. The liquid should thicken to the consistency of thin cream. If it is too thick it might burn, so thin it out with some water.

Remove the squash and sweet potato from the oven and add to the pot.

Bring the stew to the boil and then cover the pot and simmer for one to two hours, until the venison is tender and the gravy has thickened to a rich consistency. Ten minutes before serving, fry the mushrooms in the remaining tablespoon of olive oil. Do not continually stir the mushrooms. Leave them to steam and then brown on one side, then turn them over and repeat for the other side. This gives a better result. When brown and cooked, add salt and pepper and add to the stew just before serving.

Serve with rice, steamed carrots and green peas.

VENISON PIE

For me, a venison pie is a venison stew served in pastry. There are two approaches: one involving puff pastry and another involving full-on shortcrust pastry encasing the entire contents of the pie.

The puff pastry version is the easiest. Simply prepare a venison stew as above and after you add the mushrooms, put the stew in a large pie dish, cover with a topping of rolled-out puff pastry (follow the instructions on the packet – no one actually makes puff pastry these days), make a few holes for the steam, baste with beaten egg and cook in an oven at 200°C for about thirty minutes. The pastry will puff up and turn golden. It looks great and the pastry substitutes for the rice.

More complex is the business of using savoury shortcrust pastry and making a proper, fully encasing pie. Although you can buy shortcrust pastry in a supermarket, homemade is usually far better, particularly if you use beef dripping, which gives a very crisp and delicious finish. For shortcrust pastry you need:

300 g plain flour
75 g butter
75 g beef dripping, broken into small granules

1 teaspoon salt
120 ml cold water (with ice cubes)
1 egg

Put the flour in a bowl with the salt. Add the beef dripping and mix with your fingers. Cut the butter into small cubes and add to the flour. Again, mix in lightly with your fingers. You are looking for a crumbly, flake-like finish that is rough, not smooth. Slowly add iced water and mix with a pastry knife or spatula until all the flour is incorporated and the mixture is firm. Quickly form the pastry into a ball with your hands, wrap in cling film and rest in the fridge for at least thirty minutes, preferably longer.

When you are ready to make the pie, roll out the pastry with a roller on a floured board into two disks both slightly bigger than the pie tin you propose to use so that the pastry hangs over the edge of the tin (I usually use a 22 cm diameter tin). The disks should be about the thickness of a coin.

Heat the oven to 200°C. First, blind bake the pie base by arranging one disk in a buttered pie tin, with the edges of the pastry hanging over. Prick the pastry all over with a fork and cook for fifteen minutes. Remove from the oven, baste with egg yolk and return to the oven for a few minutes to turn golden then remove the tin from the oven.

Fill the base with venison stew that has particularly thick and creamy gravy. Even though the prebaked base can take quite a bit of moisture without going soggy, too much liquid will collapse it. Arrange the second pastry disk on top to form the pie lid and press down the edges to seal. Make a hole about 1 cm across in the centre to allow steam to escape and put the pie back in the oven for about thirty-five minutes. At thirty minutes take it out, baste with egg for a golden finish and return to the oven for the remaining five minutes.

One quantity of venison stew makes two venison pies.

At the other end of the spectrum from a venison pie is venison carpaccio, effectively a raw meat dish. In my opinion, very high-quality venison loin makes better carpaccio than the finest fillet of beef. I think it is the very low fat content that contributes to venison's amenability to this famous Italian dish. Cold fat is not necessarily a pleasant thing to eat. A classic Italian-style carpaccio recipe follows, but there is another carpaccio recipe in the chapter on wild strawberries at page 298, where the concept is adapted to create a very English dish using very English ingredients.

VENISON CARPACCIO

Get hold of the very best-quality venison loin available. Although successful carpaccio can be made with any venison loin, fallow deer often seems to produce the best result.

Cover the loin in good-quality olive oil and then roll in a mixture of sea salt flakes, freshly ground black pepper and finely chopped fresh herbs (thyme, oregano, parsley and a little rosemary) to form a crust.

*Heat a cast iron frying pan to a really high temperature. Add a tablespoon of olive oil and as it starts smoking, add the loin. **Very briefly** brown the loin all over, including the ends. This should not take more than one and a half minutes tops. You are trying to get a thin, browned and caramelised layer on an otherwise raw piece of meat.*

Allow the meat to cool and then put it in the deep freeze until it firms up to a point where it can be very thinly sliced with a sharp knife (almost 'shaved'). This takes an hour or two in an ordinary deep freeze.

Slice the meat into very thin slices and create a layer of slices on the plates from which it will be eaten. It does not pay to move very thin pieces of meat around more than once – they break up.

Dress with finest-quality extra virgin cold-pressed olive oil, generous shavings of high-quality parmesan cheese, a scattering of pickled nonpareil capers, droplets of high-quality balsamic vinegar, some fresh rocket leaves and a couple of pinches each of sea salt and black pepper.

Venison carpaccio is an opportunity for very rich red wines although it should be noted that a very wide range of wines, both red and white, will match perfectly well, including German Spätlese Riesling and vintage champagne. If you can afford it, it is difficult to beat the power and depth of good Hermitage or Côte Rôtie. If you want to stay true to origin, then that bottle of Barolo you have been hiding for twenty years would also be a treat. For us ordinary folk, a McLaren Vale Shiraz from Australia will work out fine.

DUCKS AND GEESE

Few things can seem as untouchable as a skein of geese passing overhead in a formation made tiny by altitude. This is true whether you are dressed in skins and carrying a stick or are attired in waterproof camouflage and armed with the latest three-inch magnum auto-loading shotgun. From the very beginning men have looked up at those distant formations and thought, *How the hell are we going to get hold of some of those?*

Geese have always been sought after, not so much for their meat, but for the pure and basically odourless fat that seeps in remarkable quantities from every part of their bodies when roasted, but particularly from a layer of fat just beneath the skin. Before the very modern era, with its plethora of oils of all types, some harvested from fruits and grains, others derived from raw crude pumped from beneath the sands of some or other desert, oil (or fat) was a problematic necessity. We take it for granted but, as mentioned earlier, you really need it for cooking, cleaning, lubricating and, in primitive places or times, lighting. In the ancient Northern European world, beyond the temperate olive-growing regions of the Mediterranean, there were generally only four sources of oil: pig fat, whale fat, waterfowl fat and milk fat (if you had domestic animals you could milk and make butter from the cream). Of these four the most useful, least malodorous and finest textured was goose fat, if you discount the remarkable oil contained in the head of the sperm whale which is still used to lubricate machine parts on space ships, there being no fabricated product combining a similar refinement with an exceptionally low freezing point.

Although killing wild geese can be challenging, it is nothing compared to the trouble involved in killing sperm whales. Of course, the way you set about killing geese is to decoy them, a solution discovered at least 2400 years ago. Few hunting experiences have the anticipatory thrill inherent in decoying waterfowl, particularly geese. You lay out your decoys, which incidentally do not have to be perfect replicas of the live birds,[11] in a realistic pattern in a likely spot and then settle yourself down under cover, which can be a preconstructed hide or simply a stand of reeds or long grass. Then you wait, keeping as still as possible. After a while, and if you selected your spot correctly, you will hear distant calls that amplify in the emptiness of the grey sky so that you hear the birds before you see them. This will set your heart thumping. If you are a highly skilled practitioner of the art, you can call back using a goose call. If you are not so skilled, rather give it a miss until you are more practised. Then you will see the birds – anything from a flight of six to a swarming multitude of dots in the far distance, depending on species. A little later, after the birds have approached somewhat closer and appear set on a high-altitude flypast, the most remarkable thing happens: you see the birds see the decoys. It is a very subtle observation and you

---

11   Successful decoys can sometimes be little more than two-dimensional cardboard cut-outs roughly the same size and shape as the bird and robustly painted appropriate colours. Of course they can also be highly realistic plastic or wooden replicas painted with pin-point precision to represent the birds in male, female and juvenile form, whichever might be appropriate and most effective. Some decoys even incorporate moving parts powered by batteries or the wind.

cannot quite pin down how you know the birds have made the crucial observation, but there is just something in the attitude of the still-tiny flock that lets you know that the game is on. This is strangely and intensely satisfying, as though fooling the flock triggers some anciently determined release of endorphins and, of course, the excitement level ratchets up another notch. Usually, the birds will now begin a cautious circling, losing altitude with each turn, searching for danger and anything whatsoever that might seem out of the ordinary. It can take the flock many minutes to complete this reconnoitre and come within range of the waiting guns. This delay, with the quarry in sight and approaching, is the undoing of many otherwise competent shotgunners. Shotguns are best aimed entirely on instinct and in the application of a much practised reflexive swing. With remarkably little training the subconscious is capable of effortlessly computing the very complex variables involved in causing a swarm of pellets ejected at high velocity from a moving barrel to intercept a target flying at an irregular range and speed. To do this consciously is more or less impossible, but observing slowly approaching waterfowl can induce the shotgunner into an attempt, with an internal dialogue that goes something like this:

'Well, they look like they are going to come in at about thirty-five yards up and either straight in or a little from left to right – should be easy. Just relax. Remember to swing through. I wonder if the wife really is having an affair. Surely not? I gave up smoking, didn't I? Hang on – what's happening now? Those birds look like they're going to be more like twenty-five yards up if they make another turn and then it will be a right-to-left swing, with them going pretty slow. Half a body-length lead should be about right. That tennis coach looks suspiciously friendly though, always hanging around with Marjorie and then the two of them glancing in my direction and giggling. Oiks! What are they doing now? Speeding up? Flock splitting!

Crikey! Should I swing on those birds to the left? No, no, the ones to the right, they're closer! Swing through. Remember to keep your left elbow in and your right knee bent. Both eyes open, remember! Maybe I should hire a private detective. But then, do I really want to know? Hey! What the hell? Where are they going now? Now it's going to be left to right at about forty-five yards and if they don't slow down it'll be at least a six-foot lead, maybe more. Here they come! Not six feet, more like three and a half. I think! Damn! Missed...'

Conscious efforts to time the shot result in interference with the smooth and untroubled application of subconscious skill. This leads to an uncertain and pokey swing and is often followed by a miss with both barrels. In this, as in most things, the cure is experience.

Geese are big birds and so the natural inclination is to fire large-size shot at them. This is usually a mistake. Several times I have peppered a goose with buckshot only to see the bird stagger in the air and then make off over the horizon, inevitably to die in agony in some distant reed bed. The anatomy of any bird is such that if you hit it in the massive chest muscles, particularly low down, you do little or no damage to its vitals regardless of the size of the shot and the bird is often capable of the most incredible feats of persistence in the face of wounds that would bring a human to a complete and screaming stop. This is totally undesirable and is unnecessary when you consider that a number six birdshot pellet (made from lead)[12] will incapacitate a goose if it hits in the neck or head or if it smashes into any of the

---

12 An exception occurs in those places where thousands of shotgunners annually fire millions of rounds at migrating geese over wetlands and lead shot has been banned because the waterfowl pick it up along with other grit for use in their gizzards and subsequently die of lead poisoning. Shot made from other metals or metal alloys is now used and because some of these, for example steel, are lighter by volume than lead, a bigger pellet size is required to be effective.

delicate wing bones. Bearing in mind that a number six birdshot cartridge contains upwards of 260 pellets whilst an equivalent load of BB (the biggest birdshot) contains around seventy pellets and a load of AAA (the smallest buckshot) contains thirty-five pellets, it is quite obvious that your chances of an effective hit are much better with the number six, as long as the birds are within the normal effective thirty-five to forty-five yard range of a shotgun, which is where the trouble lies. Geese are so big that they look as though they are well within effective range when they are in fact seventy, eighty or even a hundred yards away. I have brought down African spurwing geese that came within range with number six shot and as spurwing are amongst the largest and toughest of all geese, if they will succumb, so will everything else. However, you do have to be careful about wounded spurwing. A spurwing gander weighs around twenty pounds and is immensely strong and fearless for a bird. There was a story going around when I first took up wing shooting that gundogs attempting to retrieve wounded spurwing from deep water are in danger of being drowned by the bird holding the dog under with one of its powerful wings. I long considered this to be apocryphal, but I actually saw it nearly happen in an epic struggle between a spurwing and a springer spaniel. That dog barely escaped with its life and thereafter, quite sensibly, refused to have anything further to do with spurwings. Wounded spurwings are also dangerous on foot, where they will employ their sharp wing spurs against all comers with a very convincing display of focused aggression. As the dog would no longer retrieve spurwing, we had to do it ourselves and this led to one of my companions having a narrow escape, being effectively chased from the field of battle by a wounded spurwing. The bird fell to the first shot but on the follow-up appeared to run unscathed through the blast of a second shot fired at close range, leaving my friend little option but to flee in humiliating disarray. That this particular goose had to be dispatched in the end with a bullet from a 7 mm Remington Magnum speaks volumes for the tenacity of spurwing geese[13].

Domestic geese are now an unusual food item, seldom seen except in upmarket food halls around Christmas time where they are purchased by foodies in search of authenticity in their 'Medieval Yuletide Fayre'-style Christmas dinners. This is because geese are not that great to eat when compared to turkeys, ducks and chickens. Goose meat is very rich and dark and a little goes a long way, which is just as well because there is surprisingly little meat on a goose, bearing in mind the size of the bird. The great advantage of having a goose for dinner in past times was the effect on the quality of the roast potatoes, but these days one can simply buy a tin of goose fat and achieve the same result. Certainly, some wild species are better to eat than others, but all are an acquired taste and probably wouldn't be eaten at all by anybody if it were not necessary to justify shooting them. All I can say about cooking wild geese is that the best examples I have tasted were young birds marinated for several hours in either gin or white wine with crushed juniper berries before being roasted. That is such a simple proposition it does not require a recipe.

Wild ducks, on the other hand, tell an entirely different story on the taste buds. Many species of wild duck, throughout the world, are excellent to eat and are worth every effort taken to secure a few for the table. In particular, the most common wild duck of all, the mallard, is delicious and is a revelation with a sauce based on oranges, explaining in one taste why

---

13 The landowner, who was watching this spectacle with deep amusement from the comfort of his pickup truck, did the honours with this goose using the hunting rifle he usually carried about with him. By the time my friend had collected himself and was ready to return to the fray, the goose was 200 yards away and it was thought easier to deploy the rifle.

canard sauce bigarade[14] and its derivatives through to gloopy, over-sweet 1970s-style *duck à l'orange*, have been popular for over 500 years. Most domestic duck species are derived from the wild mallard and it is not difficult to understand how that domestication came about. Every year in spring several pairs of wild mallard arrive and take up residence on the garden pond and the females lay large clutches of eggs. From the moment they arrive, these ducks are trying to be domestic, lounging on the front lawn in the sunshine and hanging about the kitchen door in the hope that someone will throw some stale bread out for them. It is as though they are 'self-domesticating' and that the bond between a particular extended family of ducks and an extended family of humans sharing the same place grows over generations. We would no more dream of shooting these ducks than we would shoot our dogs, but we might very well think of capturing a few, clipping their flight feathers and ensuring a supply of duck eggs for the future, particularly when the numbers swell to several dozen after the ducklings hatch. They stay with us all summer while the ducklings mature and we share with them the tragedies of predation by foxes and other mischances of duck life. By September they revert to being wild ducks again and disappear to join flocks and presumably have a wild time, feeding on stubble fields, roosting on estuaries and finding a mate for the following year's breeding. It is at this time that mallards are shot and are at their best from the eating point of view. A simple and modernised recipe for classic *canard sauce bigarade* follows, in my view the cleverest duck recipe ever invented:

---

14 Originally a Florentine dish called *papero alla melarancia* imported into France in the sixteenth century along with Caterina de Medici, who incidentally brought forty personal chefs with her just to ensure that her meals would be up to standard.

CANARD SAUCE BIGARADE

(Serves 4)

2 fresh wild mallards, plucked and drawn and not hung at all
2 teaspoons groundnut oil
Freshly ground black pepper
Sea salt flakes
400 ml duck stock (or vegetable stock if you don't wish to go to
the trouble of making duck stock, which is simply duck carcasses
boiled up with the usual array of stock vegetables)
Juice of 2 Seville oranges (if you use other, sweeter varieties of
orange you are not making sauce bigarade but duck à l'orange –
very nice, but not in the same league)
Zest of 1 Seville orange, cut into a fine julienne and blanched
50 ml Cointreau orange liqueur
2 tablespoons cider vinegar
1 tablespoon Demerara sugar
1 teaspoon cornflour

Place the ducks in a roasting dish, lightly cover with groundnut oil and sprinkle with sea salt and black pepper. Roast in a preheated oven at 190°C for thirty-five to forty minutes.

While the ducks are roasting, make the sauce as follows. Put the vinegar, orange juice and sugar in a non-stick pan with two tablespoons of fat from the roasting ducks (or from a tin of domestic goose fat) and heat until the sugar melts and the mixture thickens slightly. Then add the stock and boil rapidly until reduced by half. Add the Cointreau. Mix the cornflour with a tablespoon of cold water and add to the sauce. The sauce should now thicken to a thin gravy-like consistency. If it does not, add another teaspoon of cornflour mixed in water. Add the blanched orange zest.

Simple, but very effective with the strong, slightly gamey flavour of the duck – the tart tang of the Seville orange, tempered by the sweetness of the liqueur and the sugar, combines beautifully *with the duck fat permeating the meat. Some people find that this sauce is not sweet enough for their taste. You can sweeten it up simply by adding more sugar, but remember you are then straying towards the duck à l'orange end of the spectrum.*

As nice as mallard are to eat, they are not the best eating duck in my view. That spot is held by the tiny common or Eurasian teal (*Anas crecca*) and its rarer cousins the blue-winged and green-winged teal (*Anas discors* and *Anas carolinensis* respectively), which taste exactly the same. Teal might very well be the finest eating game bird there is and it is right up there with woodcock when it comes to culinary enthusiasm in the breast of the hunter. I and others I know hunt teal (and woodcock) with a completely dedicated focus, as though we are hunting jars of Beluga caviar, so delicious is this bird. Weighing only 330 grams on average and being smaller than a wood pigeon, the speedy little teal is a challenging shot as it zips in to land on a flight pond in the half-light of dusk. Unlike some other ducks, teal usually don't circle higher up before coming in to land and so there is often no warning of their approach at all. As with all waterfowl, a retrieving dog is essential when shooting teal. Often the teal fall stone dead into the undergrowth where you are very unlikely to find them in the dark without a dog. That such a treat should end up as fox food is disappointing to say the least.

Like many very fine things to eat, teal should be prepared as simply as possible and do not benefit from any rich or complex sauce. My favourite is:

ROAST TEAL WITH FRESH CEPS

(Serves 2)
2 teal
220 g fresh ceps
Salt and freshly ground white pepper

2 teaspoons groundnut oil
25 g unsalted butter
1 small onion, finely chopped
1 thin leek, finely chopped
1 stick celery, finely chopped
1 small carrot, finely chopped
1 clove garlic, crushed
120 ml red wine vinegar
150 ml chicken stock
40 ml good olive oil
15 ml pumpkin seed oil

Remove the legs from the teal and cut off the parson's nose end of the carcasses. Roughly chop up the legs and set aside. Season the teal with salt and white pepper. Heat the groundnut oil in a roasting pan, add half the butter and then briefly sear the ducks on all sides until lightly browned. Roast at 240°C for ten minutes, then transfer to a warm place to rest for a further ten minutes. Remove the breasts from the teal and keep warm.

Roughly chop the carcasses and return to the roasting pan together with the chopped-up legs. Brown over a high heat and then add the chopped vegetables and lightly brown those too. Pour off the fat and add red wine vinegar to deglaze. Reduce until the vinegar is almost gone. Add stock and garlic and further reduce until only a third remains. Strain this through a fine sieve.

Thinly slice the ceps and fry them briefly in the remaining butter with a little salt and pepper. Make a bed of rocket on each plate and spoon the ceps into the centre. Thinly slice the duck breasts and lay the slices over the ceps. Create a dressing by whisking the olive and pumpkin seed oils into the stock whilst gently heating for a short time. Pour dressing over the duck and serve immediately with a bottle of young, but good, red Burgundy or a New Zealand Pinot Noir.

ELAND

Each year a dear friend and I would arrange a trip into the Karoo for purposes of restocking the freezers with game for the coming summer months. The Karoo is a large semi-desert area in South Africa stretching from just inland of the Cape coastal mountains north to the grasslands of the Free State. It is an extremely alluring region of enormous vistas, rocky scrub, distant mountains and colourful people, with a special herb-scented solitude that is quite unforgettable. My friend usually brought along his two sons, then teenagers, and the whole exercise would start with three or four days of grey-wing francolin shooting over pointers in the mountains between Craddock and Graaf-Reinet, interspersed with some casual guineafowl shooting in the more densely forested ravines that snake up the mountainsides from the floors of the major valleys. We would then move down onto the plain and shoot a few springbok or would stay in the foothills pursuing mountain reedbuck. Both of these are excellent to eat and a combination of them, together with the game birds, a few waterfowl and a warthog, substitutes almost entirely for all types of commercially farmed meat.

One year we were sitting around the fire in the lounge of a Karoo hunting lodge, having just arrived that afternoon from bird shooting higher up the valley, when the conversation turned to the fabulous eating qualities of eland antelope. Now, anyone who has ever eaten eland will confirm that its flesh is indeed excellent and in the antelope-meat stakes is rivalled only by prime cuts of young springbok, devotees being about equally split on which one takes first prize. However, the problem with an eland is that a small one weighs 900 pounds and a large male can weigh as much as 2000 pounds and that is a huge quantity of meat for ordinary family consumption. Our host, the manager of the private hunting reserve we were to enjoy over the next few days, poured another round of *witblitz*[15] and settled into a long tale about the legendary quality of the eland on this particular land and the exceptional aesthetic attributes of hunting them in the rolling, scrub-covered foothills leading up into the high mountains of the Sneeuberge. Normally this sort of thing would not have worked on my friend, whose ear had been bent on many occasions by persuasive game farmers to no effect, but on this trip he had brought along a new rifle of some exotic calibre and he was itching to try it out on something a bit bigger than a ninety-pound springbok. This made him susceptible, and before the evening was over the concept of securing an eland had firmly taken hold in my friend's mind.

The next morning at breakfast further discussions were a little more subdued. It was revealed that although there were indeed eland to be had on the reserve, actually shooting one was not that easy. Apparently, unless you found them in properly broken ground, the problem was that they could see you coming from about five miles out and trotted off at a pace impossible to match on foot. Eland are the slowest of all antelope with a top galloping speed of only twenty-five miles per hour, at which pace they tire quickly, but they can maintain a steady trot of fourteen miles per hour for four or five hours and usually head uphill into

15 Literal translation is 'white lightning'. *Witblitz* is a clear Cape husk brandy of eye-watering strength, somewhat like Italian *grappa* or Turkish *raki*, but without the refinement.

the mountains. This is too much, even if you are on horseback, because if eland have any idea they are being followed they seem to keep going to the full extent of their stamina before stopping. A horse is only good for a couple of hours without stopping at about ten miles per hour, so at the end of two and a half hours you are ten miles behind the eland.

The upshot of this more sober discussion was a decision that if anyone – father, sons or me – should happen upon an eland of potentially good eating quality then the shot should be taken and the cost would be borne by my friend, as he had decided he *must* have an eland to cover meat requirements for various birthday parties and anniversaries later in the year. I was happy to agree to this. Although I was planning to hunt mountain reedbuck that day, I was armed with my trusty .308 Winchester[16] which, with 180-grain bullets of robust construction, will fell any thin-skinned game whatsoever, up to and including a 2000-pound eland bull, as long as the bullet is correctly placed. Decision made, we all headed off in our various separate directions, each accompanied by a local

---

16 The American .308 Winchester calibre is the 'sporting' or 'commercial' firearm upon which the 7.62 mm cartridge used by the military forces of the Nato alliance and many other countries is based. There are very slight differences in size between a .308 and a 7.62 mm cartridge, but both cartridges will chamber in either weapon. The 7.62 mm cartridge replaced the .303 British and 30-06 Springfield cartridges used by the British and American forces in the Second World War, but is essentially a very similar moderate velocity '.30 calibre' medium rifle. Whatever its shortcomings as a military cartridge (essentially, it is unnecessarily powerful for use in standard assault rifles and has been replaced by the much smaller and faster 5.56 mm, although it is still used in machine guns), it is an excellent all-round hunting calibre. With good, reasonably heavy bullets it will deal with anything except the very thick-skinned animals (elephant, rhino, hippo and buffalo). More lions have been killed with .30 calibre rifles than with anything else, particularly the .303, because army surplus rifles were often issued to game departments of countries in, or formerly in, the British Empire. A .308 is equally effective against lions.

tracker, as is the custom on commercial hunting reserves in Southern Africa[17].

My tracker that day was the most authentic-looking San person I have ever seen. Little more than five feet tall and with glistening, copper-coloured skin, he possessed the hallmark 'peppercorn' hair of his people above a classic wide-cheeked, almost oriental, face. The effect was enhanced by his wearing a leather 'waistcoat' often favoured by San people, together with a traditional antelope-skin pouch over a tatty loincloth. I asked him (in Afrikaans) where he was from and he said 'I am from here, sir'. This was a surprising answer because I understood the San had been driven out of the Karoo more than 150 years ago. However, it turned out that he had been born on the reserve, as had the previous four generations of his family. His great-great-grandmother had been captured during a raid in the Drakensberg during the mid-nineteenth century and had been enslaved along with a small San family group who became the property of the then owner of a small sheep farm. The family group, inter-marrying along the way with a few men and women from local indigenous tribes, had simply stayed on the land, almost as part of the land, as it had transformed over the decades from a scattering of poor sheep farms into a prosperous Afrikaans farming community buoyed up by the wool booms of both world wars and then into the terminal decline of continually split land holdings caused by the testamentary laws of the Dutch Reformed Church. In the end, the most successful farmer had bought out all the rest and had 'inherited' this little group of San-origin people, who worked as labourers on the farm. In turn, the

---

17   As well as being very useful in preventing you getting lost, in locating shootable game and in dealing with it afterwards, particularly if an animal is wounded and must be followed up, trackers are the eyes and ears of the owner (or manager) – an essential element when the arrangement is that you pay a fee for each animal you shoot at and hit, regardless of whether or not you then subsequently recover it.

successful farmer had been bought out by a rich tycoon from Johannesburg who put together a vast hunting reserve for his own pleasure and as a commercial venture. The San family now worked for this concern as trackers and general labourers and continued to live with their families in the collection of stone huts they had occupied for over a hundred years.

This tracker, whose name was Elias, was the real thing, displaying all the bushcraft skills for which the San are famous and which are the hallmark of an upbringing in the bush under the practical tutelage of an older expert and without the distractions of a formal academic education. He led me up into the hills in pursuit of mountain reedbuck with great facility and we had soon disappeared into a remarkable landscape of rich grassland hummocks interspersed with densely forested ravines. We were busy making our cautious way up one of these hummocks when we heard the first shot – a distant crack followed by a distinct thump. 'A hit – big antelope – eland,'[18] commented my companion. I smiled, happy that my friend had his supply of party meat secure. Some minutes later, however, there came a second crack and thump. 'Two elands in the bag!'[19] The tracker's face broke into a radiant, partially toothless smile. I had to grin myself. Two eland – a minimum of 1000 pounds of meat, once dressed – was now the happy responsibility of my friend. His lovely wife was going to have something to say about that. I was just explaining the ramifications of this overabundance of good fortune to Elias when there was a third crack and a somewhat more hollow-sounding thump.

---

18 For Afrikaans-speaking readers, what he actually said was 'Raak skoot – groot bok – eland'. It sounds better in Afrikaans. It is amazing how much an experienced tracker can tell from the sound of the bullet strike. They can often tell the size of the animal struck and in what part of the anatomy it has been hit.

19 'Twee elande raakgeskiet!'

'Wounded antelope!'[20] was Elias' comment. 'Another eland?' I asked. 'Yes, I think so, sir. That or a mountain zebra.' There was no way any of us were going to shoot a mountain zebra, so it had to be another eland. I now began to fear for my friend's solvency, not to mention his physical safety once his wife found out he had depleted the family resources by the equivalent of a small holiday flat at the beach (eland are not cheap). And to add to the problems, the third one was wounded and probably well on its way to Lesotho by now. Just at that moment came the fourth shot, a crack merging into a thump indicating a shot at very close range. 'That's it! They have him,' exclaimed Elias, once again beaming in toothless pleasure.

Three eland! The ramifications were enormous. Five new chest freezers had to be purchased and getting what turned out to be well over half a ton of meat home proved challenging to say the least. Naturally, the inevitable had happened. My friend and both his sons had independently come upon shootable eland just standing around in suitably broken country in three different locations many miles apart. The terrain was such that sound did not travel well and so nobody had heard any shots other than their own. Elias and I had heard all the shots because we were very much higher in the foothills and the sound had carried to us clearly.

From my point of view, this superabundance of eland had one happy consequence: I was given a large chunk of meat from the hump of a young bull and I have to say it was spectacular to eat. Meat from the hump of an eland is the only antelope meat I have encountered that is marbled with delicious fat. Thus, when fried as a steak it turns out much like beef rib-eye or like the French cut *côte de boeuf*. It is, of course, equally appealing as a roast, enjoying a particular succulence and greasiness unusual in game meat. Eland meat is quite widely available in Europe, particularly in Germany, because semi-domestic eland are

---

20 '*Kwesbok!*'

'farmed' for meat in various parts of Africa, in much the same way that red and fallow deer are farmed in Britain. If you can get hold of some, it is highly recommended.

The last word in this section must be about Elias. He very skilfully found me a fine mountain reedbuck and I shot it stone dead after a difficult stalk. This was extremely satisfactory and his rare indigenous appearance and primitive dress had enhanced the aesthetic experience of hunting in an awesomely beautiful and fully restored environment. Everything seemed saturated with history. I felt I had been transported back at least 200 years and basked in the figurative glow of this startling authenticity.

Then Elias reached into his traditional skin pouch and took out his cell phone and a GPS device to phone in our position for the recovery vehicle.

FROGS

Clearly, the first person to contemplate eating a frog must have been quite hungry. Frogs do not engage the culinary imagination in quite the same way that, say, ripe fruit or fillet steak does. Nevertheless, I have no doubt that our distant ancestors were often abroad in the swamps and pools looking for the free lunch provided by molluscs and other stationary provender, and that in the course of such wanderings someone, somewhere, caught a frog. Overcoming a natural reticence when it comes to creatures with hairless or featherless bodies, our peckish swamp-searcher would have discovered that even though they look slimy and wet, frogs are in fact warm and dry to the touch. After bashing the frog on the head and skinning it, he would then have found that the only place on a small frog that has any meat worth bothering with is the back legs. Maybe he then ate the legs raw, or if this all happened after the use of fire had begun, he grilled them. Either way, he would have found that the flesh was sweet and pleasant, reminiscent of the delicate flesh of a small bird and in every way a completely worthwhile morsel. Perhaps he then returned to his home in the Lascaux caves and spread the news, thereby causing hundreds of generations of future French persons to become indelibly associated with the practice of eating frogs.

In fairness, this delicacy is not limited only to France, and many different cultures all over the world eat frogs of various sorts. Frogs are eaten in Thailand, Vietnam, Indonesia, Portugal, Spain, Slovenia, Greece, the southern states of the USA, much of Africa and, most famously, in the Cantonese cuisine of China. Indeed, archaeological evidence has come to light recently that establishes that frogs were eaten in Britain around 8000 years ago, perhaps revealing that the pejorative term 'frog' more properly belongs to the English as European originators of the practice rather than to the French as its perpetuators.

The frog commonly eaten in Europe is the 'edible frog' (*Pelophylax kl. esculentus*), also known as the common water frog or green frog. Interestingly, the edible frog is the fertile hybrid of the pool frog (*Pelophylax lessonae*) and the marsh frog (*Pelophylax ridibundus*). This hybrid is a naturally occurring phenomenon, which via some fairly complex biology is able to breed with its originator species and thus produces, in some situations, little pool frogs, little marsh frogs *and* little edible frogs. I am sure that harvesters of wild frogs do not much distinguish between these three species, nor care much about the complex biology, so it is probably fair to say that any small green frogs inhabiting pools of fresh water in Europe have always been, and still are, the subject of capture and consumption.

As an object of foraging efforts, frogs are one of those things that require expertise in identification because many species are poisonous to some extent and so you can't just go around sampling frogs you happen to come across unless you are happy to experience the occasional gastric disaster. Speaking globally, almost all frogs are toxic in the sense that they exude some or other noxious substance onto their skins as a defence against predators. Whether this has an immediately fatal effect or is something of little or no concern depends on many uncertain factors to do with the species of frog involved and the amount of toxin consumed. Little research has been done in this field because it is extremely difficult to find volunteers happy to spend time licking frogs, with the possible exception of toad-licking which is apparently popular in certain circles in view of the psychoactive element found in the poisonous secretions of many toads.

Long before I personally took a bite out of a frog's leg, a frog took a bite out of my leg. I grew up near a 'vlei', a term which in Southern Africa refers to a clay marsh that is usually a dry pan covered with short grass, but which in the rainy season turns into a quagmire that could swallow a battalion of tiger tanks without so much as a muddy burp. The vlei was criss-crossed with footpaths which my ten-year-old friends and I would use to get to various areas with decent dove shooting. One damp morning as we tramped along one of the paths a most terrifying event occurred. As my foot came down alongside one of the numerous tufts of marsh grass that lined the path, a gnarled green entity with a back about the size of a dinner plate jumped out with a hissing snarl and fastened itself to my lower leg. Boy, did I scream! I leapt back, dragging the creature with me and promptly fell over, upon which the creature let go, leaving impressive half-moon marks just above my ankle, like a mini shark bite seeping scarlet trickles into my tennis shoe. Far from being intimidated in any way, my assailant was ready to continue hostilities and again jumped forward with a malevolent hiss, but of course by now I was wriggling out of the way with great alacrity and its second strike missed the mark by some distance. By this stage it had become clear that this alarming apparition was some sort of giant frog of a species and size we had not encountered before and in the way of small boys everywhere, we were unable to resist further provoking it by poking it with sticks. Although fairly phlegmatic about this new amusement in a squat and brooding way, now and then it would catch the end of one of the sticks with a lightning quick lunge, and with an impressive crunch, would hang on determinedly like a bulldog.

This was definitely not a creature one wanted anywhere near one's fingers or toes and I felt fortunate to have escaped with insignificant injuries. Investigating matters later with the aid of a book on African amphibians, it turned out that my attacker was probably an African bullfrog of exceptional size and great age. The African bullfrog is the second largest frog in the world and is known to be aggressive in certain circumstances. Although we had never encountered one before, it is in fact a common and popular edible species and is enjoyed by many indigenous peoples in Sub-Saharan Africa. It was referred to by the Victorian explorer Dr Livingstone (he of the 'I presume'), in his book *Missionary Travels and Researches in South Africa* (1857), where he states:

'*These enormous frogs, which, when cooked, look like chickens, are supposed by the natives to fall down from thunder-clouds, because after a heavy thunder-shower, the pools, which are filled and retain water a few days, become instantly alive with this loud-croaking and pugnacious game.*'

He goes on to describe the flesh as being excellent, although he does not reveal how they were prepared or cooked. I suspect if they looked like chickens, they must have been roasted. The African bullfrog, *Pyexicephalus adspersus*, can weigh over two kilograms and the males can be as much as twenty-four centimetres long, with a very broad body and rounded head. When excited or threatened it can puff itself up in an attempt to intimidate. It sure intimidated me! In the dry season it cocoons itself in the deep mud and remains immobile in a state of virtually suspended animation until the next rains, when it suddenly emerges as though by magic.

In my limited personal experience the best way to prepare frogs' legs is to fry them – gently in butter or more robustly in deep vegetable oil after first coating them with batter or breadcrumbs – which is the way they are prepared almost everywhere they are eaten. The meat is exceptionally tender and subtle in flavour and tastes much like you hope a quail will taste but doesn't. For an exotic example of the concept in the Louisiana style, here is a recipe:

SOUTHERN FRIED FROGS' LEGS

(Serves 6)
1 kg frogs' legs, skinned and separated
2 eggs
2 tablespoons mayonnaise
Tabasco sauce
1 tablespoon corn starch
Juice of 1 lemon
½ teaspoon baking powder
150 g all-purpose flour
150 g white breadcrumbs
Salt and pepper
Sunflower oil

Mix the eggs, mayonnaise, corn starch, baking powder, lemon juice, several dashes of Tabasco and some salt and pepper together in a large bowl to make a creamy paste. Add the frogs' legs and make sure all the legs are thoroughly coated with the marinade. Chill in the refrigerator for around an hour.

Place the flour and breadcrumbs into a large plastic bag. Remove the legs from the marinade and shake to remove any excess. Put two or three legs at a time into the plastic bag and shake until the legs are well coated. Deep-fry the legs in hot sunflower oil until dark golden brown (no more than two minutes). Serve immediately.

GAME FISH

Strictly speaking 'game fish' refers to any fish that anglers attempt to catch for sport, but the term has different connotations in different places.

In Britain 'game fish' means salmonid species in fresh water, being Atlantic salmon, trout and, more recently, grayling[21]. In the rest of the world the term 'game fish' is generally taken to refer to sea fish of the streamlined, predatory type that are usually, although not necessarily, pelagic and which are usually caught by deploying some form of moving lure or swimming live bait. These will include bill fish of all types, toothy members

---

21 All other freshwater fish in Britain are designated as being 'coarse fish'. This distinction holds regardless of the method of capture of the fish, although it is usually assumed that salmonids will be pursued primarily by means of fly fishing or perhaps, in exceptional circumstances, by spinning, both of these activities being described as 'game angling', in contrast to all other methods which are designated as being 'coarse angling'. It follows, therefore, that if you catch a salmon on a worm or a maggot, the salmon will still be a 'game fish', but you will have caught it whilst 'coarse angling'. Similarly, a fly fisherman plying his fly rod in pursuit of salmonids on the lower reaches of some stream might catch a 'coarse fish' as an incidental event, in which case he is nevertheless a 'game angler'. However, if he targets and catches the coarse fish on purpose, then he is a 'coarse angler' notwithstanding that he is fly fishing. See?

of the mackerel family, tuna of various sorts, trevally (king fish), blue fish, striped bass, tarpon, bonefish, barracudas and so on – the lions, tigers, leopards and wolves of the sea. It is in this latter sense that I use the term 'game fish' in this section.

Angling for game fish from a deep sea vessel, so-called 'big game angling', is considered by many to be the pinnacle of angling as a sport. It is indeed exceptionally pleasant in calm, tropical conditions from the comfort of a well-appointed and high-powered boat, but there is generally little angling skill required of the person holding the rod, who is usually a paying customer and who simply does battle with any fish that might be hooked on the exotic array of hardware being dragged behind the boat. It is the captain of the vessel who knows, or should know, what lures to use, how far behind the boat they should be deployed, at what speed the boat should travel and where the boat should go. I suppose that in terms of it being a team effort, collectively there is a fair level of skill, but the most significant contribution by the dude in the fighting chair is to have paid the daily rate, often a very significant sum.

There is great fascination in the ancillary things experienced during a day of deep sea fishing. The sea manifests an infinite variation of colour, texture and mood – at its best in the tropics where the translucent and gently undulating water spreads limitlessly before the boat's sparkling bow wave. The gentle lift and fall of the craft is mesmeric and you are soon cocooned in solitary consideration of some fine philosophical point while you wait for the adrenaline spike of a hit. You notice the whales, the turtles, the whirring flash of the flying fish and the distant clouds of birds, but in a sleepy, happy way, as though it is all not quite yet in the present tense.

The reverie is broken by the proximity of bait fish, rolling, bucking and chopping up the surface. Often there are layers of mayhem – finger-length anchovies shatter the surface and ignite in the tropical sun; dark-backed bonito porpoise through the foam in pursuit, while the big yellow-fin tuna soar into the melee with such intense muscularity you can almost hear the thud of their tails. Around the edges might lurk a prodigious cobia or a marlin looking for a chance at a more meaningful mouthful, and always there are sharks below or on their way, drawn by the vibrations of such extremity. Through this the captain steers the boat, the thrumming Rapala lures shivering their intense colours through the water and the big, plunging Kona Heads flashing out their message in squid-tongue. You are rapt with attention and anticipation. How can the fish resist? Often they don't and the reels sing out with the happiest sound in angling. A strike! We're in! Sashimi for supper!

Landing these hard, bright fish can be a brawny task, but if the tackle is appropriate there is little the fish can do. The drag on the reel is set so that the line releases well before its breaking strain is reached and as long as the hooks hold, the fish will eventually shudder to a standstill against the inexorable pressure of the disc drag and, if it runs far, a long length of sunken line bowing out through the sea like a monofilament parachute. Unless there are jagged reefs to dive into or the tackle and fish are grossly mismatched (in which case you can run out of line more quickly than the boat can follow the fish), the result is usually inevitable. The result is less inevitable when dealing with fish that jump from the water with a rattling savagery, somersaulting end to end in copious expenditure of energy. This is the potentially ruinous high-risk strategy adopted by marlin, sailfish, dorado, tarpon and others, where the fish goes all-in on a series of leaps that either result in immediate freedom or exhaust any real hope of escape. It often works and the lure is flung free, to the enduring frustration of the angler whose hopes had been raised.

Of course, it does not always go well. Sometimes there are bad days. The worst are when the weather forecast has been misread or is just simply wrong. Being caught in bad weather out at sea in a small boat is not fun. The chromed magnificence of the boat with its counter-rotating four-stroke engines, commodious lockers and carpeted deck that seemed so invincible when tied up at the dock, now feels insufficient in the grey heave of the looming sea. Cold spray whips over the bow in ejaculations of stinging pellets and nausea crimps the belly. You are reminded of your insignificance. The pitch and roll on the long beat back to harbour is literally bruising and nobody quarrels about wearing a life jacket – cold, wet, fishless and with puke all over your new boating shoes. What a way to spend £500.

The most heroic game fishing is from the shore. The guys who succeed at this all share a significant skill: they can cast. Whether you are talking about the man up to his waist in lucent water on a tropical sand flat wielding his fly rod for bonefish, or the leather-booted and salt-grimed rock and surf expert with his fourteen-foot carbon graphite smoke-pole and five-ounce white metal spoon, these people can get the lure to the fish. Everyone else doesn't really have a chance. There are many game fish that come within range of a good cast from the shore from time to time and some do so quite regularly, but the shore-based angler has the very grave difficulty of relative immobility and this severely curtails opportunity. And when, against all odds, a fish is finally hooked, the angler has the nightmare of shallow water obstructions to deal with, requiring a clear and experienced head and some measure of luck if the fish is to be landed. In my book, shore-caught game fish count at least twice what boat-caught game fish do.

From a culinary point of view game fish tend to share certain characteristics, such that one can draw a rough distinction between 'game fish', 'bottom feeders' and 'rock fish' based primarily on the texture of their flesh. In the case of game fish that texture is usually described as 'dry', by which it is meant that on cooking, the tightly muscled and densely fibred flesh separates into large flakes that are firm in the mouth and require chewing, notwithstanding that the fish may have high oil content. In another sense the word 'dry' also conveys the same meaning it sometimes carries in the context of wine, being something like 'astringent' or even 'abrasive', although game fish often have a most excellent flavour that balances this element. It's just that the flavour is not conveyed in a limpid or soft medium, as is often the case with bottom feeders like sole or plaice, and is heavy on umami elements rather than on the fragrant, honeyed background notes often encountered in crustaceans and in some rock fish.

The texture and flavour of game fish when very fresh lends itself particularly well to being eaten raw sashimi-style with soy and wasabi. Unlike the position with sushi, you can make acceptable sashimi yourself by simply cutting the fish into thin, bite-sized slices with a sharp knife. The less oily game fish are also very tasty served as a ceviche, a Central American marinated style that is less daunting to the uninitiated than the patent rawness of sashimi. The following is a good and extremely simple ceviche recipe, particularly suitable for Spanish mackerel (also known as barracouta):

BARRACOUTA CEVICHE

For the marinated fish:

500 g very fresh raw fillet of Spanish mackerel (barracouta)
Juice of 8 limes or 6 lemons
Zest of 1 lime or ½ a lemon
Small bunch chives, chopped
1 teaspoon nonpareil capers
Salt and black pepper

For the accompanying salad:

1 avocado
1 small red onion
1 red pepper

1 green pepper
1 chilli
Small bunch mint leaves
Olive oil

Ensure that there are no bones in the fish whatsoever. Remove any skin. Remove any red 'blood line' flesh. Slice the fish into 1 cm-thick slices and lay out on a large plate so that the slices do not cover each other. Pour lime/lemon juice over the fish slices and then turn the slices to ensure the fish is evenly covered with juice. Sprinkle the lime/lemon zest, the chopped chives and the capers over the fish. Cover and place in the refrigerator for twenty minutes.

While the fish marinates, small-dice all the salad ingredients, mix with a splash of good olive oil and a sprinkling of salt, then divide between the serving plates.

After twenty minutes serve the fish on top of the salad with a further sprinkling of salt and a good few twists of freshly ground black pepper. Very good with brown bread, butter and a cold beer.

A word of warning: parasites naturally occur in fish and some of these parasites can be harmful to humans if the fish is eaten raw. There are basically three types of parasites that can cause concern: nematodes (round worms), cestodes (tapeworms) and trematodes (flukes). Such parasites may be present in larval form and either cannot be seen with the naked eye at all or are so small as to be easily missed. It is a rare thing to be infected and there are medicinal cures for most of them, but some can make you really sick or can even kill you. I actually knew someone who was infected by worms of a very rare species that affects the brain. He went slowly mad over several years and was persistently misdiagnosed by a series of doctors until a specialist in tropical medicine reviewed a scan and recognised the minute but tell-tale corridors through his brain created by these worms. There was nothing anyone could do for him and he died shortly thereafter. All these parasites are killed by thorough cooking (internal temperature of 63°C for a minimum of fifteen seconds) or by freezing to a temperature of -20°C for seven days (which is colder than many domestic freezers can manage, note). In some countries fresh fish must be frozen before commercial use in raw preparations and although safer, this must affect the flavour and texture of things like sushi, sashimi and ceviche.

Game fish are also excellent cooked over coals on a barbecue after marinating for a while in an appropriate marinade. The marinade can be successfully made from a wide range of ingredients depending upon the effect you wish to create, and full licence to the barbecue chef's creativity can be granted because game fish is a forgiving medium suitable for flights of fancy. My favourite marinade for game fish, particularly marlin, is as follows:

MARLIN MARINADE

(For 1 kg of marlin)
300 ml soy sauce
Juice and zest of 1 lime
1 tablespoon grated fresh ginger
1 tablespoon grated fresh garlic
1 tablespoon mild curry powder
1 teaspoon sweet paprika
4 tablespoons honey or syrup
25 ml cider or rice vinegar

Mix the marinade ingredients in a bowl. Ensure the honey/syrup has dissolved fully. Add the fish and cover. Place in a refrigerator for a minimum of one hour, preferably overnight.

GUINEAFOWL

The guineafowl is well known in both Europe and America as a domestic fowl, sharing farmyards with chickens and being available for sale in supermarkets. It was first domesticated several thousand years ago and was known in ancient Egypt and in both classical Greece and Rome. The Romans were probably responsible for its initial distribution across Europe as a poultry species and it spread from there to America in the early sixteenth century. At the same time, turkeys were exported to Europe from the New World and a great confusion arose in the minds of the general public as to which bird was which. Interestingly, some think that when reference is made to turkeys in the works of William Shakespeare[22], what Shakespeare meant was guineafowl. These domestic birds are as far away from wild guineafowl as the chicken is from the red jungle fowl. An intensively reared supermarket guineafowl tastes like a vaguely gamey chicken, but lacks the succulent golden fat of the chicken on the one hand and the uniquely delicious flavour of the wild guineafowl on the other – an unhappy compromise in a bird that seems uncomfortably domesticated.

There are good, organic, free-range, domestic guineafowl available, however, and as with many foods, the best come from

22   *Henry V* [V, 1]; *Twelfth Night* [II, 5]; *Henry IV, Part 1* [II, 1].

France. These are well worth eating and have a unique flavour, as well as a vastly increased fat content when compared to the wild variety, although it is far short of the fat content of a chicken. There is something about this flavour that always reminds me of Mozambique. During colonial times the Portuguese settlers in Mozambique brought with them a laid-back, continental attitude that permitted a degree of casual decadence unthinkable in Calvinistic, deeply conservative South Africa. They even had strip clubs in the big towns and every shop sold wine and beer and rough local cigarettes, even to fourteen-year-old holidaymakers. They also had very exotic foods – a melange of continental European, local African, Arab[23] and Goanese[24] influences. The most memorable of these was 'peri-peri', which I have referred to in some earlier chapters and which is a very spicy sauce made from a special variety of African bird's eye chilli, paprika, lemon juice, olive oil, garlic and numerous other sundry additions depending upon the traditions and preferences of the maker. No two peri-peri sauces were (or are) exactly the same and fierce rivalry existed between housewives and restaurants as to whose peri-peri was best. Peri-peri is primarily used with prawns and with chicken, both of these being basted with the sauce whilst being grilled over charcoal, although it is also used to good effect in certain beef stew recipes and with chicken livers. The result is often spectacular and every restaurant or eating establishment in the entire country served it. You could not get far enough off the beaten track so as to be unable to find a peri-peri meal. Even when travelling through the God-forsaken coastal plain on the way to the beach (on a 400-mile road in bad repair, dull grey

---

23 Arab traders had been doing business in Mozambique for at least 1000 years before the Portuguese conquest of the area in the fourteenth century and continued doing business for several centuries thereafter.

24 The state of Goa on the Indian coast was also a Portuguese colony for centuries and many Goanese people immigrated to Mozambique as labourers, soldiers and administrators over a period of 450 years.

scrub bush, temperature 40°C, one hundred percent humidity, malaria a virtual certainty if you had forgotten to take your pills), you would come upon some landmark hundreds of miles from anywhere, a bridge say, and there would be a dilapidated and tiny general store with a scattering of scruffy tables and chairs outside under a covering or convenient thorn tree. If you stopped for a break or maybe a cold beer[25], the Portuguese proprietor and his shy, usually African, wife (or wives) would greet you enthusiastically and try to talk you into a peri-peri chicken meal. It was usually worth succumbing to this and, taking the cold beers, we would sit down in the dusty shade. What invariably happened next was a crowd of coffee-coloured children hurtling around the corner in pursuit of a gaggle of scrawny but extremely athletic bush chickens. Talk about free-range. Man, those chickens could run. But then, so could those children – free-range children! The chase would disappear out of sight into the bush accompanied by continuous shouting and shrieking, punctuated now and then by a strangled squawk as some unfortunate chicken zigged when it should have zagged. This could go on for over an hour if the party was a large one requiring many chickens, but eventually the children would emerge from the bush carrying their limp and bedraggled victims, headless necks dripping blood in long splashes down thin brown legs.

At least another hour would pass before plates of peri-peri chicken were triumphantly deposited onto the tables, accompanied always by mounds of deep-fried potato chips. Grilled to a crisp brown, the peri-peri sauce mingles and caramelises with the skin of the chicken. Golden juice and olive

---

25 In that climate and under those conditions, everybody over the age of twelve drank beer. Those under twelve drank bottled *limonada*. It was one or the other because there was no bottled water and you cannot drink wine if the temperature is 40°C. Local sources of water were usually infected with cholera or typhoid or both.

oil, flecked red with crushed spices, pools in the plates and soaks into the potato chips. When you tear into the chicken the stark white flesh is dry and tough and stringy, but it is delicious and has a particular flavour in combination with the peri-peri that you just cannot duplicate with any shop-bought chicken, no matter how good or bad its quality or how free range it might or might not be. What does approximate this flavour though is a good, free-range domestic guineafowl. I do not know why, but I suspect it has to do with the fat content of a domestic guineafowl being similar to that of a scrawny bush chicken. It might also be that domestic guineafowl are slower growing than chickens and are thus older when slaughtered. Even the biggest of commercially produced free-range chickens is only about fourteen weeks old when killed and the average supermarket chicken is only about six weeks old. Those Mozambique bush chickens were probably several years old. Whatever the reason for the similarity, it is well worth trying:

BARBECUED PERI-PERI GUINEAFOWL

Cut the guineafowl into quarters. Place the quarters into a dish and squeeze the juice of two lemons over them. Sprinkle with salt and pepper and a little dried thyme, cover and leave in the refrigerator for an hour or so. Then liberally baste the pieces with peri-peri sauce and leave to stand out of the refrigerator for thirty minutes. If you can get a bottle of genuine Mozambique or South African peri-peri[26] sauce, this will be the best. You can sometimes

---

26 Many Portuguese people moved to South Africa from Mozambique during the civil war and established a large community in Johannesburg. Peri-peri subsequently became very popular in South Africa in every community, and peri-peri, both as a dried spice powder and as a prepared liquid sauce, is commercially produced there. Although not as good as the genuine article in Mozambique, some of these commercial preparations are a close approximation.

get it in the speciality South African shops that have sprung up in both the UK and the USA. If you cannot get it, then you will have to make your own:

PERI-PERI SAUCE

A handful of dried bird's eye chillies (how many depends on how hot you like the sauce), crushed
1 tablespoon ground paprika
1 onion, finely grated
2 cloves fresh garlic, finely grated
Juice of 1 lemon
100 ml olive oil
50 g butter, cut into 6 pieces
Salt

Heat up the olive oil in a saucepan. Add the grated onion and fry for two minutes. Add the grated garlic, crushed chillies and paprika and fry for a further minute. Add the lemon juice and immediately remove from the heat. Add the butter piece by piece, stirring into the sauce as it melts. Add salt to taste. Reheat the sauce only if necessary and then very gently. Too much heat after the butter has been added causes the butter to separate and most of the flavour gets trapped in the milk solids. The sauce is then difficult to use and will not re-emulsify regardless of what you do.

Grill the guineafowl on a charcoal barbecue, basting liberally with the sauce now and then. Be careful. The oil and fat in the sauce is explosive if the coals are too hot (or the grill is positioned too low) and the guineafowl will soon burn and blacken. What you are looking for is a crisp golden finish over thoroughly cooked, slightly dry meat. This takes constant attention and almost continuous turning of the guineafowl pieces. Save some of the sauce for the very end and give the pieces *a final baste after they have come off the grill. For authenticity, serve this with chips and the Sub-Saharan African version of a Portuguese-style green salad (lettuce, tomato, mild white onion rings, black olives) dressed with olive oil and white spirit vinegar. There is nothing more suitable, or traditional, than a slightly effervescent Portuguese Vinho Verde to wash down this meal, but be careful of the hangover if you overdo it. Lager beer is also very good.*

Wild guineafowl of several species inhabit almost all of Africa and are often very numerous, due to their compatibility with human agriculture. They are great crop raiders and thrive anywhere that grain crops are grown. In the bush areas guineafowl also flourish and small flocks of them are found in almost all types of terrain. From the shooting point of view, they occupy the same place in Africa that the pheasant does in Europe, being the numerous and large game bird most often pursued. However, unlike the pheasant in Europe, wild guineafowl are never reared in captivity, are always genuinely wild and are not generally driven by beaters over waiting guns, although circumstances sometimes permit a drive.

Usually guineafowl must be pursued and outmanoeuvred. A flock is sighted on a distant hillside. Through the bush the guns stride, brushing through the scrub and ignoring the thorn scratches. By the time the guns get to the hill the birds have moved. There they are – about a hundred yards ahead, dark bodies weaving through the thin cover, heads bobbing above the grass. The guns pick up the pace. So do the birds. Stumbling and sweating across the broken ground, the guns do their best to catch up. Everyone is filled with total excitement and increasing anxiety – a well-known phenomenon in guineafowl shooting this; 'guinea fever'[27] it is called – and it afflicts some men, most boys and all dogs. Onwards charge the guns. Now the birds seem to be getting fewer as they go along. Finally, the guns are brought to a halt by a *donga* (small ravine) filled with a fierce tangle of bush. No birds. They have simply disappeared. Guineafowl do this. Their primary defence mechanism is to run away and then hide and they are very good at both. What they do when alarmed is all set off together as a flock and if they are pursued, individuals peel off now and then along the way and hide in small bushes or grass tussocks as the opportunity arises. The main flock then acts as a decoy, leading the predator onward and past the hidden members. In this way the flock gets smaller and smaller as the race progresses until finally you are chasing three birds out of an original forty or fifty. The last three usually manage to disappear too and you are left chasing nothing, which makes you feel frustrated and a little stupid. Of course this only happens when the ground cover is thin enough to permit long-distance running by a bird the size of a lean chicken. In most bush areas it is plenty thin enough. On the other hand, if the cover is thick, then the guineafowl tend to get a bit thick too. They have a strange faith that if they cannot see you then you cannot be there. So if they run into very thick grass, for example,

---

27 'There is just something about a large flock of guineafowl that produces an over-excited craziness in the hunter. Perhaps it is the large number of birds, for guineafowl are found in flocks of anything from twenty to a hundred or so birds. Certainly, this is what defeats the dogs. Several dozen guineafowl criss-crossing one another and running about produce the nasal equivalent of a cacophony for a dog. He does not know which scent to follow, is continually sidetracked by new scent and ends up getting absolutely and totally confused. Add to this the visual temptation of tantalising glimpses of an escaping quarry running hard through the grass and what you get is a dog that completely loses the plot. Off he goes, foaming at the mouth and yipping hysterically, usually followed by a red-faced owner, also foaming and yipping and occasionally blowing meaningless blasts on his training whistle. Chaos, but fun.

they tend to just sit in it and then it is quite simple to get close to them, whereupon they flush like a proper game bird and often get shot. The trick to guineafowl shooting, indeed its greatest pleasure, is that a plan has to be made by the participants to get the guineafowl into shootable terrain or position. This is true whether you are two or twenty participants and the plans are extremely *ad hoc*, infinitely entertaining and have only a speculative chance of success, which is very satisfying when it comes off.

As is clear from the above, wild guineafowl are running-type birds. They seem to feel the same way aviophobics do about flying: it is something you do only as a last resort. This affects their edibility in an obvious way: the legs and thighs are tough as hell, but the breasts are succulent and tender. More than once when reading European cookbooks, I have encountered the comment that wild guineafowl are inedible. The authors must have been eating the legs because the breasts are about the most edible thing you can lay your hands on in the bush. I know people who do not really shoot at all, who actually disapprove of the activity, but who nevertheless blast away at the guineafowl, salivating all the way.

I have cooked hundreds and hundreds of wild guineafowl in many dozens of different ways. In fact, wild guineafowl breasts can be used as a substitute for chicken in any of the thousands of chicken recipes with good result. But to do this is to cheat yourself out of one of life's uniquely subtle and delicious flavours. After all that experimentation over a period of forty years, I now cook wild guineafowl breasts in only one very simple way:

CRUMBED BREASTS OF GUINEAFOWL

(Serves 2, if you are lucky. Easily eaten by 1.)
Breasts of 1 wild guineafowl

50 g white flour
Two generous handfuls of freshly toasted white breadcrumbs
100 g ghee[28]
Salt
Freshly (and finely) ground black pepper
1 egg
1 lemon

Give the guineafowl breasts a few thumps with a meat mallet to flatten them out a bit. Drench the breasts in the flour. Beat the egg and then dip the breasts in it. Put the breadcrumbs in a large plastic bag together with the salt and pepper. Put the egged breasts into the plastic bag, close and shake vigorously until the breasts are well covered with breadcrumbs. Remove from the bag and place them on a covered plate in the refrigerator for two to three hours.

Heat the ghee in a frying pan. Get it to a good hot temperature. Fry the breasts in the ghee until the breadcrumbs are golden brown and the meat is cooked through. This does not take long. Serve immediately with a squeeze of lemon juice. The flavour is unique and very addictive.

---

28   Ghee is the Indian form of clarified butter and is often made from buffalo butter. Ordinary fresh and unsalted cow's butter gives a better result. It is very simple to make. Take 500 g of unsalted butter and heat it in a saucepan. The butter melts and then boils. The water content in the butter separates and boils off as steam. Simultaneously the milk proteins also separate from the clear butterfat. The butterfat rises to the top and the solid milk proteins precipitate to the bottom of the saucepan. It is ready when all the water has boiled away and no more steam comes off. Then you had better be quick because the milk solids burn in a flash at this stage. Take the saucepan off the heat and put it in a sink of cold water to stop the cooking process. Once it has cooled a little, carefully pour the butterfat off the top into a container – this is the ghee. Discard the milk solids. Ghee is wonderful stuff. It keeps for months even if not refrigerated and can be heated to very high temperatures without burning. It gives a pleasant, vaguely caramel flavour to anything cooked in it.

So what do you do with all the leftover legs and thighs? Unfortunately, they are beyond redemption. I use them to make game bird stock, for which purpose they are fine. If mixed with a whole lot of other things, they also make reasonable soup.

HARE

The European brown hare is one of the great game animals from a culinary point of view. It has delicious meat and in some places is regarded as a sumptuous treat suitable for the most special of occasions. Particularly in the rural regions of France, Italy and Greece, procuring a hare is in itself a special occasion, resulting in widespread excitement throughout the village and considerable manoeuvring for an invitation to lunch. This is not least because in those places there are roughly three hunters to every hare and even the most dedicated of hunters does not expect to get more than one or two in the course of a whole year.

In Britain there are still plenty of hares, to the point that in some areas they are considered almost an agricultural pest. They are also the subject of the ancient sport of hare coursing, an activity that is now illegal in Britain following the Hunting Act of 2004. Not that the law has completely eliminated hare coursing. A certain sector of society, recognisable by multifarious tattoos, shaved heads and a penchant for the companionship of pit bull terriers, still illegally engages in hare coursing as a gambling blood sport over the weekends, where 'lurchers' (usually border collie/greyhound cross-breeds) competitively pursue hares over someone else's land. Indeed, the participants in this activity can be so anti-social and threatening that some landowners attempt to exterminate hares on their land simply to avoid ever having to confront these aggressive criminals[29]. Exterminating a species to prevent it being poached seems profoundly weird, but suppose the Hell's Angels arrived at your house every Saturday, parked their motorcycles all over your lawn and proceeded to hunt down the goldfish in your pond with pet sharks. Bet it wouldn't take you long to remove the goldfish and concrete over the pond!

It always strikes me as odd that there should be such a difference in the appreciation of the culinary merits of a game animal in different places. In Britain very few people actually ever eat hare at all (which is why there are plenty of hares) and when they do, they often eat it after it has been hung for quite some time, which is the traditional approach. If you hang a hare, ungutted, for a week or more it becomes very gamey and although some people really like it that way and it will be tender, it will be too strong for most. There is, in my view, no need to hang a hare at all, which is the Mediterranean, warm climate, approach. I like the clean, subtle flavour of fresh hare and just accept that some parts of the animal are too tough to roast or pan fry successfully. However, the saddle of a prime, reasonably young hare shot in October or November has tender meat that rivals the finest fillet of venison and it should be treated in exactly the same way, as follows:

DEBONED SADDLE OF HARE

(Serves 2)
One deboned saddle of hare, producing two slim steaks each
weighing around 100 g
High-quality oil (I like extra virgin olive)
Salt and pepper

---

29 This is a terrible indictment of the authorities in the UK, who seem powerless in the face of low-level theft of game and fish all over the place.

The simplest of all game meals to prepare. Rub oil all over the steaks. Generously coat with salt. Fry on a very hot cast iron griddle or in a frying pan until medium-rare – about two minutes on each side. Sprinkle with freshly ground black pepper, then cover and rest the meat for ten minutes. Serve with fried mushrooms and a bottle of Barolo. It is completely stunning. A 100 g steak may not seem like much, but it is in fact a completely satisfactory amount of hare for one adult. For some reason, hare is very filling – the only thing I know that is more filling than hare is zebra. The rest of the hare should be treated in accordance with the second recipe below.

The above recipe is only suitable for a hare that has been cleanly shot. Hares are often quarry for shotgunners who take snapshots at them when they bolt out from their 'forms', as their daytime sleeping nests are called. This can result in a hare that has been peppered with shot and which leaks intestinal fluids onto the saddle meat, thereby tainting it. From a culinary point of view, it is much better to hunt a hare with a rifle and aim for the head. Air rifle hunters out after rabbits are often tempted by hares, which seem gigantic in comparison to a rabbit and which excite them in much the same way that an eland or a moose excites a venison hunter. Although an air rifle of the sort usually used for rabbits[30] is quite capable of killing a hare with a neck shot or a heart shot at twenty-five yards, this cannot be recommended, even for expert marksmen. The temptation to have a go at forty or even fifty yards is overwhelming and at those ranges such an air rifle is inadequate. The better rifle for hares is the .22 rimfire or one of the very powerful air rifles that require a firearms licence.

In Britain 'jugged hare' is the iconic game dish that many have heard of but virtually nobody has tried. The term 'jugged' is

---

30 Rabbits in Britain are usually hunted with an air rifle having a muzzle energy of less than twelve foot-pounds, for which no firearms licence is required, see page 238 below.

medieval speak for 'stewed' and originally referred to a cooking method where a whole hare cut into pieces was placed in an earthenware 'jug' or container that was then placed in a basin of water before being put in the oven. This is simply a slow cooking method, a bit like the modern *sous vide* method using a water bath. A signal feature of jugged hare (and of the French equivalent *civet de lièvre*) is the use of the hare's blood. Hares have plenty of thick, almost granular, dark ruby blood and this is usually stirred into the gravy as a considerable enrichment just before serving or may even be served separately and everything is washed down with a large glass of port. This has got to be one of the richest, most pungent and most indigestible meals there is, particularly if the hare is well hung. Personally, I prefer the Greek approach of stewing a hare with onions in a *stifado* and in particular like the Cretan version that uses the oxidised and sherry-like local wine of the western mountains. As that wine is impossible to get anywhere but in Western Crete, I substitute fino sherry in the following recipe:

HARE STIFADO

(Serves 4)
A whole fresh hare, minus the saddle steaks, jointed

For the marinade:
500 ml dry fino sherry
1 large onion, sliced
4 cloves garlic, sliced
5 bay leaves
2 teaspoons salted Greek capers
1 tablespoon black peppercorns

For the stifado:
250 ml dry fino sherry
150 ml good olive oil

350 ml passata
1 large onion, chopped
20 small or 10 large shallots, peeled
4 cloves garlic, sliced
5 bay leaves
2 heaped teaspoons salted Greek capers
1 teaspoon dried Cretan oregano
1 teaspoon dried thyme
Salt and freshly ground black pepper

First, joint the hare and roughly cut the saddle bones into three large pieces (the saddle meat will undoubtedly have been removed and eaten as steak). Place the hare and all the marinade ingredients into a bowl, ensuring that the hare is covered by the liquid. If 500 ml of sherry is not enough, use a bit more or top up with a little water. Marinate for around twelve hours, stirring things up now and then.

Remove the meat from the marinade. At this point either reserve the marinade and use its ingredients in the stifado, or you can discard the marinade and use fresh ingredients. I prefer to use fresh ingredients as specified above because I think you get a more intense and clearer flavour.

Heat the olive oil in a large cast iron casserole. Brown the hare pieces and remove. Fry the chopped onion in the casserole until it is soft and just starting to turn golden. Return the hare to the casserole and add the capers, dried herbs, bay leaves and sherry. Place a sheet of foil over the casserole and then put on the lid (the foil is for a tighter fit). Place in an oven at 180°C for one hour so that the hare pot-roasts. Do not open the lid to check during the roasting time, just have faith.

After one hour, remove the casserole from the oven. At this point I like to take the hare out of the pot, cut or pick all the meat from the bones and discard the bones. In the traditional Greek hare stifado, the bones would be retained. Return the hare meat to *the casserole and add the passata, shallots, garlic, salt and pepper. Replace the foil and the lid and return to the oven at a reduced temperature of 160ºC.*

Cook for at least another two hours, until the hare is tender, the gravy thickened and the shallots are soft. You can check now and then during this second stage of cooking to make sure all is going well. If things seem to be getting a bit dry, add some more sherry.

This is a really tasty dish and in Crete it would be served with chips. Elsewhere in Greece it would be rice. Personally, I prefer it with good Italian polenta into which a handful of grated cheddar cheese and a large dollop of butter have been melted. It is a great opportunity for a chilled bottle of very good Manzanilla or, if you are in Western Crete, a jug of that local mountain wine which one buys directly from the barrel.

KUDU

The kudu was the unicorn of my youth – a grey ghost of an antelope, beautiful, with secretive habits that easily turn it into a local myth rather than a real flesh and blood animal, or so it seems. The bulls are magnificent, with high curling horns and shaggy throat on a large, but delicate-looking frame. The cows are smaller, slimmer, with huge ears that can hear the faintest whisper of a boot against the dry winter grass at 200 paces. Kudu are amongst the spookiest of all antelope and hunting one successfully requires a high level of hunting skill. As a result, they are often the last antelope remaining on farms in developing agricultural areas in Sub-Saharan Africa, notwithstanding their relatively large size. Kudu thus represent pretty much the most advanced example of the integrated defence system used by antelope, consisting of a triumvirate of senses working in unison. Primary among these defensive senses is the sense of smell. As humans with very limited olfactory abilities, it is difficult to grasp how advanced this sense is in antelope (and in many other creatures). It is more like our sense of sight in many ways, revealing huge quantities of biological information in vast detail up close and detecting basic, but immensely valuable, facts at a distance from a few sparse molecules drifting on the breeze. To hunt antelope effectively the hunter must understand that scent molecules slew off the human body in a constant cloud that is then carried downwind in an ever expanding cone that allows detection at a distance of at least a mile, probably more. It is therefore imperative to hunt 'into the wind' or at the very least, across the wind so that there is a chance of getting within range of the antelope before being scented. A light breeze suits antelope the best. Under these conditions the breeze wafts a continuous smorgasbord of aromas towards them such that they can identify with considerable accuracy what is happening upwind and can accordingly concentrate on visually checking what might be approaching from downwind. This all changes if they smell a predator approaching from upwind, which they can discern from the increase in concentration of molecules reaching them from the relevant direction. They will then look and listen in that direction, seeking confirmation of what their noses are telling them. Antelope in areas relatively heavily populated by humans do not immediately run away upon scenting a human. To do so would result in continuous running with no time to eat or sleep. But, if a human is smelt and the smell gets stronger, indicating an approach, antelope might very well run or move away before confirming that approach by sight, particularly if there has been intensive hunting in the area, and they will definitely bolt at the slightest movement or sound indicating an uncomfortable proximity of a human.

Antelope also have very different sight to that experienced by humans. They have dichromatic vision and thus see the world in varying shades of grey with very limited, if any, colour vision. The positioning and structure of an antelope's eye differs radically from that of a human with the effect that antelope see a more diffuse, but almost 360-degree, picture in which movement is discerned far more readily than detail and which is particularly effective in low light conditions. This makes it very difficult to sneak up on antelope and particularly difficult to sneak up on those that hang out in herds or family groups because there is always one with its head up looking in your direction. Thus even if you approach from downwind and the antelope do not smell you at all, there is an excellent chance of being seen first and before you can get into a position to get off a shot. This is particularly true if your movements are hurried and upright. Bipedal humans have a very distinctive motion with their relatively lanky frames and scissor-like leg movement. It is thus necessary to keep movement slow and low and crawl along on all fours if the cover is thin or non-existent. This business about movement cannot be overemphasised. On a number of occasions I have stood or sat out in the open and had both antelope and deer that were initially out of sight wander right up to me because I was downwind and kept completely still. It seemed I was for all practical purposes invisible to them as long as I didn't move.

Hearing is also important to antelope, particularly those that spend most of their time in thick bush where lines of sight are limited. These antelope, which include kudu, have relatively large ears to enable them to funnel sound more effectively and they can hear things from a remarkably long way off. Depending on its identity, sound on its own is not necessarily enough to cause antelope to flee. The bush is a noisy place, with many creatures crashing and snapping their way through the undergrowth in the course of their daily activities. Such natural sounds do not generally alarm, more particularly because the antelope's main cause for concern is usually big cats and they are lethally silent most of the time. However, noise of any sort will focus attention and, of course, if the sound is identifiably human or is that of the human's favourite compatriot in the chase, the dog, then the game will instantly be up and the antelope will hurriedly depart for some neighbouring country. Nothing is more disruptive or alarming in the bush than the sound of a human voice and the rule when hunting is no talking at all or at most a low whisper. Other particularly unnatural sounds that always alarm animals within earshot are the distinctively metallic slither of a rifle bolt and the piercing snick of a safety catch being released.

This exceptionally effective defence system with its three overlapping senses corroborating one another is very difficult for the hunter to overcome in benign conditions and is particularly difficult in conditions of inconsistent or swirling wind, for obvious reasons. Interestingly, strong wind is capable of more or less defeating the system entirely on its own. In a strong wind scent molecules are dispersed widely and quickly so that even a predator approaching from upwind might escape detection; the branches of trees and bushes thrash about violently concealing any movement and the roar of the gale effectively drowns out any suspicious sounds. Consequently, antelope are very 'jumpy' in a strong wind and often compensate for the sensory loss by continually running from place to place in a state of intense paranoia.

I started hunting on jaunts away from boarding school with farming schoolmates. To start with, my mates and I had little appreciation of the sophistication of antelope defence systems and nobody really took the time to teach us anything. Once we had graduated beyond the doves-and-pigeons-with-air-rifles stage and were allowed about the farm with powerful weapons like twelve-bore shotguns, it was not long before we were instructed to try and shoot something bigger for staff rations or for biltong. For this purpose we were usually handed a .303 rifle with open sights and a handful of cartridges. These .303 rifles were invariably army surplus Lee-Enfields, which were sold off to the public for nominal sums when the 7.62 mm Fabrique Nationale assault rifles were introduced in the 1960s. They were excellent, accurate bolt-action rifles with ten-round magazines and peep sights providing for ranges up to 300 yards. Under bush conditions, though, the absence of magnification meant that the effective range was limited to a hundred yards at the very most, simply because at longer ranges unseen sticks and twigs always seemed to get in the way and bullet deflection was a major problem. Bullet placement was also a problem because no matter how good your eyesight and how slender the front sight, at ranges beyond eighty yards or so with open sights you are effectively aiming at the front end of the animal in a general way rather than at some definitely lethal spot, like just behind the shoulder. With practice you can get quite effective because you develop a feeling for where the bullet will go that transcends the limitations of unassisted vision, but the telescopic sight is a great and merciful invention that has much enhanced accuracy for the average hunter[31].

Our initial efforts at antelope hunting were clumsy to say the least and we felt plagued by ill fortune. There is a paragraph in *Jock of the Bushveld* that admirably captures the frustrating experience of being a novice hunter blundering ignorantly about the bush failing to see, let alone shoot, any antelope:

'Game there was in plenty, no doubt, but it did not come my way. Days went by with, once or twice, the sight of some small buck just as it disappeared, and many times the noise of something in the bush, or the sound of galloping feet. Others brought their contributions to the pot daily, and there seemed no reason in the world why I alone should fail – no reason except sheer bad luck! It is difficult to believe you have made mistakes when you do not know enough to recognise them, and have no idea of the extent of your own ignorance; and then bad luck is such an easy and such a flattering explanation!...'[32]

First success came from chance encounters with grassland species. Often when bird shooting with shotguns for francolin

---

31 For several decades in the mid-twentieth century the public felt quite strongly that hunting with telescopic sights was 'unsporting' and gave the animal no chance of escape. What telescopic sights do is dramatically reduce the number of wounded animals and so they are an unqualified improvement, regardless of 'sporting' considerations.

32 *Jock of the Bushveld* by Sir Percy Fitzpatrick, first published in 1922 and in print ever since. Extract is at page 24 of the first edition.

we would walk quietly and slowly through open, grassy areas and would, by chance, flush steenbok or oribi, literally from underfoot. We learned that if you covered these areas by approaching from downwind, these little knee-high antelope would often elect to lie hidden in the grass just like a game bird rather than instantly fleeing. If you then slowly and methodically worked out the cover like a spaniel, their nerve would sometimes fail and they would streak away. We took to loading SSG buckshot into the choke barrels of our double-barrelled shotguns and bowling these little fellows over on the run, much like a European hunter bowls over a hare. But success with the rifle continued to elude us for some time. Even though we came to grasp the concept of scent and wind direction, what let us down was the way we moved through the bush – much too fast and with the impetuosity of youth. This would lead to what seemed like tantalisingly close encounters with impala, wildebeest, hartebeest and so on, but always with the animals alarmed and snorting and moving away at great pace. It was not until we had mastered the art of the slow approach and the crawling stalk that we began to enjoy the odd success now and then. In truth, you cannot move too slowly through the bush and the slower you go, the more you see and the less you are seen, but that is a hard lesson for a teenager.

Throughout this formative stage of our development as hunters, the kudu represented a sort of Holy Grail to us. There were plenty of kudu on the farms we hunted, but you rarely saw one during daylight hours. They held to the broken ground, the densely forested ravines and the most inaccessible corners of the farm where hunting them was spectacularly difficult. Kudu have an ability to remain absolutely motionless and this, coupled to the striped grey camouflage of its coat, renders it practically invisible in dense bush. Thus, no matter how carefully downwind and slow your approach, the kudu almost always sees you or hears you before you see it and then, with a loud dog-like bark of alarm, plunges silently into the twisted confusion of grey branches and disappears. Eight times out of ten you do not see the kudu at all and the only indication that it was ever there is the echoing alarm bark. Sometimes though, if your eyesight is well attuned to the bush and you are accustomed to seeing parts of an animal rather than the whole thing, you might see the kudu just as it sees you and in the three or four seconds that might pass before the kudu resolves to leap into invisibility, you have the chance of a shot. Needless to say, until your nerves are steadied by experience and your reflexes honed by practice, the prospect of you pulling that shot off are remote.

Notwithstanding weeks and weeks of effort, I never managed to shoot a kudu during my school days. I came close on several occasions and a couple of my school friends succeeded, but I never managed to aim and fire the rifle in the time allowed by the kudu. I shot several kudu later in my life, but by then the intensity of my desire had faded somewhat and the joy of success was tempered by regret that a creature so magnificent and ethereal should have died by my hand.

Kudu are reasonably good to eat in a general sort of way, with a fillet of kudu being superior to the fillet of most other medium- or large-size antelope. Where kudu really come into their own, in a culinary sense, is in the making of biltong. In my view, and in the view of many biltong aficionados, there is no finer biltong than kudu biltong. Biltong is wind-dried meat and is the universally popular savoury snack of Sub-Saharan Africa. Its origins are uncertain and everybody likes to claim a hand in its development because it is very well liked by all sectors of the community. It seems unlikely that the original San inhabitants of Southern Africa dried meat in any great quantity or at all, bearing in mind their predominantly mobile lifestyle and physical capability of consuming all meat available in one sitting, but everyone else most certainly did. The indigenous tribes invading from the north were known to dry the meat of both game and cattle and the European settlers and their slaves arriving at the Cape were armed with all the knowledge of meat preservation developed in their Dutch, French and Malay homelands. It is thus no surprise that biltong seems to be an amalgam of traditions, with the meat being semi-pickled in vinegar and dusted with salt and spices before being wind-dried (as opposed to sun-dried), something originally done by hanging the strips on thorn trees in the shade during the bushveld winter, when the air is so dry that it desiccates your lips into painful cracks in less than half a day. Whilst I am something of a traditionalist when it comes to biltong and prefer, if possible, my biltong made outdoors in the old style because I think it gains some subtle additional flavour, most biltong is now made commercially in artificial environments specifically set up for its manufacture. On a smaller scale, there are also many 'biltong makers'[33] now for sale to facilitate biltong making at home, regardless of where home is. Biltong has spread all over the world with the South African diaspora of recent years and can now be found almost everywhere.

The following is a traditional biltong recipe. These days one finds all sorts of things added to biltong to increase or vary its flavour, in particular barbecue spices and chilli in various forms. This is fine if we are talking about standard beef biltong. However, to add any of these things to kudu biltong would be a tragedy and would probably destroy the unique flavour. Almost any meat, other than pork, can be made into acceptable biltong, including chicken and the meat of game birds.

---

33 Biltong makers can be as simple as a wooden box with a light bulb to dry out the air. They can also be very sophisticated cabinets with built-in fans, electrical elements, hygrometers and thermostats.

TRADITIONAL BILTONG

5 kg meat
300 ml vinegar (red wine or malt)
400 g coarse salt
250 g brown sugar
2 tablespoons bicarbonate of soda
250 g coriander seeds, crushed
2 tablespoons black peppercorns, cracked

Cut the meat into strips between one and three inches wide and an inch or so thick; cut **with** the normal grain of the meat.

Dip each strip into the vinegar and then layer in a bowl. Reserve what remains of the vinegar. Cover the bowl and leave for thirty minutes.

Mix the salt, sugar and bicarbonate of soda. Remove the meat from the bowl and cover each strip thoroughly with the mixture. Once again layer the strips into a bowl, sprinkling a covering of the mixture over each layer so that the meat is effectively buried in the salt/sugar/bicarb. Cover and leave in a refrigerator for three to nine hours, depending on the thickness of the strips.

Mix the crushed coriander seeds and black pepper.

Remove the meat from the refrigerator and, using the reserved vinegar, wipe down each strip to completely remove all of the salt/sugar/bicarb mixture. This step is crucial otherwise the biltong will be excessively salty.

Cover the strips with the pepper and coriander mix. This can be achieved conveniently by putting the mix into a large plastic bag, adding the strips a few at a time and then shaking and massaging the meat in the bag. This gets the spices to imbed into the meat somewhat.

Hang the strips in a biltong maker (or on galvanised iron hooks outdoors in a fly-proof cage, if you are in the bushveld in winter) for between three and twenty days, depending on how dry

you prefer your biltong. Beef biltong is good when quite young and
pink. Kudu biltong is best when totally dry and hard.

I have noticed that British and French people, generally speaking, do not much warm to biltong, particularly if they come to it later in life and not as a child. They can taste a certain background putrification they say, which is undetectable to a Southern African person. Southern Africans enjoy biltong from a very young age. Indeed, a stick of dry biltong is thought to be an excellent remedy for a teething child and you see little toddlers tottering around gumming away on dry sticks of biltong with every evidence of enjoyment. If you think about this in the context of inflamed gums and salt in wounds it is little surprise that Southern Africans enjoy a certain culinary robustness in later life, much like the robustness engendered on the iron-hard rugby fields by playing junior school rugby barefoot on frosty mornings. With apologies to my English friends who I know hate this story, I must tell you about the occasion upon which I was seated beside an indignant and obstreperous lady during a dinner given at a ruinously expensive English private school. Upon discovering that I recently hailed from South Africa, she immediately attacked me about the roughness and barbarity of South African school children. Apparently, a rugby team from the English school had travelled to South Africa on tour and after some days of acclimatisation, had taken to the field against the host school for the first match. After just twenty minutes, so many of the visiting English players had been injured and had been carried from the field that there were insufficient players left to continue the match. In fact, so severe were the injuries and consequent fearful shock amongst the players that the tour had to be abandoned – making it probably the shortest rugby tour in history. I tried to look contrite about this, but I fear I may not have succeeded.

By contrast, Italian and Spanish people take to biltong very readily. This probably has something to do with the widespread consumption of dry-cured hams in those countries. After all, a *jamón Ibericó* or *prosciutto di Parma* is nothing more than a salt-cured, air-dried chunk of meat, although of course with much greater subtlety and finesse than can ever be achieved in biltong.

LOCUSTS

The invitation to lunch was a privilege not often accorded to outside folk, but the presentation of the freshly tanned leopard skin was a special occasion. The old chief was doubly delighted – delighted to receive the skin and delighted that the constant toll of calves, sheep and dogs killed by this old cat had finally ceased. As slayers of the beast we were in high regard and even more so for having handed the skin over to the chief to whom it technically and traditionally belonged as representative of the clan who had requested that we hunt it and on whose land it had been killed. There is a possibility that this cat was a man-eater, technically speaking. A toddler had gone missing from the village some months previously and there was a suggestion that this aged leopard might have had something to do with it. Personally, I very much doubt it. The toddler had entirely vanished – no tracks, no corpse, nothing. Usually that means so-called 'muti murder' – kidnap and murder of a young child for purposes of making magic medicine from body parts. Incidentally, for those of you who are shocked at the demise of a leopard, leopards in Southern Africa are not even vaguely endangered, regardless of their global Sites status, and this one was shot in terms of a permit issued by the Department of Environment and Nature Conservation.

Lunch was a fully traditional affair held outside in the shade of a large acacia tree, with the chief and his guests, including us, seated on skins and cushions laid out on the meticulously swept and compacted earth courtyard before the chief's house. Festivities commenced with the passing round of communal cartons of 'Chibuku Shake-Shake', as the commercially produced traditional beer of Africa is known. Although I have occasionally drunk it, I never got used to this beverage. If you close your eyes and just concentrate on the flavour then it is very much like any other beer, but it is the texture and appearance I could never adjust to. It both looks and feels in the mouth like watery, grey oatmeal porridge. It is in fact a thin, fermenting sorghum porridge and it gets stronger the older it is, starting off at a very mild one percent alcohol when it leaves the brewery and progressing upwards from there to around six or seven percent a week or so later. It is reputed to continue fermenting in the stomach of the drinker, but this doubtful proposition is probably apocryphal. People do get spectacularly drunk on it, but then they consume huge quantities on occasion. Food was then served – also very traditional: large bowls of maize meal porridge prepared to a stiff and slightly sticky consistency for eating with the fingers together with iron pots filled with braised meat and wild greens in gravy and as a side dish, platters of deep-fried fresh locusts. These were all placed before us so we could help ourselves.

This was the first and only occasion upon which I have eaten locusts and they really were not bad at all – close your eyes and imagine eating a small piece of buttery chicken schnitzel with the consistency and crunch of an unshelled deep-fried shrimp and you have a fair approximation of the sensations and flavours involved. If there was some way you could shell a locust then they really might take off as a culinary treat, but the anatomy and distribution of fleshy parts on a locust do not allow this. Nevertheless, locusts are eaten all over Africa, in parts of the

Middle East and across much of Southeast Asia. They are a fine source of nutrition, with protein being over fifty percent of dry weight (which is more protein than a cow) and fat being twelve percent. They are very low in carbohydrates and would make an excellent snack for those on a diet, but noticeably those who eat locusts are seldom overweight. It seems locusts have been eaten for a very long time. They are frequently mentioned in the Bible and other religious texts emanating from the Middle East as both a boon and a curse. John the Baptist was said to subsist in the wild on a combination of locusts and wild honey and clearly locusts came to the rescue of hungry folk from time to time. As a curse, though, they are famous for being integral to the threats of plague made by Moses in his efforts to free his people from the yoke of Egyptian slavery and receive more than one mention in the gruesome context of Revelations.

Locusts in a large swarm are astonishingly destructive. The ones I was eating in the African bush were the migratory locust (*Locusta migratoria*), whilst the biblical locust of the Middle East is the desert locust (*Schistocera gregaria*), but nevertheless both species share the peculiar characteristic of being polyphenic, meaning that they are capable of transitioning from a solitary form, or phenotype, to another that is gregarious. This seems to occur in response to suddenly increasing population density and an abundance of food, such as might happen when a period of good rains follows a severe drought. As the transition from one form to the other proceeds, progressive generations alter in appearance from the brown-with-green coloration of the solitary form to the brown-with-yellow coloration of the slightly smaller gregarious form. These days the transition is noticed and the authorities notified so that steps can be taken to prevent the accumulation of truly massive swarms, which in the old days could cover several hundred square kilometres, with forty to sixty million insects per square kilometre. Each insect consumes its body weight in green foliage per day, so a 250 square kilometre swarm would consume upwards of fifteen million kilograms of food per day, literally leaving a swath of bare earth behind it as it tumbled across the landscape at the mercy of the wind, blocking out the sun and generally presaging an apocalyptic shortage of food and other miseries for the people unfortunate enough to be in its path. These days there are few people left who have seen such a thing, but it is apparently quite dreadful. The principal step the authorities take to prevent this from happening today is to liberally spray incipient locust swarms with powerful insecticides, so if you are ever minded to collect a few locusts for the pot, bear in mind they might be easy to catch because they are loaded down with poisons and on the verge of collapse.

As locusts are the only kosher insect and thus may be enjoyed by Jewish folk whenever the mood might take them, here is a recipe for fried locusts by the famous Jerusalem chef Moshe Basson:

MOSHE BASSON'S
CRISP GRASSHOPPERS

About 25 locusts
2 litres of vegetable stock with a little turmeric added to it
4 tablespoons flour
1 teaspoon salt
2 teaspoons dried chilli flakes
1 teaspoon ground coriander
1 teaspoon dry garlic granules
1 egg

Throw the locusts in the boiling stock, whole. Cook for about three minutes. Drain the locusts and let them cool somewhat, then twist off their heads: this will also pull out the black, threadlike viscera.

Remove the wings and small legs.

Make a seasoned flour with the flour, salt, chilli powder, ground coriander, dried garlic granules and a little black pepper.

Roll the precooked locusts in a beaten whole egg and then roll them in the seasoned flour. Shake excess flour off.

Fry in olive oil for one and a half to two minutes, till the colour turns golden brown.

Serve with a lemony tahini sauce, or a za'atar pesto made more lemony than usual.

Crunch! Mazel tov!

MOPANE WORMS

If you imagine a Nik Nak, only longer and more hollow and dark brown, and then picture yourself crunching down on it and the greasy, powdery savoury suddenly filling your mouth with a dust dry and acrid flavour, then you will have come close to appreciating what it is like to bite into a dried mopane worm. It is not recommended, at least not by me, although people sometimes do it and it is more popular in some places than in others. Generally, though, dried mopane worms are not eaten as a snack but are reconstituted by rehydration before being used in a savoury stew or fried with onions.

Mopane worms are the caterpillar of the very large African emperor moth (*Gonimbrasia belina*) whose eggs hatch in great profusion in summer in the dry semi-desert and bushveld areas of Southern Africa, mainly on mopane trees (hence the name), but also on other types of tree so they are widespread and not limited only to areas of mopane forest. As the larva grows, it moults four times and in the end is a large grey, black and yellow caterpillar about four inches long with a plump, segmented body ringed with spiky tufts of hair. It really does not look appetising and the first people to eat mopane worms must have been starving. Once they reach the fifth laval stage the caterpillars are hand-picked in the wild, mainly by women and children, and there is a certain etiquette involved. Caterpillars out in the bush are not considered to belong to the landowner and can be collected by any passer-by, but those on trees near to a house are not collected without the permission of the householder. This is because young caterpillars may have been moved from the bush to these nearby trees to facilitate collection once mature. When picked, the caterpillars are processed by being pinched at the tail end to open the skin, then squeezed like a tube of toothpaste or pushed together lengthwise like a concertina to expel the green, slimy guts. The worm is then flicked violently to cast off the ruptured innards, leaving the surrounding skin and flesh intact. This is then either eaten fresh in one or other traditional recipe or is preserved for later use by drying or smoking over a low hardwood fire. Today mopane worms are also tinned in brine by various commercial concerns.

Mopane worms are sold all over the world and must be one of the most widely distributed African 'bush tucker' items available, regardless of the fact that traditionally they are very much a subsistence food on their home continent and are only eaten by very poor rural folk who lack culinary choices. Having said that, millions of people in Southern Africa eat mopane worms every year and they make a significant contribution to protein consumption. As for the rest of the world, I suppose it must be the novelty 'shock' value of eating such a peculiar item that has helped to spread them about all over the place. Perhaps mopane worms are in fact making a transition from subsistence food to luxury item as has happened in the past with things like oysters. Some people find that the taste of stewed or fried mopane worms reminds them of honey-barbecued chicken and they are most enthusiastic about them. The flesh is yellow and quite succulent, particularly when the fresh item is used. Personally, I have not much enjoyed them on the few occasions that I have eaten them, but must confess that on all of those occasions they have been buried away in a rich tomato-based stew with so much chilli that one could have happily included chopped tennis shoes into the mix without noticing the difference.

In case you come across a packet of dried mopane worms somewhere, here is a recipe:

MOPANE WORM STEW

(Serves 4)
500 g dried mopane worms
4 tomatoes, diced or a 420 g can of chopped tomatoes
2 onions, diced
1 teaspoon turmeric
4 fresh chillies, finely chopped
3 cloves of garlic, finely chopped
1 tablespoon fresh ginger, finely chopped
3 tablespoons groundnut oil

Soak the dried worms in water for three to four hours to reconstitute. Fry the onions in the groundnut oil on a medium heat until translucent. Add turmeric, chillies, garlic and ginger. Fry for about five minutes. Add the tomatoes and cook on low for about twenty minutes until the spices are well blended. Add the drained worms and cook until they have softened a bit but are still a little crunchy. Add salt and pepper to taste. Serve with maize meal porridge cooked to a thick and sticky consistency (like Italian polenta, which you could use instead).

MUSHROOMS

British people have a deeply ingrained fear of wild mushrooms that has somehow become part of British culture. They believe that collecting and eating wild mushrooms is about the most dangerous thing you can do outdoors in the otherwise benign and gentle British countryside and they are correct, if you are talking about ignorant people. However, it is not compulsory to remain ignorant. There are excellent, well-illustrated books available[34], not to mention comprehensive courses run by experts, that will get you out there collecting a dozen or so edible species with very little danger at all, provided you employ a little common sense. But the danger aspect lingers like a vague shadow in the mind of the Briton, even when he or she knows exactly what mushrooms to collect, and this adds spice to the process of gathering and eating them. It's a strange thrill – probably much like the kick a Japanese person gets out of eating

---

34 The best book for comprehensive identification of European mushrooms using brilliant photography is Roger Phillips' *Mushrooms*, published by Macmillan. The best for getting you started and explaining the basics is Patrick Harding's *Mushroom Hunting* published by Collins.

fugu[35]. A further consequence of this British reticence is that most mushroom habitats in Britain receive almost no attention from private mushroom collectors and are under little pressure except from the odd eccentric hunter-gatherer type like me and from foreign commercial collectors[36]. This really is not the case anywhere else in Europe where the woods are full of mushroom hunters from mid-summer through to the end of autumn, sometimes achieving such density in the forests near places like Paris or Rome that they appear to be standing around in groups under the trees ready to pounce the instant any mushroom breaks cover.

I began my mushroom-collecting career as a small child and we limited ourselves to African field mushrooms of two distinct varieties that occurred on vlei grassland near our home in Zimbabwe. My father was in charge of mushroom expeditions and my mother, being English, refused to have anything to do with it. 'Someone has to be able to drive you all to the hospital,' she would tell us and would expand upon the horrors of the medical process known as the 'stomach pump', much to our macabre and youthful glee. The mushrooms would emerge immediately following (or sometimes, actually during) heavy rain. They emerged fast, were of light structure and quickly developed into classic-looking Agaricus mushrooms with white caps and pink

---

35 Fugu is the Japanese name for pufferfish of various species. Fugu contains lethal amounts of the poison tetrodotoxin, especially in the fish's liver, ovaries and eyes. The poison, a sodium channel blocker, paralyses the muscles while the victim stays fully conscious. The victim is unable to breathe and eventually dies from asphyxiation. Fugu poison is 1200 times stronger than cyanide and there is no antidote. Obviously, very careful preparation of these fish to remove the poisonous parts before eating is essential.

36 There has recently been an irritating increase in commercial mushroom pickers who descend on a woodland in force and clean it out in a few hours. Consequently, some areas in Britain have been closed entirely to mushroom collecting by the environmental authorities.

gills. My father would be quick off the mark if it was over the weekend and an expedition would set forth immediately, clad in plastic raincoats and armed with baskets and paper packets. If you could walk, you could come, so kids were included from the age of about eighteen months. We considered it huge fun and collected hundreds of mushrooms on each occasion. Of course, we also became expert at the identification of these two species, both by sight and by the fresh and very distinct mushroom aroma they would give off. It always seemed incredible to us that anyone could misidentify these mushrooms given what they smelled like and we constantly reassured ourselves by smelling each one collected. Once the hunt was over we would return home and a mushroom feast would ensue. We prepared and served these mushrooms in only one way: on toast after being fried in butter with a sprinkling of salt and pepper. This was the only way these mushrooms could be prepared because they were very fragile and collapsed into a grey mush almost instantly heat was applied to them. This does not happen with European field mushrooms, so I presume these were of a different species regardless of a very similar appearance. They were delicious.

The field mushrooms of my youth were the only mushrooms I ever personally collected in Africa. We simply did not know of any other edible species, although there are apparently many, with a big overlap of European species that either also occur in Africa naturally or have been accidentally imported along with European tree species. However, I did eat one other wild African mushroom many years later when I lived for some time on the Southern Cape coast of South Africa. Occasionally, in early autumn, a local greengrocer would stock a huge wild mushroom about twice the size of a dinner plate. It looked very similar to a European parasol mushroom, only much bigger, having a large, very lightly scaled, white-gilled cap with a dark central hump. I was assured by the storekeeper that it was not a parasol, but a species of termite mushroom (genus *Termitomyces*) collected by local people off termite mounds deep in the indigenous coastal forest near Knysna. These were by far the most delicious mushrooms I have ever enjoyed. They really were spectacular when simply fried in a little butter with a sprinkling of salt and a squeeze of lemon juice, being reminiscent of a delicate veal roast in the Italian *al limone* style. A keen following for these mushrooms soon developed amongst the greengrocer's customers, such that it was seldom possible to get hold of them more than once or twice a year. I tried to discover where to find these mushrooms in the wild, but was met with a solid, silent wall of resistance to my finding out anything at all. Unfortunately, the greengrocer has now closed down and I have not heard of these mushrooms being available for many years. Termite mushrooms are a popular edible further north in Africa and in the case of the species *Termitomyces giganticus,* are reputed to reach a cap size over three feet in diameter and weigh many pounds. There is a photograph of one circulating on the internet that shows a young boy on an African roadside somewhere holding one up like an umbrella. It is huge and has elicited many comments about the photograph potentially having been Photoshopped, but it is in fact within the parameters expressed by official mycological authorities for the giant termite mushroom. I start salivating every time I look at the picture.

When I moved to England I again became interested in wild mushrooms, spurred on by the abundance in the local woods and the sight of my neighbour (of Polish extraction) harvesting huge basketfuls, which he then mainly dried or pickled for year-round consumption or simply dried and hung up from beams in his kitchen as a decoration. I bought some books, made a study of the subject and have become a fairly confident identifier of the common species of fungi found in Southern England, particularly the good edible ones and also the deadly poisonous varieties. That is the thing, you see: it is not necessary to learn every single one of the five million or so species of fungus that are believed to exist. All you need to learn are the ones that you want to collect and the dangerous ones that you need to avoid confusing with the ones you want to collect. In my case, in Surrey, there are less than two dozen species I think are worth eating and only half a dozen or so poisonous species that could create confusion. A few words about some of these follow, mainly in a culinary context:

MORELS

After truffles, morels are undoubtedly the most sought-after wild mushrooms. Those who know where to find morels are amongst the most secretive of all hunter-gatherers. If you are out in the woods in late March or early April and you see a figure dressed in camouflage, carrying a basket and slinking cautiously from tree to tree you have probably stumbled upon a morel hunter. There is no point in trying to follow, unless you too are dressed like a sniper and have not been observed. In all recorded history, no morel hunter has ever knowingly revealed a secret morel location. From a flavour point of view, morels contribute a distinct, but very subtle and refined, umami[37] element to any dish in which they are used. They are thus an exceptionally good addition to any stew or soup and incorporate into a cream-based sauce with remarkable effect. Morels benefit from prolonged, gentle cooking and, almost uniquely amongst mushrooms, become more flavoursome and delicious the longer they are cooked (within reason). They also dry very easily, turning

---

37 The term 'umami' refers to the relatively recently identified fifth basic human taste sensation (the others being sweetness, sourness, bitterness and saltiness), and was coined by the Japanese chemist Kikunae Ikeda in 1908. Although the term is often translated as meaning 'savoury', the word 'deliciousness' would be closer to what Kikunae Ikeda had in mind. It is that delectable savoury quality in roasted meats, rich sauces and concentrated vegetable essences that makes us salivate in anticipation – very difficult to put into words, but we all know exactly what it means.

black, shrinking significantly and losing all volatile hydrazines in the process. These hydrazines are poisonous, so do not eat raw or partially cooked fresh morels. Dried morels can be easily reconstituted by soaking in warm water whereupon they resume a size and texture that is almost indistinguishable from fresh ones. Morels are commercially collected in Europe, India, Pakistan and North America and are freely available in dried form all over the world. They are not cheap.

CEPS AND OTHER EDIBLE BOLETES

Boletes give more joy to the woodland mushroom hunter than all the other mushrooms put together. They fruit in late summer through to the end of autumn, are numerous in both variety and quantity and are amongst the easiest of all mushrooms to identify safely. This is because boletes have dense, sponge-like, tubular pores on the underside of their caps and not the familiar gills found in other types of mushrooms. Although there are a few poisonous boletes, all the poisonous ones have orange or red pores and so an easily remembered safety rule can be formulated for boletes: only collect the ones with white or yellow pores. The most prized of the boletes is *Boletus edulis*, now universally known in Britain as a 'cep' in adoption and adaption of the French word *cèpe*. After truffles and morels, ceps are the most sought-after mushrooms in the world and are famous everywhere they occur, being known as *fungi porcini* (piglet mushrooms) in Italy, *steinpiltz* (stone mushrooms) in Germany and as king boletes in America. Their old English name was 'penny bun' in reference to the colour and shape of the cap. If you find a young, fresh cep, as yet unmolested by slugs or maggots, then slice it thinly and fry the slices briefly in a very hot pan with a dash of good olive oil and a sprinkling of salt and pepper. Serve on a bed of rocket with generous shavings of the best Parmigiano Reggiano you can find, another dash of olive oil, some crusty fresh bread and a bottle of aged Barolo or Barbaresco. This is a great classic combination of flavours and never fails to delight. If the cep really is very young and blemishless, then it can be served raw in this dish for a slightly different textural experience and a lighter flavour. If you cannot find ceps, then there are other common boletes that are very nearly as good: the summer bolete, the oak bolete, the bay bolete, the orange birch bolete and so on. In my experience, the lighter the colour of the spongy pores, i.e. from pale cream to light yellow, the better the bolete will be to eat[38]. Boletes also dry very well and dried ceps are freely available in supermarkets and grocery stores all over the world. Like morels, dried ceps introduce a marked umami flavour into any dish where they are used, but this flavour is more robust than that of morels. I use them extensively in stocks, sauces and soups where they bring a depth of flavour difficult to emulate without using the concentrated and caramelised meat juices found at the bottom of the roasting pan when dry roasting meat. They are thus very popular with my vegetarian family who have difficulty getting that type of savoury flavour from any other source. Unlike morels, dried ceps do not reconstitute on soaking to a texture or flavour anything like the fresh item, being very slippery and very strong tasting. I thus often discard them after soaking them for half an hour or so in whatever stock or sauce I am constructing. I find this imparts more than enough flavour for most purposes.

PARASOLS

If it were not for the deliciousness of parasols, I would be able to say 'don't touch mushrooms with white gills'. But, parasols have white gills and are very worthwhile, so that potential rule

---

38 Beware, though, the bitter bolete which has pale cream pores. It is not poisonous but is unpleasant to eat and is the ruin of any dish into which it has accidentally been included.

is out of the window[39]. The reason for wanting to exclude white gills is because two of the most deadly mushrooms, the deathcap and the destroying angel, both have white gills. Although both these lethal mushrooms occur in roughly the same wooded areas where parasols might be found, I doubt that many have been mistaken for parasols because apart from the white gills there is little resemblance. Instead, the confusion seems to occur with Agaricus mushrooms and so this topic is continued in the section on field mushrooms below. Also, don't collect parasols that have caps less than eight centimetres across. There are a number of small parasol relatives that are poisonous, but all have cap diameters of less than eight centimetres.

There are two commonly encountered edible parasol species: *Macrolepiota procera*, known simply as the 'parasol mushroom' in Europe, and *Chlorophylum (formerly Macrolepiota) rhacodes*, known to all as the 'shaggy parasol'. Some folk are upset-stomach allergic to shaggy parasols, so don't serve them at a dinner party and try a small quantity first, just to make sure into which camp you fall. Both are excellent to eat and are best prepared by simply frying in a little butter. They have firm, dry, very tasty flesh that is probably best enjoyed all on its own, but which would happily accompany any fried or grilled meat whatsoever.

CHANTERELLES (GIROLLES)

Bright orangey-yellow and smelling distinctly of apricots, I am always delighted to encounter chanterelles. They grow in troops on mossy woodland hillsides in autumn, usually in association with deciduous trees (oak, chestnut, hazel), but sometimes also with conifers. They will appear in the same spots year

---

39   Other edible white-gilled mushrooms include various *Russula* species (including the well-known 'charcoal burner') and the St George's mushroom. These are insufficiently tasty to stand in the way of a potentially life-saving rule.

after year so there is often some secrecy attaching to precisely where chanterelles may be found. With their vibrant colour and attractive texture, neither of which are degraded by cooking, chanterelles are beautiful to look at and easy to use in almost any dish calling for mushrooms. Personally, I think they are at their best simply fried in butter until tender and then incorporated into a generous omelette together with some grated summer truffle. The truffle lifts the egg into a different dimension where it partners more positively with the chanterelles to create a dish of memorable luxury.

Unfortunately, chanterelles can be confused with four poisonous lookalikes: the false chanterelle, the jack o'lantern, the deadly webcap and the fool's webcap. The confusion seems to arise mainly from similar colour and size because these lookalikes are very different from true chanterelles in gill structure and aroma. Chanterelles do not have gills in the conventional sense, having primitive wrinkles on the underside of the cap instead. The false chanterelle (*Hygrophoropsis aurantiaca*) is more of an upset-stomach risk and culinary disappointment than anything deadly; some people actually consider it edible, but it can cause alarming symptoms like hallucinations in some cases. The jack o'lantern (*Omphalotus illudens*), which contains such an exotic array of chemicals it can glow in the dark, will definitely do you no good if you eat it, but it is so rare you are unlikely to have the opportunity for confusion. The real killers are the deadly webcap (*Cortinarius rubellus*) and the closely related fool's webcap (*Cortinarius orellanus*), which have been responsible for the deaths of many people, particularly in Central Europe. Even if you survive eating a dish of these webcaps, your kidneys will not and you can look forward to a life on dialysis until a kidney donor can be found. Chanterelles are thus not a good idea for the novice collector.

WOOD HEDGEHOG
(PIED DE MOUTON)

I often find wood hedgehogs amongst moss in beech woods when out in the autumn looking for boletes. Every bit as delicious as chanterelles and with a similar appearance from above, wood hedgehogs are one of the safest mushrooms for a beginner to collect. This is because instead of gills or the chanterelle's wrinkles, hedgehogs have a mass of closely packed and brittle vertical spines on the underside of the cream- to yellow-orange-coloured caps, reminiscent of the spines on a hedgehog's back. You have to be a real idiot and probably deserve to be removed from the gene pool if you misidentify a poisonous mushroom as a wood hedgehog.

The spines of wood hedgehogs are easily broken and so they should be treated very gently if you want to preserve this feature in the final cooked mushrooms. Some chefs remove the spines entirely before cooking, claiming that they impart a bitter flavour, but I have found this is true only of old specimens. I think prime, young hedgehogs are better served with spines intact for a very exotic appearance. The French name *pied de mouton* or 'sheep's foot' is derived from the stout, solid stem often being attached to the cap towards one side like a hoof. Excellent in virtually any dish requiring mushrooms, hedgehogs also pickle very well.

PUFFBALLS

Another mushroom that is easy for the beginner to identify in both its woodland and grassland forms. With species varying in size from a large marble, through golf ball and hockey ball sizes, to the huge, football-sized giant puffball, you cannot really mistake these mushrooms for anything else, particularly once you slice into them. It is simple: if the interior is firm and bright white and is surrounded by a skin no thicker than a fingernail, then you have found a young and very edible puffball. If it has a thick skin or is discoloured inside (anything from pale yellow to dark purple-brown) you have found an earthball or a puffball too old to eat. Be particularly careful of any you find that contain a miniature mushroom inside. These are not puffballs at all and you have probably collected an immature Amanita species. Amanitas emerge from within a volva that looks a little like a puffball before the mushroom actually emerges. The Amanita genus contains some of the most deadly poisonous mushrooms, so always cut into a puffball before cooking.

Puffballs are a unique and subtle flavour experience. They do not really taste like other mushrooms at all, being reminiscent of sweetbreads more than anything else, particularly in texture. You can simply fry slices in butter with a little crushed garlic and then add a squeeze of lemon juice and a sprinkling of salt and pepper, but they are at their best in my view when thin slices (particularly from a giant puffball) are dipped in flour, egg and breadcrumbs prior to frying in oil or butter. The resulting mushroom 'schnitzels' are then served with a garlic mayonnaise (classic Mediterranean aioli works well), lemon wedges and a green salad. A chilled bottle of Muscadet then transforms the whole thing into a memorable and highly unusual feast.

CHICKEN OF THE WOODS

Considered a delicacy in Germany and North America, this soft-textured bracket fungus with its beguiling bright yellow and orange coloration is virtually unknown to the general public in Britain, notwithstanding that it can frequently be found growing on oak and sweet chestnut trees. It is at its best in early summer when new fan-shaped fruit bodies are produced that are succulent and tender. By the end of summer, these tend to become pale, tough and dry and are not worth collecting.

The flesh of a young bracket when cut into strips, blanched and then fried in butter has both a texture and flavour that is strikingly similar to chicken breast. In fact, if the fried strips are mixed into a light curry mayonnaise sauce (as in Coronation Chicken) and are then served on buttered crusty bread, everyone is fooled. A word of caution: chicken of the woods contains thermolabile poisons and should not be eaten raw. Even after the elimination of these poisons by cooking, some people are allergic and may suffer stomach upset, nausea, swollen lips or skin rash. Try a small amount the first time you eat it.

ST GEORGE'S MUSHROOM

For most mushroom hunters, the St George's mushroom is the first edible mushroom to appear each year, fruiting around about St George's Day, the 23rd of April. Apart from morels, no other mushrooms fruit this early so there is little prospect of mixing this white-capped, white-gilled and white-spored mushroom up with one of the white-capped, white-gilled and white-spored deadly species like the destroying angel and the deathcap. These deadly species fruit in late summer and in autumn long after the St George's mushrooms have come and gone. Perhaps the only risk of confusion comes in May when the poisonous red-staining inocybe could conceivably be misidentified as a St George's mushroom, notwithstanding that it has yellow gills, flesh that turns red on being cut or bruised and smells strongly of rotting fruit.

St George's mushrooms are something you either love or hate. They smell strongly of meal or freshly milled flour and young specimens are heavy with water which exudes plentifully when cooked. People who like them often stew them in chicken stock with wine and herbs and then finish the dish with cream or yogurt and serve it with rice. Personally, I find St George's mushrooms very difficult to digest and so they are not my favourite. However, my family love them and enthusiastically collect them every spring. Those that are not eaten fresh are dried and used in stews and soups later in the year. They impart a mild savoury flavour when dried and do not impact my digestion at all in this form. Clearly, whatever disagrees with me is volatile and evaporates during the drying process.

CAULIFLOWER FUNGUS

Relatively rare and found at the base of coniferous trees, particularly scots pine in my experience, the cauliflower fungus is a real treat for those who recognise what they have found. No other mushroom is quite as nutty and sweet-flavoured as a nice young cauliflower with its appealing soft, yet slightly crunchy texture and pale, sinuous, flattened, folded and brain-like mass of flesh, particularly when sliced and fried in foaming salted butter. Cauliflower fungus is usually a little under football-sized, but can grow much bigger, up to as much as forty pounds on occasion. A really big one could feed literally dozens of people.

I prefer to eat fried cauliflower fungus all on its own, perhaps with a dash of double cream and a sprinkling of parsley, but it is also extremely good with fillets of firm white fish, such as tilapia or cod. It looks absolutely spectacular on the plate.

JELLY EAR

A close relative of, and workable substitute for, the famous wood ear mushroom used extensively in oriental cuisines, the jelly ear is easy to find, easy to collect, easy to dry, easy to rehydrate and, when very thinly sliced, makes a noticeable difference to the flavour of any stir-fry in which it is included. It's one of those subtle things – you can't really taste it as such in the stir-fry, but you notice a difference in the flavour if it is not included. The jelly ear is sometimes also called the Jew's ear, but that is now considered politically incorrect and insensitive by some, not to mention that the derivation of the name from the myth that Judas Iscariot hanged himself from an elder tree (the principal host of jelly ears) is tortuous to say the least.

Jelly ears can also be used to soothe a sore throat. Simply make an infusion by pouring boiling water over either fresh or dried jelly ears and then gargle with the liquid once it has cooled down a little. I have tried this and it does work, although sucking on a Strepsil is probably more effective.

BEEFSTEAK FUNGUS

A mushroom where you get precisely what it says on the tin, at least in the context of appearances. This bracket fungus grows on the trunks or broken branches of old oak[40] or sweet chestnut trees and looks exactly like a chunk of beef when young, although some are reminded of ox-tongue or liver. It even bleeds red, blood-like fluid when you cut into it. However, that is where the resemblance to a juicy cut of beef ends, unfortunately.

Some people really like this fungus, notwithstanding its high level of tannins, but I am not one of them. It is usually soaked for an extended period in water or milk before being blanched and then stewed or barbecued. The flesh turns black during cooking.

FIELD MUSHROOMS (AGARICUS SPECIES)

Ironically, the mushrooms that are most likely to cause identification errors and potentially fatal poisoning are the mushrooms many erroneously believe are the safest to collect. The Agaricus mushrooms, which include the famous field

---

40 Beefsteak fungus (*Fistulina hepatica*) causes the heartwood of the oak to discolour, creating the highly sought-after and expensive so-called 'brown oak' popular in furniture manufacture.

mushroom (*Agaricus campestrus*) and the wild progenitor of the ubiquitous domestic mushroom (*Agaricus bisporus*)[41], fall into this category. There are at least seven species of wild Agaricus mushrooms that are most excellent to eat. There are a few other species that, although not deadly, are poisonous. Telling one from the other is sometimes very difficult because they all share common features: free gills, pink when young, later brown, with a chocolate-brown spore print; a button stage, where a veil covers the immature gills; a mature stage with an open, fleshy cap and ringed stem; a light white to cream to brown cap colour, sometimes flecked with brown scales, sometimes not. But, sorting out Agaricus mushrooms one from another is not where the big danger lies. The big danger lies in the fundamental shape of the Agaricus mushroom and its generally pale coloration being similar to the shape and colour (at least to profoundly ignorant eyes) of lethal members of the Amanita genus, particularly the deathcap. This is especially true of woodland species of Agaricus that might be growing in similar habitats to those favoured by Amanita species, which are mycorrhizal and limited to woodland habitats, although beware the phenomenon of a woodland mushroom growing thirty metres out into the middle of a field because the roots of its host tree spread out that far into the meadow. Simply put, people sometimes collect deathcaps and destroying angels believing them to be Agaricus mushrooms, with fatal consequences if the error is not picked up by an expert before consumption.

Wild edible Agaricus mushrooms are delicious – all of them, without exception, are far better to eat than commercially produced *Agaricus bisporus*. It is difficult to beat the simple pleasure of returning home from a successful foray into nearby

---

41 Notwithstanding the large variety of shapes, sizes and cap colours and a variety of names – 'chestnut mushroom', 'Portobello mushroom' etc. – all commercially grown Agaricus mushrooms are derived from *Agaricus bisporus*, ironically quite a rare mushroom in the wild.

fields with a good basket of field mushrooms and then simply frying them in butter with a generous sprinkling of salt and pepper and then serving them on thick slices of toasted bread. The toast soaks up the salty butter and creates a perfect backdrop to the flavour of the mushrooms. You suddenly realise what the fuss is all about and how far the flavour of commercially grown mushrooms has fallen from the heights achieved by the wild ones. By comparison, commercial mushrooms are barely worth eating.

OYSTER MUSHROOMS

These days, oyster mushrooms of various species and colours are commercially cultivated and are available in supermarkets all year round. The species *Pleurotus ostreatus,* the ordinary silver-grey oyster mushroom, can also be found in the wild in Britain, growing all year round on tree trunks, cut logs, stumps and broken branches of mainly beech trees, but also on other broad-leaved timber.

Wild oysters are often found in some abundance and it is always a satisfying find. Although one strongly feels that wild oyster mushrooms should taste better than shop-bought ones, in fact they do not. They are a popular ingredient in stir-fries.

BLEWITS

As a food-oriented person, there are very few things that I do not eat. However, I cannot abide, stand or tolerate tripe in any form. It follows, therefore, that I really do not warm to blewits because they taste and feel in the mouth almost exactly like tripe and also carry with them a peculiar background perfume, as though the tripe had been prepared by an elderly lady wearing an excessive amount of floral eau de cologne. But many people in Britain do not agree with me, particularly in the Midlands, where blewits of both field and wood species are commonly collected in the wild and sold at stalls in open-air markets. Indeed, field blewits are now cultivated commercially for the restaurant trade and are commonly added to casseroles and other dishes advertised as containing wild mushrooms.

Fresh young blewits are very attractive mushrooms with their fleshy in-rolled caps, violet sinuate gills and lilac-streaked stems. They fruit latest of all edible mushrooms, from late September through to Christmas, and are relatively abundant, particularly the wood blewit which appears amongst vegetation in deciduous and coniferous woods and in parks and gardens. In September and October it is possible to confuse blewits with poisonous violet-coloured species of *Cortinarius*, but as winter gets a grip on the landscape, blewits are left as the fungal last man standing.

I have consciously not included fully comprehensive information on how to correctly identify the mushrooms mentioned above in my short comments on each edible species. This is because if you want to get involved in the tremendously satisfying pursuit of collecting wild edible mushrooms you *have to* learn how to identify them scientifically and properly using the comprehensive photographic guides available and by strictly following all the identification procedures recommended by the expert mycologists who painstakingly put these guides together. At least, you have to do this until you are so familiar with each species, including the poisonous lookalikes, that you are one hundred percent certain of your identification every time. There are no shortcuts to safe identification, and traditional rules derived from folklore are positively dangerous. The following 'old wives' tales' concerning distinguishing edible from poisonous mushrooms are all completely wrong and cannot be relied upon:

- Cooking a poisonous mushroom with a silver spoon will blacken the spoon.
- The cap of a poisonous mushroom cannot be peeled.
- Mushrooms that change colour on handling are all poisonous.
- Mushrooms with a mild smell and taste are edible.
- A mushroom eaten by an animal must be safe.
- Mushrooms collected from grassland are safe.
- All mushrooms growing on wood are safe.
- Poisonous mushrooms can be made safe by par-boiling them.
- Drying a mushroom destroys its toxins.
- All mushrooms that exude a milky fluid from the gills are poisonous.
- Poisonous fungi are all brightly coloured, while white ones are edible.

All total rubbish!

The consequences of eating a deadly poisonous mushroom are horrific. Here is an extract concerning the deathcap from Roger Phillips' book that I find quite chilling:

'This is the most deadly fungus in the British Isles, and despite years of detailed research into the toxins it contains, no antidote exists against their effects on the human body. Poisoning by deathcap is characterized by a delay of 6 to 24 hours between ingestion and onset of symptoms, during which time the cells of the liver and kidneys are attacked. However, if a gastroirritant has also been consumed, for example as the result of eating a mixed collection of mushrooms, the delay in gastric upset may not occur, and this vital diagnostic evidence will be masked. The next stage is one of prolonged and violent vomiting and diarrhoea accompanied by severe abdominal pains, lasting for a day or more. Typically this is followed by an apparent recovery, when the victim may be released from hospital or think *their ordeal over, but death results from kidney and liver failure within a few days.'*

If you get to hospital very, very quickly, are correctly diagnosed instantly and are very, very lucky you might survive. Most probably you will not. Mortality in cases of this type of poisoning is over ninety percent. However, as dreadful as all this is, it is not true that you can be poisoned by simply touching a poisonous mushroom or that the temporary inclusion of a poisonous specimen in a basket of edibles will contaminate all the other mushrooms. You have to eat a good mouthful, say fifty grams or so, before you will be poisoned properly and lethally. In fact attention-seeking, 'bad boy' type mycologists have been seen to taste small quantities of deathcap or destroying angel just to see what they taste like and to impress girls.

Of course some people, generally live-fast-and-die-young or counter-culture types, go out of their way to collect (or buy) essentially poisonous mushrooms in order to enjoy their psychotropic effects. For decades now (and probably for thousands of years before that) people have enjoyed the hallucinogenic effects of the alkaloids psilocybin and psilocin found in *Psilocybe semilanceata,* a small, brown fungus with a narrow, cone-shaped cap, traditionally named the 'liberty cap' and commonly occurring on grassland pasture, lawns and playing fields in Britain in late summer and autumn. Consumption of this fungus in fresh, dried or powdered form induces auditory and visual hallucinations, enhances the senses of touch and smell and generally produces a 'trip' not dissimilar to that produced by LSD. The common name changed from 'liberty cap' to 'magic mushroom' in the decades following the 1960s and, predictably, the mushrooms were ultimately classified as a class-A drug and were prohibited by the authorities. Although this closed down the 'shroom' shops that had opened up in places like Camden, the magic mushrooms that emerge on my lawn appear contemptuous of the Home Office and continue to spring up wherever the hell they like.

Another toxic fungus sometimes consumed by humans is the fly agaric[42], *Amanita muscaria*, the classic red and white-spotted toadstool often depicted in children's fairytale books. The fly agaric contains the toxins muscimol and ibotenic acid which cause heightened sensory perception, misjudgements of size and distance and general falling-down-type drunkenness. Saami shamans and other folk from Siberia and Lapland have long consumed this fungus in specially prepared dried form as part of shamanistic rituals or simply in search of a good time. It is also very popular with various deer species and in particular reindeer, which seem unable to resist the stuff. Another peculiar feature of *muscaria* consumption is that the intoxicating quality is imparted to the liquid excretions, in other words urine, of the consumer and so if another person drinks that urine, they also become inebriated. This is the obvious source of the term 'get pissed', which clearly originated in more robust and less fastidious times and is testament to how determined humans can be when it comes to recreational intoxication. It is also interesting to note that the poet Clement Clarke Moore was probably influenced by the *muscaria*-induced antics of Saami shamans in his famous poem *A Visit from St. Nicholas* that starts 'Twas the night before Christmas...', in which the traditionally sober, saintly and slightly grim figure of St Nicholas is portrayed as a portly and clearly inebriated figure of fun, dressed in the colours of the fly agaric, flying high through the sky on a sleigh pulled by reindeer, occasionally crashing on rooftops and engaging in chimney-descending antics. On a serious note, though, consuming fly agaric could kill you if you don't know what you are doing, so unless you are a Saami shaman, do not try it.

---

42 *Amanita muscaria* is called 'fly agaric' because it was traditionally broken up into a plate of milk and used to stupefy flies – useful if fly numbers get out of hand in the autumn.

Few things are more satisfying to the hunter-gatherer than collecting edible wild mushrooms and the pleasure is multiplied considerably by realising how expensive they are to buy, if you can buy them at all. I was recently in Fortnum and Mason in the West End of London and was interested to note that the value of my previous day's haul of fresh ceps was over £200. This represents the equivalent of over twenty-six hours of work at the current (2017) minimum wage. Not bad for a forty-five-minute stroll in a beautiful woodland.

MUSSELS

Mussels can kill you, and not in the way you think. All over the world various species of marine mussels cling in vast beds to rocks in the inter-tidal zone. These beds, which can contain thousands of individual mussels cemented to the rock by means of their byssal threads, are generally arranged in such a way that the mussels lie side-by-side with their elongated, wedge-shaped shells closely packed and with the sharp edge of the wedge facing outwards like a blade. Now, if the sea happens to be rough and you happen to fall into the sea within the inter-tidal zone, then the chances are that you are going to end up being smashed up against the mussel beds. These will cut you to pieces and will prevent you from climbing out by simultaneously slicing your fingers and being too slippery to grip. This is absolutely horrifying for bystanders to watch and is beyond terrifying for the victim. The sea smashes the victim onto the mussel bed. You can actually see the flesh being sliced up through the clothing. The wave then retreats, leaving the victim scrabbling frantically for purchase, hands and knees reddening with blood. Then the next wave crashes into the victim, lifting him off the mussel bed and into deeper water trailing a long, brown smudge of gore. The third wave then smashes the victim back onto the mussel bed and so it goes on, until either the victim drowns and disappears from sight beneath the roiling foam or is somehow rescued by the bystanders. So, whilst the mussel is probably the easiest of all the marine foods to gather and is the blackberry of the beach zone, collecting them can involve hazards well beyond anything that might be encountered in a hedgerow. As with anything to do with the sea, caution and discretion are advised, particularly because the biggest, juiciest mussels tend to be the most inaccessible ones and those are usually found on the seaward side of the inter-tidal zone next to the deep and dangerous water. It is not true that the smaller ones are sweeter, as some who collect their mussels close to the beach suggest.

Huge prehistoric middens scattered about the world testify to the long popularity of mussels as a part of the human diet. Some of these middens contain millions of shells and are evidence that in some places, and at some times, mussels (usually along with oysters and limpets) have served as the staple food of entire communities for extended periods. This makes perfect sense in ancient societies with primitive technologies because these molluscs are highly nutritious, can be collected with little or no equipment and can be eaten raw, so it is not even necessary to have mastered fire. Even if you have fire, they can be cooked in the shell and so no fire-proof utensils are necessary either. In fact, one of the most satisfying ways to enjoy wild mussels is to cook them then and there on a beach fire. Although a small, portable sandwich grid is convenient for this, it is not essential and a flat rock in the fire or similar contrivance (use your initiative) for keeping the mussels from tipping over is just as effective. The mussels are, or should be, alive immediately before cooking and thus clamped firmly shut when first placed on the fire. They cook quickly, upon which the shell opens revealing the inner flesh. Leave them on the fire for a bit to allow the juices to concentrate a little, the flesh to contract and for a slightly smoky flavour to develop. Then take them off, pull open the shell and slurp the flesh out with a combination of your teeth and tongue.

This is a primordially satisfying thing to do.

One of the most important aspects of preparing freshly collected wild mussels is to deal with the 'beard', as the dense mat of byssal threads emerging from the shell is called. These byssal threads are often inundated with sand and other small items of marine detritus and if not removed, this gritty stuff will get into the mussels during the cooking process[43]. It is often said that mussels should be soaked for some hours in a bucket of seawater before being cooked in order that they can 'spit out the sand'. This is more or less nonsense. Mussels do not usually take in much sand during normal feeding and thus usually do not need to spit any out. Most of the sand comes from the byssal threads and from grit that might be adhering to the outside of the shell, which should be scrubbed off before cooking. To remove the beard, you basically take the mussel by surprise. Wait until the mussel relaxes and the shell opens slightly. Lift the mussel gently and then firmly tug out the beard with one decisive movement. The mussel will react by clamping shut, but if you have pulled enough of the beard out by the time this happens, the entire beard and a little of the attaching sinew will snap free. Cook the mussel immediately because this process will cause the mussel to die much more quickly than would otherwise be the case. If the mussel does not clamp shut firmly during the removing of the beard, the mussel is already dead and should be discarded. This is a much better way of ensuring that the mussels are alive immediately before cooking than the usual recommendation that any mussel that does not open during cooking should be discarded[44]. Although most mussels do in fact open during

---

43 Shop-bought mussels are usually grown on ropes in deeper water and away from the sand so this problem is much less pronounced with them.

44 According to marine biologist Dr Nick Ruello, discarding unopened mussels after cooking is erroneous advice originating in old, poorly researched cookbooks. Somehow, the principle has become an assumed truism for all shellfish. His research unequivocally establishes that it is nonsense.

cooking, those that remain shut were not necessarily dead before the heat was applied. Similarly, those that open were not necessarily alive – something you can prove to yourself by buying vacuum-packed mussels in a supermarket. These are definitely not alive, have closed shells when you remove them from the packaging and open up upon cooking.

Perhaps the most famous mussel dish of all is *moules-frites*, a Belgian classic enjoyed all over the world, but particularly on both the Mediterranean and Atlantic coasts of France and the North Sea coast of Belgium and Holland. It is an extremely simple dish in which a large bowl of steamed mussels on the shell is served, together with the liquor generated by the steaming process, with a separate and usually generous portion of French fries. There are a number of ways in which the mussels are prepared for this dish, dependent on where you are and the proclivities of the particular chef in charge. *Moules marinière* (steamed in white wine, shallots, parsley and butter) is probably the most common, but *moules natures* (steamed with celery, leeks and butter), *moules à la crème* (as for *moules marinière*, but with the liquor resulting from the steaming process being thickened with cream and a little flour) and *moules à la bière* (steamed with beer and various aromatics instead of white wine) are also popular. I find the accompanying sauce produced by all these mussel recipes to be a little bland, particularly as an accompaniment to French fries. Doubtless, if you are accustomed to mayonnaise with your French fries then all is well, but being of essentially British stock, I prefer something a little more acidic. I accept, however, that the 'fish-n-chips' approach of drenching everything in brown malt vinegar is too robust for the flavour of the mussels. The following recipe is my solution to this conundrum:

MOULES AFRIQUE DU SUD

1.5 kg fresh mussels, washed, scrubbed and debearded
250 g unsalted butter
1 tablespoon olive oil
8–12 large cloves garlic, peeled and thinly sliced
Bunch of fresh flat-leaf parsley, chopped
250 ml dry white wine
Juice of 1 or 2 lemons, to taste
Salt and black pepper

Heat the olive oil and butter in a large, heavy-bottomed pot until the butter is foaming. Add the sliced garlic. Pay very close attention to the garlic while it cooks. Like onions, garlic can be lightly caramelised into a wonderful, slightly sweet savoury. This takes very little time over a high heat, literally a minute or so. Thirty seconds longer and it is burnt and acrid, which ruins this dish. Just as the garlic reaches the correct translucent and lightly golden state, dump the parsley into the pot, stir it around for about fifteen seconds and then add the white wine. Bring everything to a boil, add the mussels to the pot and put on the lid. Steam the mussels for about five minutes until they open. Remove the mussels and strain the liquid in the pot. Add the lemon juice to the strained liquid together with salt and pepper to taste. Divide the mussels into serving bowls and then pour the liquid over the top. The mussels will still taste like mussels, but the liquid is one of the nicest things to dip a French fry into that you will ever experience.

Some people lose their nerve when preparing this dish and cut back on the quantity of garlic. Don't do this. This dish requires the fearless use of garlic to achieve its full potential.

NETTLES

If you are a totally urban person who never ventures into the countryside under any circumstances, unless forced, one of the first things that will happen to you as you stroll through the unfamiliar rural idyll of the British countryside[45] is a sudden and excruciating pain. It might afflict a hand or a bare arm or, if wearing shorts, the pale and unlovely flesh of your winter-tanned legs. You will jump and swear and leap about looking for the author of this agony, but no angry, buzzing culprit will be evident. You will stare at the blistering skin of the afflicted part with mystified anxiety and will utter some more expletives. Someone will then explain to you that you have brushed up against a nettle and that you will most likely survive. However, you will immediately take extremely careful note of what a nettle looks like and will forever after seek to avoid contact with another one, probably unsuccessfully. As strange as it may seem, it is not possible to explain to someone before they venture out into the unknown hazards of the hedgerow that they might encounter nettles. Yes, yes, they will say with a smile and a glazed look in their eyes, but they will not have taken in your warning. This is because the concept of an innocuous-looking

---

45 Or the countryside of elsewhere in Europe, Asia, North Africa or Western North America.

green plant inflicting such pain in return for mere contact is quite radical.

The mechanism used by nettles to inflict this painful deterrent is very sophisticated. The underside of the leaves and the stems of the plant are covered by extremely sharp, hollow hairs called *trichomes* that are like tiny hypodermic needles. When touched these penetrate the skin and inject a combination of histamine, formic acid and other chemicals, causing a severe stinging pain. Compared to other widespread and common plants, this physical defence mechanism seems wildly excessive – as though mice had been armed with machineguns. Not only do hairless creatures like humans avidly concentrate on avoiding nettles, but ruminants of every sort find that trying to eat nettles is an unhappy experience. As a consequence, nettles flourish mightily wherever they occur and are generally left undisturbed by all but keen gardeners armed with strimmers and thick gardening gloves. It invites the enquiry: what do nettles have that requires such heavyweight protection?

It turns out nettles have a great deal, most of which we have forgotten about in this age of globalisation and readily available leaf vegetables from Kenya or South Korea. On the culinary side, young green nettle leaves make a really tasty spinach-like green mush tasting something like a mixture of spinach and cucumber. It is very easy to make by simply treating it as though it is spinach, wilting down the leaves in a pot with a little water over a good heat and then draining, chopping and adding butter and salt and pepper. This can then be used as a vegetable side dish or can form the base of a soup or pesto to which other ingredients can be added. You have to use gloves to collect the leaves, to pluck them off the stalk and to get them into the pot, but once they have been cooked they are harmless. The *trichomes* break down and largely disintegrate, and the volatile irritants are destroyed or evaporated by cooking. Getting people to believe this is the main obstacle to the use of this free and abundant vegetable growing at the bottom of the garden. Note, however, that nettles should not be eaten after they have entered the flowering and seed-setting stage when their leaves develop grit-like cystoliths which, if eaten, can irritate the urinary tract[46].

Nettles are also used for flavouring the famous Cornish Yarg cheese, and nettle beer is said to be popular in England, although I must say that I have been living here for seventeen years and have never heard it mentioned in conversation or ever seen it offered for sale. I suspect it is brewed exclusively for the tourist market and is probably something foisted upon elderly couples over here from Wisconsin on a cultural tour of the West Country, probably together with a slice of Cornish Yarg. Historically speaking, nettles have also been used to make a linen-like cloth for at least 2000 years through a retting process much like that used for flax. This cloth substitutes perfectly well for cotton fabrics and was used extensively for German army uniforms during the First World War due to shortages of other fabrics.

Medicinally, nettles in both fresh form or dried to make a herbal tea are said to be an astringent, diuretic, tonic, anodyne, pectoral, rubefacient, styptic, anthelmintic, nutritive, alterative, hemetic, anti-rheumatic, anti-allergenic, anti-lithic/lithotriptic, haemostatic, stimulant, decongestant, herpatic, febrifuge, kidney depurative/nephritic, galactagogue, hypoglycemic, expectorant and anti-spasmodic. Personally, I have no idea if any of that is true or to what extent it might achieve these ends. However, it seems plain that if this useful plant had leaves you could dry and smoke to narcotic effect then it would rival cannabis as a one-size-fits-all, multi-purpose miracle vegetable/herb/weed/crop/intoxicant. Doubtless it would then be designated as a Class A drug and could join magic mushrooms in widespread disregard for the edicts of the Home Office.

---

46 Note also that as the leaves and stalks dry out with the approach of winter, the capacity to sting diminishes considerably, to the point that ruminants can start to eat the plant. Consequently, nettle stalks make reasonable hay for winter feed.

OCTOPUS

The boy stood on the beach alongside a small wooden dinghy and looked out over the translucent water of the lagoon. He held a small rod and reel in one hand and a packet of bait prawns in the other. From beneath his feet the white sand stretched out under the water for a short way before a green carpet of eel grass dropped down into the dark blue of the channel. Being a small boy, he was not allowed to take the dinghy out onto the silver expanse of the lagoon, but because the deep channel ran near to the beach, he was allowed to paddle the dingy out a short way, drop the sand anchor and fish directly into the channel. The boy slid the old boat out over the sand, pulling himself in over the transom just as the water reached above his bony knees. Grappling with one of the heavy wooden oars, he managed to guide the boat to the edge of the channel and just as the current began to catch the bow he scuttled forward and dropped the anchor. The boat swung to a stop as the anchor caught and held. Satisfied, the boy turned his attention to his tackle and attached a light nylon trace with a swivel and a small hook beneath a running ball sinker on the main line. In this way the sinker would be free to shift up and down the main line above the swivel and any fish taking the bait would pull the line through the sinker and be unable to feel its weight. A prawn was threaded onto the hook and secured in place by a tight winding of thin elastic thread. Flicking out the sinker and prawn into the middle of the channel, the boy watched the bait disappear into the dark water and settled back to wait. Surely a bite would not take long, he thought, as he relaxed into a complicated daydream.

A strong pull on the line woke the boy from his reverie. He struck smartly and then leaned back, the rod arching forward almost into the water. Whatever was on the end of the line gave a hard kick and then everything went solid, as though the line were caught on a rock. The boy maintained the pressure and felt an elastic stretching in the obstruction, but the line remained taut. He tugged the rod one way, then the other and then pulled hard back straight up over his head. Suddenly the line went slack and the boy nearly fell over backwards into the bottom of the boat. He reeled in the line furiously trying to take up the slack, but before he could make contact something thumped into the underside of the boat, causing it to rock from side to side. The boy stopped reeling in surprise. That had never happened before. He was about to shift position so as to peer over the side when over the starboard gunwhale came a thick and writhing octopus arm, its huge suckers sticking to the wood and the thin end questing like a searching snake. The boy felt a surge of adrenaline, yet before he could call out or reach into the bottom of the boat for a weapon of some sort, another octopus arm came thumping over, but this time on the port side, scattering the bait prawns and wrapping around the wooden seat. Hardly able to believe the sight of the whole boat being embraced by the biggest octopus anyone had ever heard of, the boy scrambled into the stern and, being a brave boy, gave thought to how to fight the monster off. He was about to grab an oar and do battle when, in a flurry of writhing limbs, the whole octopus heaved itself up onto the bow of the boat. The boy's nerve broke and with a scream he flung himself into the water and swam for the shore. Apparently, so fast did he move his arms and legs that when he reached the beach, the back of his shirt and shorts were still perfectly dry. When telling of the incident afterwards the boy said that the sight of the octopus's eyes lifting up over the gunwhale now haunted him and he had decided to give up fishing and move to the mountains as soon as he was old enough to determine his own fate.

I know, I know. The first time I heard this story I was also suckered into the narrative before realising it was utter nonsense – a quintessential tall tale. It was told to me decades ago by a well-known seafront raconteur who claimed he was the boy in question and managed to keep a straight face throughout, but could not quite supress the bright twinkle in his eye. It was thus a surprise to learn that there is at least one species of octopus that grows big enough to lend the story some prospect of veracity. The Pacific octopus averages thirty pounds in weight with an armspan of fourteen feet, but the largest ever credibly recorded boasted a weight of 300 pounds and an armspan of thirty feet – plenty big enough to hug a small boat to its bosom and then climb aboard and eat a small boy.

Apart from the lethal blue-ringed octopus which can deliver a serious dose of tetrodotoxin[47] to the unwary or over-familiar bather in Australian waters, most octopuses are small enough to handle quite easily and are generally regarded as harmless creatures, notwithstanding a sharp beak capable of delivering a painful nip and an injection of venom. Apart from the blue-ringed octopus, this venom has little or no effect on humans, fortunately. In my ignorant younger days on the Southern African coast, I and other angling types often caught small octopuses in rock pools in the inter-tidal zone by the simple method of attaching a red rag or strips of red rubber tubing to the hook end of a gaff and then shaking it about in the water. Any octopus in the pool would perceive the rag or red rubber as

---

47   Tetrodotoxin is the same poison found in fugu mentioned earlier. It is not
      a nice way to go.

a competing octopus and would launch itself forth into battle. It was then a simple matter to hook the octopus on the gaff, lift it out of the water and bash it into submission on the rocks[48]. We used these octopuses as bait and had no serious thought of eating them, although we vaguely understood that Portuguese people liked to eat them in a stew. They made good, tough bait, very resistant to the attentions of small nibbling fish, and thus were a popular choice when targeting larger fish, which need to be given an opportunity to find and then swallow a big bait before it is torn to shreds by the tiddlers.

There came a day when I gave up catching octopuses for bait after hearing a touching story about a close relationship between a diver and an octopus in the quiet waters of a Southern Cape lagoon. The diver and the octopus would meet underwater each day and would play a game together, where the man would hide a bright silver coin inside an old sunken bucket and the octopus would find it and return it to the man. I just felt that such a creature should not be used for bait. I first met the diver in question one evening whilst enjoying a drink with friends at the local yacht club. This tanned and handsome chap in his late thirties, with long hair swept back into a ponytail, was much admired by the ladies present and also appeared to be the owner of the most magnificent deep sea fishing boat I think I have ever seen – a towering chrome and fibreglass delight equipped with every conceivable gadget and two huge four-stroke engines, all of the finest quality money can buy. He was recently married to a lady somewhat older than himself and he was a genuinely personable character. We got on well and some weeks later I received an invitation to dinner at a magnificent waterfront

---

48 If you left the dead octopus on the gaff hook and then swished it about in another rock pool, it was even more effective at tempting out another octopus. If the pool did not in fact contain an octopus, then it would contain rock crabs which would immediately climb out of the water and could also be caught for use as bait.

property lately purchased by his wife. A fine and entertaining dinner ensued, but the most memorable part of the evening was to see a brass plaque prominently displayed in the hallway of the house which read:

In loving memory of Harold, without whom
all this would not have been possible

Harold, of course, was the lady's first husband who had worked excessively hard as a business executive in Johannesburg and had died of a heart attack a few years short of what would undoubtedly have been a comfortable retirement. I have never been able to work out whether this plaque was one of the most touchingly honest acknowledgements I have ever seen or was a cynical attempt at slightly embarrassed humour. Be that as it may, the idyllic enjoyment of Harold's riches by the happy couple did not last long and they parted company less than a year later.

It was not until I started to holiday occasionally in the Mediterranean that I properly discovered octopus as really delicious seafood. The Greeks do it best. On the Rodopos Peninsula in Northwestern Crete there is a little village which has a tiny cove-enclosed pebble beach reached by way of a rough gravel road that plunges precipitously down to the sea through terraced vegetable gardens and grazing goats. At the beach there is a little *kafenia*, an establishment too small to be called a taverna, which nestles up against the cliff just back from the water's edge. It is nothing but a few tables outside under a basic shade roof attached to a tiny room the size of a caravan with a service hatch and a glass-fronted refrigerator containing soft drinks and ice-cold Mythos beer. Cooking is done outside over a barbecue constructed from an old forty-four-gallon drum sawn in half lengthways. It is a family concern, with the women and girls of several generations doing all the cooking and waitressing, a son, tanned and long-haired, who then looked to be in his early twenties, doing the catching of octopus by diving amongst the nearby rocks or further out from a small boat, and men of more mature age sitting at a table in the shade drinking coffee and engaging in 'management'. The octopuses are hung out to dry on a wire strung along the side of the shade roof and also benefit from the shade of a conveniently jutting section of cliff face. The menu is limited to grilled octopus, spicy homemade sausages, Greek salad and French fries, but it is the freshest, most local food I have ever eaten in a restaurant. Very few ingredients are preprepared. If you order a Greek salad, a small girl hurtles off up the hill to the terraced vegetable gardens above and returns with ripe tomatoes, green peppers, cucumber and red onions, all picked right then and warm from the sun rather than the usual refrigerated chill. These are then cut up in the usual way and served with the family's home-produced olive oil, fresh oregano picked from the hillside above you and a thick slice of feta-like cheese made from the milk of the goats you passed on the way down to the beach. If you order grilled octopus, the son selects one he judges sufficiently dried from the wire alongside and then grills it over charcoal on the oil drum barbecue. This is then served with a vinegar and olive oil dressing and a scattering of a different oregano, also collected off the hillside. Both the salad and the octopus are simply magnificent – locally considered the best in the whole of Greece. The place is totally famous and is patronised over the weekend by wealthy Greek families from the relatively nearby town of Chania. They make a day out of it and arrive in large, shiny speedboats that they anchor off the cove. The people then jump off the boats and swim in to shore. During the week, though, a tourist might get a table if you get there early enough. Regardless of the fame, the *kafenia* doesn't change and the prices remain reasonable, which is extraordinary. Also, if the octopus is finished, it is finished and they don't substitute a frozen octopus from who knows where, as I suspect is the practice in every other Greek taverna I have ever been in.

Octopus really does need to be wind-dried first for a few hours if it is to achieve its full potential when grilled and this is simply not possible everywhere. The Greek islands in summer offer some of the best conditions for this with moderate temperatures, low humidity and a breeze off the sea. Other places where I have tried it have had too much humidity, which resulted in the octopus going off rather than quickly curing into an end result that both caramelises well over the coals and remains soft and white on the inside. Omit the wind-drying and the octopus will still be edible, but will retain a sort of wet, salty springiness that inhibits the grilling process and produces a far more rubbery finish. If you are not able to wind-dry your octopus, then it is better to serve it in a stew or to marinate it and serve it as a sort of carpaccio. Both of these methods produce a very pleasant result and are very popular all around the world, but are a distant second to grilling in my view. Recipes for stewed octopus and octopus carpaccio follow:

STEWED OCTOPUS

750 g octopus, either small or large, cleaned
4 tablespoons olive oil
4 cloves garlic, finely chopped
6 fresh ripe tomatoes, peeled and chopped
350 ml white wine
2 tablespoons brown Muscovado sugar
2 tablespoons chopped fresh dill
4 tablespoons chopped fresh parsley
1 tablespoon chilli flakes
2 tablespoons capers
Salt and freshly ground white pepper

Bring a large pot of salty water to a boil. Toss the octopus into the boiling water, return to a boil and cook for one to two minutes, then remove. Discard the water.

Cut the octopus into large pieces and sauté in olive oil over medium-high heat for two to three minutes. Add the chopped garlic and sauté for another minute or two.

Add the wine and bring to a boil over high heat. Stir well and let it reduce for three to four minutes. Add the tomatoes and chilli flakes and bring to a simmer. Add about a teaspoon of salt and the sugar. Mix well, cover the pot and simmer.

After thirty minutes, add the capers, plus half the dill and half the parsley.

Continue simmering until the octopus is tender, usually between forty-five minutes and one and a half hours. When you think you are about ten minutes away from being done, take the lid off the pot and reduce the sauce a little.

To serve, add the remaining dill and parsley, a sprinkling of white pepper and more salt if needed. Excellent with pasta or crusty bread and works either hot or at room temperature. If serving at room temperature, add a little more olive oil before serving.

OCTOPUS CARPACCIO

A 1 litre plastic mineral water bottle
1.2 kg octopus
1 carrot
2 stalks celery
1 onion
1 teaspoon black peppercorns
6 juniper berries
2 tablespoons red wine vinegar
4 fresh bay leaves
Parsley
1 clove garlic, crushed
Salt and black pepper
Extra virgin olive oil
Juice of 1 lemon

This is a recipe from giallozafferano.it, Italy's top food website. It is delicious. The method described below is demonstrated in a YouTube video that is well worth watching before you attempt the dish.

First, prepare the octopus. If the octopus is not cleaned, slice into the head and empty out everything inside. Then remove the eyes and the beak. Slice on each side of the eyes to remove a wedge of flesh containing each eye. Normally, when you remove the eyes you will see the beak just below and you can cut the beak out using a small knife. Wash the octopus thoroughly under cold running water.

Make a stock by placing the carrot, celery stalks, the onion cut in half, the peppercorns, juniper berries, bay leaves and vinegar into a pot with enough water to just cover the octopus. Add a teaspoon of salt. Bring to a simmer.

Before cooking the octopus and in order to create a more pleasing aesthetic appearance, the octopus's legs should be curled. This is achieved by repeatedly dipping the octopus's legs into the simmering stock and then removing them until little by little they curl to the required extent. Once the ends of the tentacles are nicely curled, submerge the entire octopus in the hot stock and simmer for about an hour over a medium heat.

Once the octopus has cooked, remove it from the pot, drain it and allow it to cool. Then cut the octopus up – remove the head and cut it in half and then cut the octopus into quarters. The octopus is now ready to be packed into the bottle. The bottle is prepared by first cutting off the tapered end, leaving the straight part. Next, poke holes into the bottom of the bottle using an awl or the end of some scissors. Put the bottle into a bowl to catch the moisture that will be squeezed out of the octopus. Put the octopus into the bottle, trying as far as possible to keep the tentacles curled in the bottle to make an attractive cross-section when cut. Press the octopus down into the bottle very firmly using a pestle or thinner bottle or something wide enough to compress the octopus without breaking it or cutting it.

Once the octopus is compressed into the bottle and the liquid has drained from the bottom, it is time to close the bottle. This is achieved by cutting the plastic into tabs vertically down to the level of the octopus, then closing the bottle by folding the tabs over into the centre and then wrapping the bottle tightly in cling film.

Chill the octopus in the refrigerator for at least twenty-four hours. Before serving, remove the octopus from the bottle, again wrap tightly in cling film and place in the freezer for twenty minutes. Then slice as you would a salami (which the compressed octopus now somewhat resembles) as thinly as possible using a very sharp knife or a slicing machine.

Serve by placing the slices of octopus on a platter and drizzling with a mixture of lemon juice in which the crushed garlic has been placed and the olive oil. Scatter a handful of chopped parsley over the top.

OSTRICH

The distant black and grey figure shimmered through the heat haze in that distinctive high-kneed, bouncy gait employed by ostriches to put distance between them and anything they perceive as being a nuisance, which on this occasion would have been me. The terrain was the hard bushveld of the Marico District in North-West South Africa and specifically on land that had once been farmed, first for crops in a bitter experiment involving clearing fields out of the thorn and rock and then failing to grow anything worthwhile; followed by cattle in a low-volume, disease-susceptible, ecologically destructive decade that had not improved the owners' fortunes; ending finally in abandonment of the farm. The land was now being allowed to revert to its original, natural state and game animals had been reintroduced in an effort to create a private hunting reserve – an increasingly lucrative and ultimately successful venture. In pursuing this vision the balance of wild creatures had to be managed and it happened that too many ostriches came into existence on the farm. These had to be thinned out and hence a request to me, as one of the first clients on the hunting reserve, to please shoot a male ostrich or two, free of charge, if the opportunity arose. That is how I came to be struggling through the heat and thorns in pursuit of a rapidly fading blob bobbing up and down in the distance.

Today ostriches are not generally perceived of as something you hunt regularly or even at all. They have been reared in captivity for hundreds of years, historically for their magnificent feathers, but more recently also for meat, which is available all over the world, and for the beautiful leather created from their skins. Moreover, although wild ostriches are common in most bush areas of Sub-Saharan Africa and were often hunted in the past, any ostrich hunting lore that might once have existed is now quite obscure and when confronted by the prospect of actually hunting one in the modern era, I found myself in personally uncharted and vicariously unguided waters. For a start, what do you shoot an ostrich with? It's a bird, of course, but a large male weighs around 280 pounds and is not a prospect for a charge of number six birdshot. Even with heavy buckshot, how do you get within forty yards of a creature that stands nine feet tall, possesses the largest eyes of any land-based vertebrate and is famous for its typically avian philosophy of flee first, ask questions later? A shotgun being clearly out of the question, a rifle of sorts was called for. For want of any better idea, I set out on my ostrich hunt armed with my .308 Winchester, a weapon I felt confident with and which would undoubtedly possess the requisite power to subdue an ostrich if I came across one. If anything, my concern was that the .308 would be too powerful for the job and would cause unjustified meat damage.

As I was soon to discover, hunting ostriches on purpose is not something that can be undertaken lightly. They really do have the most incredibly acute eyesight and seem to realise that you are hunting them the instant they catch sight of you. This takes you by surprise because normally when you are out after other game, they are cautious of you but far from panic-stricken, often allowing you to come well within range whilst you are busy stalking some other creature. But somehow if they are the principal target they know, from body language or something, and become extremely skittish, continually moving away at speed and keeping hundreds of yards between you and them. This is very tiring. In fact, most ostriches get taken as a casual adjunct to a hunt for antelope, where the decision to shoot the ostrich is a spontaneous matter encouraged upon the client by an opportunistic professional hunter or tracker. Most hunters, and particularly trophy hunters, are not overly inspired by the prospect of an ostrich as a trophy – lacks glamour seemingly, although Americans out for a 'safari of a lifetime' do shoot them and have them shoulder mounted and shipped back home. Probably, an ostrich mount is considered exotic and has greater appeal in Texas.

Having flushed my first ostrich into a rapidly disappearing dot on the horizon, I adopted new tactics. Climbing to the top of a ridge of hills that traversed the reserve, I perched on a high rock in sweaty exhaustion and surveyed the adjoining plain with binoculars. Sure enough, several groups of ostriches were visible, all peacefully grazing away in a restful manner over 1000 yards away. Noting the position of each group, I decided upon a progressive approach that would take me up onto each group in such a way that if I was spotted and the birds bolted, they would hopefully not disturb the other groups. Taking a long swig of water from my rapidly diminishing supply, I slid down the rock and set off.

Well, so much for plans. To curtail a long and somewhat tortured tale of heat, sweat and thorns, what happened with each group I approached was one of two things. If the bush was thick then I would manage to stay out of sight and get quite close, sometimes inside a hundred yards, but without exception the birds would see me before I saw them and would instantly set off at a fast run, disappearing rapidly into the acacia thorn and giving no chance of a shot. If the terrain was more open then, no matter how slowly and carefully I approached, they would note my presence at about 300 yards and even if I crawled on hands and knees, would be moving off steadily before the range had closed to

250 yards. These distant birds made me crave a different rifle. As excellent as the .308 is in almost all respects, the one thing it does not do well is handle ranges beyond about 200 yards. Beyond 200 yards the relatively heavy bullets commonly used for bushveld hunting (168 to 200 grains) drop off appreciably in a banana-like trajectory that is very hard for the hunter to manage. A much better bet for such long ranges are very much higher-velocity rifles like the .300 Winchester Magnum, the 7 mm Remington Magnum or the scorching hot .270 Weatherby Magnum which have much flatter trajectories with similar bullet weights and are feasible right out to 300 yards and beyond if a powerful scope is used. Generally, I am not very keen on long-range sniping at game. Unless you are very practised at it, there is so much that can go wrong and the target is reduced to such a relatively tiny size that you are often taking a grave risk of wounding rather than killing, but on this occasion such a weapon might have saved me from a very long and hot afternoon of fruitless pursuit.

I never did manage to stalk an ostrich successfully. I did manage to shoot one, though. As the light began to fade I made my way to a waterhole where I knew a borehole producing fresh, clean water was located. After slaking my considerable thirst I sat down under a bush to rest awhile and enjoy a quiet smoke before making my way back to camp. While I sat there contemplating the frustrations of the day and enjoying the vivid African sunset, a prime male ostrich emerged from the bush some fifty yards away, obviously also intent on a drink and completely oblivious to my presence. While I don't usually shoot animals at waterholes, this was really a culling exercise so I made an exception. Taking aim at a point just in front of the leg and in the middle of the body, I fired and the ostrich immediately collapsed on the spot with a sort of forward falling flounce. By the time I had walked up to it, it was dead. From this I have the impression that ostriches are quite soft and could probably be hunted with any rifle from the centre-fire .22s upwards, as long as you hit the bird in the vitals (the front part, beneath the neck and in the forward chest part of the body, not behind the legs and low into the extensive gut).

Ostrich meat is very lean and prone to toughness and although I have tried it in many recipes, it works best if briefly cooked over a high heat to produce a medium-rare finish like a beef steak. It is then tender and very palatable. My favourite is:

OSTRICH STROGANOFF

400 g ostrich steaks
300 g chestnut button mushrooms
Olive oil
1 medium onion, sliced
3 cloves garlic, grated
1 tablespoon sweet paprika
1 lemon
50 ml brandy
6 tablespoons double cream or crème fraîche
Bunch of flat-leaf parsley
Salt and freshly ground black pepper

Slice the mushrooms in half. Heat two tablespoons of olive oil in a deep frying pan and fry the onion and garlic briefly. Add the mushrooms and cook for a few minutes. Remove the mushrooms, onion and garlic mixture from the pan.

Slice the ostrich steaks into strips about 1 cm thick. Squeeze lemon juice over them and then toss them in salt, pepper and paprika. Heat another tablespoon of olive oil in the pan. Fry the steaks for one to two minutes over a high heat – you want them nicely browned but still very rare on the inside. Add the brandy to the steak and flame briefly. Return the mushrooms, onions and garlic to the pan. Add the cream, bring rapidly to the boil and as soon as it thickens slightly, check the seasoning, add a handful of chopped parsley and serve immediately with basmati rice and a green salad.

OYSTERS

Oysters are supposed to be romantic. If you collect them yourself from a warm and effervescent sea and then share them right there on the rocks in the sunshine with a bikini-clad nymph, salt water beading on golden, sun-freckled skin then they are, by God, most definitely romantic. Wash them down with a bottle of chilled Verve Clicquot and enjoy the transient delights of youth. The alleged aphrodisiacal qualities of the oysters will hardly be necessary.

I once sought to employ oysters in a great seduction. A fine and very attractive girl came to my attention and accepted an invitation to dinner at my flat. *Right*, I thought, *here is my chance*. At great expense, for I was then a very junior member of the legal profession, I purchased several dozen wild coastal oysters, a loaf of fine French bread and a couple of bottles of Laurent Perrier rosé champagne. Lengthy and detailed were my preparations, for I wished to make a good impression. All was set: candlelight flickered, soft music played and an ambience of sophisticated perfection prevailed. My guest arrived and was duly impressed. We got on well and soon I was able to present the oysters and champagne with an appropriate flourish.

'Oooh!' said this delightful girl. 'Oysters, my favourite!' Then with considerable focus she wolfed down most of the oysters accompanied by large slices of buttered bread and great draughts of champagne. *Nothing wrong with her appetite*, I thought.

In a short time the feast was over and my guest moved into a comfortable position on the couch whilst I cleared away the dishes. *Now for the main act*, I thought as I cleaned up in the kitchen and washed my hands. Returning to the living room with a mounting sense of anticipation, I found not a willing and pliable siren, but a happily sleeping young woman, a smiling look of great contentment on her face, hands clasped over a little pot belly. It was really quite beautiful and there was nothing I could do but cover her with a blanket and go off to my lonely bed. So much for my career as a Don Juan, although my situation was later redeemed[49].

There are over a hundred different varieties of edible 'oyster' drawn from at least five species, not all of them true oysters, but precise definition of taxonomic character is obscured by the vagaries of commercial cultivation and consequent marketing. Commercial cultivators try to create proprietary 'brands' of oysters and are not at all forthcoming about precisely what they are up to, biologically speaking. This does not make much difference to those of us who simply like eating them. Try them all and see which ones you like best. Perhaps the most significant culinary divide is between oysters that are collected in the wild and those that are cultivated. As a very general statement, wild oysters tend to be larger, meatier and creamier in texture than those that are cultivated. I love wild oysters for exactly those characteristics. However, many people find the wild ones to be just too much oyster for comfort and prefer the leaner, cleaner and, some would say, more sophisticated flavour and texture of the cultivated ones – sort of like the difference between a nude by Rubens and a ballet dancer by Degas. Perhaps more significant than the origin of the particular oyster is how it has been treated

---

49   At time of writing I have been happily married to this girl for thirty-one years.

and how much time has elapsed since it was harvested. One of the commercially attractive features of oysters is a very long shelf life as a live mollusc after harvesting, up to four weeks if refrigerated, and this can create a huge variation in the quality of oysters from the same source because the longer they are kept out of seawater the less appealing they become to eat. Another very big factor is how long elapses between the time the oyster is opened and the time you eat it. Many restaurants make a mistake with this. Oysters are fiddly and time-consuming to open, particularly if the person doing the opening is the most junior member of staff and does not have much experience, and so restaurants tend to open all the oysters they anticipate selling well in advance and then keep them on ice in the refrigerator. This simply ruins them[50]. Oysters die rapidly after opening and the flavour and 'plumpness' factor so important to enjoying them diminishes exponentially with the passage of time after opening, reducing by half after about thirty minutes and then by half again every twenty minutes or so until all that is left is a slightly leathery and flavourless dead vestige of what was a really delicious live thing mere hours previously. It is at this point that they are usually served to the customers. Owners of restaurants where this happens must reflect on whether they are in business to provide pleasure to customers or convenience to staff. It's a tragic waste. In my view a restaurant that advertises fresh oysters is obliged to serve you oysters that are still alive. You can tell whether an oyster is alive very easily. Oysters are invariably served with lemon wedges or with a vinegar-based sauce of some sort. Drip a little lemon juice or sauce onto the oyster's flesh. If it is alive its flesh will visibly contract upon contact with the acidic liquid. If they are not alive, send them back for they will probably be disappointing and might even be dangerous, for oysters go off quickly once opened. An oyster that has started

---

50 If you freeze them immediately after opening, however, they are quite palatable when defrosted.

to go off has a distinctly peppery, metallic flavour that fills the mouth with unpleasantness. Spit it out! If you swallow you are doomed to days of gastric unhappiness and might even end up in hospital.

It is fun to collect your own oysters if you find yourself in a place where wild oysters occur. These days, even in obscure destinations, the oyster beds near the shore have almost always been hammered and so your best chance will be slightly further out. Obviously, a calm sea is necessary and a low spring tide will be the most productive time. You don't need much equipment: mask, weight belt, fins, net bag and a robust diving knife or sharpened metal bar capable of wrenching the oysters off the rock. Oysters cement themselves to the rock and to each other very firmly and so a strong implement is needed to lever them off. Many places restrict the size of the implement in an effort to save the oyster beds from the worst excesses of destruction inflicted by people let loose with large crowbars. The weight belt is essential if you are diving for oysters in more than three feet of water. Without the belt it is very difficult to achieve the requisite leverage because as you try to press down on the implement your body tends to rise towards the surface. Once you have collected a few dozen oysters you then face the challenge of opening them yourself. The same challenge faces you if you buy unopened cultivated oysters (which you should). Advice on this aspect follows:

HOW TO OPEN AN OYSTER

Like most things these days, the best way to learn how to open an oyster is to have a quick look at one of the many YouTube videos that demonstrate the art. However, a few words about the more obscure aspects. For a start, you really do need the right equipment: a proper oyster shucking knife and a robust kitchen towel. An oyster shucking knife is a specially designed knife with a short, robust and pointed blade. Expert oyster shuckers prefer to wriggle this knife into the joint between the two shell halves, then twist to release the suction before sweeping the blade forward pressed tight up against the uppermost shell half so as to sever the ligament that attaches the flesh to the shell. This is much more easily said than done. Particularly on wild oysters, the hinge between the two shells is the thickest, strongest and often a very irregular part of the shell. Experts like to open at that spot because it is the tidiest and because the shell is so strong at that point it does not flake off shards of shell into the flesh as sometimes happens when you open at other points. For an amateur it is better to select a spot somewhat forward of the hinge where you can usually get the point of the knife under the edge of the shell more easily. Once you have opened your first oyster you will understand the design of the oyster shucking knife – oysters are very difficult to open with other types of knife and there is a grave danger of snapping the blade or of stabbing yourself.

The kitchen towel is also something it is very difficult to do without. Oyster shells have sharp edges and are very uncomfortable to grip with an unprotected hand. A glove could be worn instead, but amateurs seldom have a glove available with sufficient thickness of fabric or padding. The force employed in using the shucking knife is considerable and the shell has to be held very firmly. I usually cradle the entire shell in the towel, doubling over the fabric along the edges to protect my fingers. The cradling has the advantage that the shell remains horizontal throughout the process and the juices are not spilled when the top shell half is removed.

Most people would agree that the best way to enjoy oysters is perfectly fresh and alive, with a little lemon juice and a bottle of good Chablis or dry champagne. I like a couple of drops of Tabasco sauce on each oyster as well, in the American style, although this once got me thrown out of a beachfront restaurant on the Côte D'Azur. On this occasion, after requesting Tabasco from the Maître d', I was subjected to a particularly scathing attack by the chef, who came all the way from the kitchen to deliver a tirade dripping with contemptuous denigration. This got my back up somewhat and I was constrained to reply that any establishment that routinely served an eye-wateringly strong sauce of red wine vinegar and chopped shallot with its fresh oysters was in no position to point fingers at Tabasco. Well, you would think I had insulted his grandmother, so vituperous did this chef become, such that in the end and in the spirit of the moment I may have suggested he stick his oysters in a dark and uncomfortable place and that if he required assistance with this I would be happy to oblige by applying my right foot to the problem. He then refused to serve us and we were escorted from the premises under dark glares from the other patrons. I genuinely believe that Tabasco is an enhancement to oysters. There is just some chemical magic that happens whereby even large dollops of Tabasco don't overwhelm the oyster, though on paper that should be what happens. If you eat oysters in the Southern States of the USA, particularly in Louisiana, then you are usually offered a choice of hot pepper sauces, each subtly different from the other. A great afternoon can be spent in a New Orleans oyster bar sampling all the varieties of oyster on offer in combination with all the different pepper sauces and all the different types of beer. By the time you have finished that, the sun will have set and you will be ready to drift gently through the sleazy romance of a humid night in the French Quarter. If you are not careful you can easily be waylaid by the strains of jazz or blues emanating from the doorways of the basement cafés and before you know it you find yourself roaring with good cheer in some gumbo joint in the swamp. The next morning you will have no idea how you got back to your hotel.

Some people don't like fresh oysters. My youngest brother, on first tasting one, likened it to a great dollop of salty snot and refused to sample another. He likes smoked oysters, however, which is of course a completely different thing. Tinned smoked oysters, particularly those immersed in cotton-seed oil, are delicious. I have tried to smoke fresh oysters in a small hot smoker several times, but the result has always been disappointing and far short of what is achieved by the commercial canning outfits. There are also two other simple cooked oyster recipes that are very worthwhile if you get to a point where you have eaten so many fresh oysters that you are bored or if you are one of those who don't like fresh oysters. They are:

OYSTERS ROCKEFELLER

1 garlic clove
1 small packet fresh baby spinach
1 small bunch watercress, stems trimmed
1 onion, roughly chopped
250 g unsalted butter at room temperature
Large handful dry breadcrumbs
2 tablespoons Pernod or other anise-flavoured liqueur
1 teaspoon fennel seeds, freshly ground
2 teaspoons Tabasco or other hot pepper sauce (Frank's etc.)
500 g rock salt
24 fresh oysters, shucked and on the half-shell
100 g freshly grated Parmesan cheese

Preheat the oven to 230°C. Wilt the spinach and watercress together in a pot. Once wilted, press as much moisture out as possible. Finely chop the garlic in a food processor. Add the wilted spinach and watercress mixture and the onion to the garlic. Process until the mixture is finely chopped. Transfer the mixture to a bowl.

Combine the butter, breadcrumbs, Pernod, ground fennel and hot sauce in the processor. Process until well blended. Return the spinach mixture to the processor. Process, using on/off turns, until the mixtures are just blended. Season with salt and pepper.

Sprinkle rock salt over a large baking sheet to a depth of half an inch. Arrange the oysters in half shells atop the rock salt. Top each oyster with one tablespoon of spinach mixture, completely covering the oyster and smoothing off with a knife. Sprinkle generously with Parmesan cheese. Bake until the spinach mixture browns on top, about eight minutes.

Great as a starter with a crisp New Zealand Sauvignon Blanc.

ANGELS ON HORSEBACK

12 fresh oysters, shucked and removed from the shell
12 broad rashers of streaky bacon, size to match size of oysters
12 toothpicks
1 lemon or 2 limes

Simplicity itself. Fry the bacon rashers until about half-cooked. Allow to cool and then wrap each oyster in a rasher of bacon and secure with a toothpick. If the oysters are large, you can cut them in half or use two rashers of bacon (increasing the quantity of bacon rashers accordingly). Grill under a high heat until the oysters are just cooked and bacon is crispy. Squeeze lemon or lime juice onto the angels and serve immediately. Totally addictive. Great with dry Amontillado sherry.

PARTRIDGE

There are 187 species of partridge in the world, occurring mainly in dry, open country throughout Southern Eurasia, Africa and Australia. They are all dumpy, short-tailed birds with a penchant for running from danger rather than flying, but suddenly bursting into a quick whirring flight if danger gets too close. They all suffer the curse of being white-fleshed and succulent from the top of the neck to the foot of the drumstick and thus are a favourite of game gourmets all over the world. They tend to hang about in family groups, or coveys as they are called, numbering from about six to as many as thirty birds and the most popular shooting species will also hold in cover for both pointing and flushing gun dogs. This makes them probably the most sought-after game birds in the world, aesthetically speaking, because they are a very challenging target both when driven and when walked-up. Only grouse are arguably more challenging and that argument is far from easily resolved.

The native partridge of the British Isles is the grey partridge. It was once a very common and widespread species, but has suffered serious decline in recent decades due to a combination of three factors. Firstly, grey partridge chicks feed almost exclusively on insects during the first few weeks of life, and the use of herbicides to control crop weeds since the 1950s has significantly reduced insect food and hence insects by as much as seventy-five percent. Secondly, mechanised agriculture has led to the destruction of thousands of hedgerows. Hedgerows generally have grass margins and these are perfect habitat for partridges. Finally, the economics of game management, driven in no small part by the decline in naturally occurring partridge populations following upon the first two factors, has led to an emphasis on pheasant rearing rather than on predator control and habitat management for partridges. As a consequence, the halcyon days of grey partridge shooting in Britain, where the annual bag exceeded two million birds, have long passed and a grey partridge shoot has become a relatively rare treat for a British shooter. At first blush these sad facts engender a kind of nostalgic bitterness, but there is a circular irony at work. Remember that it was the agricultural machinations of mankind in the creation of the hedgerows and in the considerable intensification and expansion of agriculture following common land enclosures, particularly in the eighteenth and nineteenth centuries, that led to a population explosion among grey partridges in the first place. What man's activities giveth they can also take away and we are probably back to more or less where we started with grey partridges in Britain.

The red-legged partridge is the famous 'French' or 'Spanish' partridge of mainland Europe, occurring mainly in France, Iberia and North-West Italy, although it has been introduced all over the place in Europe and in England, where it is raised in captivity for later release like pheasants and has also established naturalised local populations here and there. Although it is an iconic and popular game bird everywhere in Europe, it reaches its apex in Spain. It is the general consensus amongst those who can afford such things that the driven partridge shoots offered by the famous Spanish shooting estates are beyond compare. These estates cover tens of thousands of acres and hold vast numbers of wild partridges. Each drive will offer hundreds, if not thousands, of birds, in all sorts of varied and challenging terrain, and so rapid is the pace of shooting that each gun has, as an absolute minimum, two shotguns, a loader and a general assistant called a *secretario* who assists in the slaughter by marking and retrieving fallen birds and keeping count of the numbers so an appropriate charge can be made by the estate. I am told that wealthy Spanish dignitaries who regularly enjoy such shooting often have a travelling team of assistants that move around to the different estates with their employer, much like a top professional golfer might travel about with a caddy, a couple of coaches, a physiotherapist and a psychologist. It is thus a common sight to see a gun literally surrounded by staff in the field and apparently it is the practice for these Spanish folk to have *six* shotguns available to them (two sets of three identical shotguns) in the field. This extraordinary abundance in the shooting is matched by supremely luxurious accommodation, wonderful food and superb wine to create a mix that is bordering on the obscene (some would say well over that border, particularly having regard to the state of the Spanish economy and the fact that many of the dignitaries are bankers) and the cost is eye-watering – three days of such shooting for you and six or seven of your mates, during which you would dispatch some 3000 partridges, would equate to the purchase price of a luxury three-bedroom holiday apartment in a golfing estate on the Costa del Sol.

Of course, things are different in the developing world. In the developing world, particularly Sub-Saharan Africa, not every square inch of land has been worked over for thousands of years. Things are still in a raw, if not exactly pristine, state. This includes the state of things for partridges, of which there are dozens of different species, usually designated as being one or other kind of 'francolin' or 'spur fowl', these terms sometimes being interchangeable depending upon which ornithological authority is holding sway. Every ecological niche seems to have its partridge species and I have encountered them in the dry vastness of the Kalahari Desert, the high mountains of the Drakensberg and Karoo, throughout the 'bush' areas, be they thorn scrub or grassland savanna, and in the shrinking luxuriance of the coastal forests. Africa is the cradle of partridge kind, the *fons et origo* of the family, and from shortly after the extinction of the dinosaurs some sixty-six million years ago, partridges have been migrating out of Africa, mutating through the normal processes of evolution, including migrating back into Africa again, until the considerable diversity of species encountered in the modern world has developed. It is accordingly a quintessentially African bird and as is the case elsewhere, some species of African partridge are compatible with, and have benefited from, the advent of expanding agriculture. Populations of these species have increased considerably, sometimes at the expense of other, less adaptable, species whose habitat has concomitantly been reduced.

The experience of shooting partridges on farms in Africa is very similar to rough shooting for partridges in Britain or Europe. With or without the assistance of gun dogs, grassland cover adjacent to crops is worked thoroughly and the birds, some of them hen-pheasant sized, flush from the cover and sometimes get shot. But it is in the bush areas that Sub-Saharan Africa boasts truly fantastic partridge shooting, it is just that nobody is interested in it. In bush areas the emphasis is very much on game viewing and on big game hunting and so the birds are left almost entirely alone and flourish undisturbed in the many private wilderness areas and in the huge national parks. This situation looks set to continue indefinitely into the future, so if you are ever on a safari for big game don't overlook what can often be the best bird shooting you will ever experience. Also, don't be put off by the professional hunter or safari operator who may well have a negative attitude. Bird shooting does not generate the big bucks, but the real reason for reticence is that

African professional hunters, with some notable exceptions, are hopeless with a shotgun and fear humiliation at the hands of a client who is supposed to be in a state of worshipful awe.

When I first started shooting partridges in South Africa some forty years ago there was an eccentric atmosphere attaching to the pursuit and it was certainly something that only a person of English cultural heritage would dream of doing. As far as the Afrikaners were concerned, running around in the bush with a shotgun trying to slay birds when the surrounding *kloofs*[51] were groaning with kudu and the reedbuck were dying of old age, was completely impossible to understand. Why go to all that effort when for the same trouble the result could be big basins of fresh meat for *braaivleis*[52] or biltong rather than a few scruffy bundles of feathers? The indigenous black person was in complete agreement with the Afrikaner on this issue right up until the point that a commercial fee had to be paid for the privilege of hunting the kudu or reedbuck, something that an Afrikaner was quite happy to do. At this point the indigenous person would ask why on earth someone would pay the price of two cows for something having less meat than one cow. It just goes to show that all white folks are crazy.

More recently partridge shooting in South Africa, particularly for the much sought-after greywing and redwing francolin of the mountainous regions, has become a highly organised and expensive activity producing rough shooting of the very highest quality, rivalling rough shooting for grouse on the moors of Scotland. I cannot afford it anymore, but back in the early 1990s when luxury bird shooting was in its inexpensive infancy, I would go greywing shooting every year with friends. Greywing occur in various mountainous areas in South Africa, but the area we preferred was in the Karoo, in the mountains between the towns of Craddock and Graaf-Reinet. The scenery

---

51   Mountain ravines

52   Barbecue

in these parts is memorably vast and once you are on top of the mountains the view is a staggering 360-degree panorama of lean, brown plains stretching out to smoky-blue mountain ranges in the distance. It is evocative and mysterious country, full of ghosts. It was once more densely populated, first by groups of San people and then, starting about 200 years ago, by Afrikaans settlers who displaced the San and occupied the more fertile mountain valleys in a progression of small farms, each with a homestead, a *kraal* for livestock and sometimes a small dam or weir on a mountain stream. Many of these structures remain, but the Afrikaners are long gone to jobs on the mines or in the big cities. Generally only the most successful family in each major valley still remains, having bought out all the rest. So the valleys are now silent and only the rushing crackle of the wind through the stands of poplar trees near the ruined homesteads breaks the hypnotic stillness. The partridge are found in grasslands near the mountain tops and are hunted using German shorthaired or English pointers. It is a harsh environment given to extremes of weather and I have walked along in my shirtsleeves sweating profusely in the sunshine and then had my shotgun barrels freeze shut in a snowstorm all in the course of the same afternoon. Getting up the mountains is a challenge for the physically unfit. The shoot operators do their best to get as far as possible with 4x4 vehicles, but in the end the gun must walk (or even worse, ride a horse), sometimes for many miles, because the dogs range prodigiously and the birds are highly mobile and have large territories. When the dogs do go on point it can sometimes take as long as ten minutes to get all the guns up and in position and amazingly, both the dogs and the birds will often sit tight for such a protracted length of time. The birds flush explosively when pushed out of the cover and as many as twenty birds fragment away in a whirring flash, always curving and always dropping down to disappear over the nearest horizon. They are really fast – the fastest of all African game birds. It takes some time to get the hang of the speed. The first time I experienced it, I was simply astounded. I just stood there open-mouthed, having failed to even lift my shotgun. But you do get it in the end and learn that at such speed only instinctive shooting can possibly prevail, so the less you think about it the better you do. Just a few days shooting at greywing makes any other game bird seem as big and ponderous as a 747 and you have to consciously slow yourself down if you are not to blow the poor thing to tatters on the second wingbeat.

It is very difficult to decide which partridge species is the best to eat. They are all good and it may well be that individual characteristics of a particular habitat make the decisive difference. A Swainson's francolin living next to a field of sunflowers and feasting on oil-saturated seeds will be better than some other species scratching a living in some meagre patch of bushveld somewhere. In Britain the grey partridge is thought to be better eating than European red-legged or Asiatic chukar species that now occupy the same space, but naturally a continental European thinks otherwise. Two recipes follow that are suitable for any partridge species anywhere:

PARTRIDGE POTJEKOS

Potjekos is a traditional South African layered stew cooked in a cast iron potje, or three-legged pot, over the coals of a slow fire. Of course it can also be cooked in an ordinary enamelled cast iron pot, in which case it is better to bake it in the oven. Potjekos is never stirred and the layers are maintained until the stew is served. Potjekos experts insist that the layering is crucial to the flavour and if you change the order of the layers or leave one out the flavour is irredeemably altered. The best pork loin to use in this dish is warthog, but warthog is hard to get even in Africa because warthogs carry swine fever and it is illegal to transport the meat. Ordinary free-range pork is a reasonable substitute. The pork is included to generate and enrich the gravy which accumulates in the bottom of the pot. The pork itself is not eaten and can be discarded – it is the partridges that are the star of this show.

(Serves 6–8)
3 or 4 partridges, cleaned and plucked
600 g pork loin
500 g potatoes, peeled and sliced
500 g onions, peeled and sliced
3 yellow peppers, deseeded and sliced
2 x 400 g tins chopped tomatoes
1 or 2 bottles fruity white wine (South African Chenin Blanc, French Vouvray, German Riesling), depending on the size of the pot
Dried thyme – a decent shake
50 ml brandy
1 tablespoon sweet paprika
Salt and freshly ground black pepper
3 tablespoons sunflower oil

Heat the oven to 180°C. Cut each of the partridges into six pieces – breasts, legs and thighs. Heat the oil in the pot and briefly brown the partridge pieces. Remove the partridge pieces from the pot. Slice the pork loin into medallions at least sufficient to cover the bottom of the pot. Brown the pork medallions on both sides. When the medallions are nice and brown, add the paprika, stir and then add the brandy. Flame the medallions in the brandy briefly. Add a good quantity of salt and pepper. This is the bottom layer of the potje. Remove the pot from the heat entirely and allow to cool. For the next layer, cover the medallions with the yellow pepper and half the onions. Place the partridge pieces on top of the yellow pepper and onions as the third layer. Sprinkle generously with thyme and more salt and pepper. The fourth layer is the tinned tomatoes and the rest of the onions, followed by the potatoes as the fifth and final layer. Top up the pot with the wine – as much as is necessary to submerge everything in liquid. Cover and bake in the oven for three hours – halfway through baking take the pot out of the oven and check on the liquid level. If the stew looks a little dry, add more wine. In the bush this dish is prepared in the morning and cooks slowly over gentle coals for as long as ten hours before being eaten for supper. The birds are moist and tender and the gravy is absolutely spectacular in combination with the potatoes. The pork loin can just be thrown away in my view, but some like to eat it, particularly cold with piccalilli the next day.

MEDITERRANEAN ROAST PARTRIDGE

You find versions of this dish all over the Mediterranean in winter. The essence is the combination of sweet wine and roast grapes with the savoury gaminess of the partridge and the salty richness of bacon. The dish takes on a regional flavour through use of regional ingredients – Vin Santo and pancetta in Southern Italy being the best in my view.

(Serves 4)
4 partridges, cleaned and plucked
3 tablespoons olive oil
100 g unsalted butter
250 g seedless grapes
100 g diced pancetta
4 cloves of garlic, peeled and crushed
Pinch of coriander or fennel seeds (or both), briefly crushed in a mortar
8 fresh sage leaves
150 ml Vin Santo
Salt and freshly ground black pepper

Preheat the oven to 220°C. Heat the olive oil in a non-stick roasting tin to a medium/high heat and then add the pancetta, coriander/fennel seeds, sage leaves and garlic. Fry for about two minutes until they start to brown. Remove the garlic and reserve. Add the partridges and turn them over in the mixture a few times to thoroughly coat them and then leave them to brown slightly on each breast. Turn the birds breast side up and pour over 100 ml of the Vin Santo, reserving the remaining 50 ml for later. Season the birds generously with salt and pepper and then transfer them to the oven to roast for twenty minutes.

Put the grapes into a bowl and drizzle with the remaining olive oil. Add a sprinkling of salt and pepper and mix well. Put into the roasting tin with the birds and roast for fifteen minutes.

Remove the roasting dish from the oven and switch the oven off. Lift the birds and the grapes into an ovenproof dish, cover with foil and return to the oven to keep warm. Place the roasting tin over a medium/high heat and return the garlic to the pan. Pour in the remaining Vin Santo and deglaze the pan to create a sauce. Add the butter and as soon as it has melted remove from the heat and strain into a serving jug. Serve the partridges surrounded by grapes and covered with the sauce. Exceptionally good with polenta and a decent bottle of Greco di Tufo or Gavi.

PHEASANT

The first pheasant I ever saw looked impossibly exotic strutting across the immaculate emerald of a colonial lawn. The African sunlight refracting on the iridescent plumage created an image of complete loveliness. *What a magnificent bird*, I thought. Sad then, that the next time I saw a pheasant in Africa it was fluttering weakly towards me above the flat tops of the thorny acacia trees, just prior to being blown into a lump of tatty feathers by an overenthusiastic neighbouring gun. The occasion of this 'driven pheasant shoot' in the African bushveld was something organised by homesick English ex-pats and their anglophile hangers-on and was far from an uplifting experience. I am sure I was invited by mistake.

Pheasants do not naturally occur in Africa and do not thrive in the African bush. In Africa they are not viable unless you raise them to adulthood in a cage and then fling them out towards the waiting guns for the first and last proper flight of their lives. This is distastefully unsatisfactory. But, if you release them anything more than about five minutes before you intend to shoot them they get eaten – by jackals, leopards, lynxes, rock pythons, hyenas and even crocodiles. This is because they are delicious and not very bright. And it is not only in Africa that pheasants are not really viable. In many of the other places where they occur they would not last long if wild populations were not annually supplemented with domestically raised stock. In fairness, in most areas in Europe and North America, these domestically raised birds are usually released into the wild at a young age and some months prior to shooting. This is workable because of acute shortages of jackals, leopards, lynxes, rock pythons, hyenas and crocodiles in those places, although foxes take a toll. Nevertheless, the domestic experience at a young age seems to permanently affect pheasants which forever after seem uncomfortably wild and a bit incongruous. They look disgruntled and bewildered and give you the feeling they would be far happier as free-range chickens. But maybe that is just because they are very far from their natural home in the forests of Asia.

Pheasants have been a very popular game and domestic bird all over the Northern Hemisphere for several thousand years for a very good reason. Properly prepared, they are one of the nicest birds, in fact one of the nicest *things,* to eat that there is. Actually, they are *two* of the nicest things to eat that there is, but more of that later. Pheasant are at their most delicious when eaten after a lengthy maturation achieved by a process known as 'hanging'. Hanging used to be more popular for all types of game birds than it is these days. It involves suspending the bird by the neck, unplucked and uncleaned in some well-ventilated place for a number of days or even weeks. The effect is a progressive tenderisation of the flesh and a considerable strengthening of the gamey flavour. This is fine if you like the gamey flavour and prefer to convert it from the subtle undertone found in fresh birds to a powerful, nostril-filling, signature feature of the ensuing meal. For most game birds the process is linear and easy to manage; the longer you hang it, the gamier it gets. But with pheasants it is different. Pheasants have a 'magic moment' during the hanging process where, for reasons multifarious and mysterious, the darkly pungent, gamey flavour converts on cooking to a rich and subtle savoury of spectacular depth and memorable originality. It is delicious beyond the ordinary meaning of that word and is startling in its dissimilarity to most people's idea of the flavour of game.

Brillat-Savarin, the eighteenth-century French provincial magistrate and grand gourmet, whose entertaining book *The Physiology of Taste*[53] has been enthusiastically in print since 1825, was in no doubt at all about the importance of pheasant cooked at the magic moment and clearly rated it as one of the greatest of culinary experiences. His recipe for pheasant has all the reckless extravagance of a more innocent age and is given with such disarming enthusiasm that one really is tempted to try it. In short, you pluck and lard a magic moment pheasant and then stuff it with a minced concoction of two boned woodcock, steamed ox-marrow, grated cheese, grated bacon, pepper, salt, herbs and a 'sufficient quantity of good truffles to produce enough stuffing to fill the interior of the pheasant'. This is then roasted on a large piece of bread upon which has been spread the woodcocks' livers and entrails, pounded with two large truffles, an anchovy, a little grated bacon and a piece of good fresh butter.

Brillat-Savarin mentions that a pheasant is ripe for cooking at a fairly advanced stage of decomposition. He is not wrong there. In my experience, the magic moment arrives just before the bird descends into collapsed putrification and it is terribly hard to judge. Leave the bird for just one day, or sometimes even a few hours; longer and it is ruined – a soggy, rotting mess that no cooking technique or flavoursome sauce can disguise. To make it more difficult, there is no consistency in the time the hanging bird will take to reach its 'esculent apogee', as Brillat-Savarin puts it. There are too many variables: the temperature, the humidity, the air-flow, the size of the bird, its condition and fat content, even the number of pellets that struck the bird; these

---

53 Jean-Anthelme Brillat-Savarin, *The Physiology of Taste*, translated by Anne Drayton 1970, first published as *La Physiologie du Gout*, 1825.

all count and can only be judged on the spot and by one blessed with the necessary divine inspiration. Generally speaking, that is not me and I have ruined a lot of pheasants trying for the magic moment. So many in fact, that I felt obliged to look in other directions for a substitute approach that would render pheasants sufficiently, if not equivalently, esculent – and I found one. Ironically, it is the *absolutely fresh* pheasant.

You cannot buy an absolutely fresh pheasant. For practical purposes, you have to go out and shoot it yourself. Absolutely fresh means drawn while the innards are still warm, which is within an hour or so of the bird being shot, and then plucked or skinned within two or three hours. The bird must then either be cooked immediately or deep frozen so that there is no maturation at all. Hardly anyone ever does this. At big driven shoots the shot birds generally spend the day piled in the back of a Land Rover. At the close of proceedings they are usually placed in a cold storage facility for some days before being transported to game processing and packaging outfits. Here they are plucked, cleaned and packaged before being distributed to retailers, mainly supermarkets. Thus the bird on the supermarket shelf is one that has had some days of maturation, but it is usually far short of the magic moment. The same goes for birds shot at little 'rough' shoots. Although these are often kept by the shooters themselves, there is a convention that they should be hung and so they end up suspended from the garage rafters for a few days before being deposited in the deep-freeze. These somewhat-hung birds are completely edible, but are disappointing. Any succulence is overcome by a gaminess that is at once too vague and too acrid. They have, as Brillat-Savarin says, 'an undistinguished taste'. But an absolutely fresh pheasant has a sweet, nutty lightness and a subtle wild undertone that is altogether delightful. It does not have the richness or depth of a magic moment pheasant, but it comes in a good second and is best thought of as a different thing entirely.

Pheasants are at their best in December and January when they have put on a layer of fat against the winter cold, but where I live in Southern England, the best pheasant meals are to be had in October because of the other ingredients that anyone can go out and gather at that time. I make quite a performance of a pheasant lunch at this time of year and everybody seems to enjoy it, particularly the confirmed and stifled urbanites from the 'Big Smoke'. I get everyone to arrive at breakfast time and tell them to bring their warm outdoor jackets and a pair of Wellington boots. When they arrive, I serve freshly made bacon sandwiches and rich coffee laced with brandy. Everybody stands around chatting in that happily relaxed and expectant mood that always precedes a cheerful outdoor activity. Then I hand out a few wicker baskets and a couple of small hessian sacks and we set off into the woods. First order of foraging business is chestnuts. Wild sweet chestnut trees grow here and there in the woods, and at this time of year, the spiky, green pods have started to fall. The nuts inside are not big, but they are fresh and when roasted have a clean, delicate taste that is far superior to the tinny pungency of the preserved, store-bought variety. We usually manage to fill a couple of small sacks without much difficulty. Then attention turns to mushrooms. There is much more on this in the section on wild mushrooms, but the mushrooms we are after are boletes, which are common in the woods in October of most years. Particularly, we look for bay boletes, which are very good with pheasant, but we usually find five or six different varieties, including the renowned cep. Once we have found a few dozen mushrooms, we head home. If the weather is good, the guests are happily employed in making a fire outside, roasting the chestnuts and drinking beer. I cook the pheasant. This is what I do:

PHEASANT WITH MUSHROOMS AND CHESTNUT STUFFING

Ingredients for stuffing (per pheasant):
3 slices of ordinary white bread
1 large onion, grated or finely chopped in a food processor
Handful of fresh sage
1 teaspoon dried herbes de Provence
A handful of roasted chestnuts, peeled and grated
1 or 2 walnut-sized black truffles, grated
Salt and freshly ground black pepper
2 tablespoons melted butter
1 large egg

Cut the crusts off the bread and then break the bread up into small pieces in a mixing bowl. Add the grated/processed onion, the handful of chopped fresh sage and a teaspoon or so of dried herbes de Provence to the bowl. Then I go outside and have a beer with the guests and in the process rescue a handful of roasted chestnuts per bird. You have to be quick about this because by now the guests will have remembered how exceptionally good fresh, roasted chestnuts are and how well they go with good English ale. Back in the kitchen, I peel the chestnuts and finely grate them into the stuffing mixture and add a pinch of salt and freshly ground white pepper. Then comes the big trick: one or two walnut-sized truffles, also finely grated into the mixture, followed by a couple of tablespoons of melted butter. The fresher and better the quality of the truffles, the better the end result, but even if you can only get hold of the bottled supermarket variety, they are essential. The mixture is bound with the single large egg. As soon as the egg hits the truffle and the butter, you will start to get a hint of the extraordinary savoury herbal effect this stuffing will have on the delicate flavour of the pheasant.

Stuff the body cavity of the pheasant with the stuffing mixture. Rub a generous quantity of very mild olive oil over the outside of *the pheasant, season lightly with salt and white pepper and place in an oven at 230°C to roast for between twenty-five and thirty-five minutes, depending on the size of the bird. You will find that pheasants are narrow and, unlike chickens, do not sit well on their backs while they are roasting, falling over onto one side. Just go with the flow and cook them on one side for about fifteen minutes and then turn them onto the other side for the remainder of the cooking time.*

Do not overcook pheasant, it is a great shame and the meat loses flavour and toughens. Have faith, the breast meat is supposed to be pink; not bloody, but just moist and pale rose. While the pheasant is roasting, prepare a mushroom sauce using the boletes. Bay boletes are best because they have a compatible nutty, fruity flavour that is not as strong as the more highly regarded ceps and summer boletes, but any of these will do fine. The sauce is also very simple: slice the mushrooms and fry them in butter with chopped shallots and a little salt and pepper. When they are cooked, add just a dash of rich Madeira and some fresh double cream. Let the cream thicken a little and you are ready to go. Serve the pheasant and mushroom sauce with roast potatoes or good rice and a simple boiled vegetable – Brussels sprouts or green beans with garlic work well.

This dish is capable of changing the way people feel about eating game on a fundamental level. It is, as my youngest son says, 'immense'. It is very rich and one pheasant for two people is more than enough. It works well with both fresh and magic moment pheasants, with the edge going to the magic moment. It is an occasion to break out a few bottles of good Burgundy. With fresh pheasants – white Burgundy. With magic moment pheasants – the best red Burgundy you can afford, but watch out for the Madeira in the mushroom sauce. I said a dash, not a gurgle – just enough to lift the fruitiness of the mushrooms to a higher level, without the Madeira remaining as a distinct flavour in the sauce. If you have overdone the Madeira, stick with the white Burgundy or, if you have really overdone it, serve rather a spicy Vouvray or even a glass of the Madeira itself.

If you can only get hold of supermarket pheasant then do not roast them. The best thing to do with them is either chop them up and put them into a pie – any chicken pie recipe will do – or use them in one of the oriental recipes below. I suppose it is because it is an oriental bird that pheasant goes so well in these recipes, both of which are well worth the effort and turn the pheasant into a tasty, exotic curiosity. This is much better than sitting at the table knowing that your guests would much rather be eating roast chicken.

PHEASANT TOM YUM

(Serves 2)
4 cups water
Breasts of 1 pheasant
4 oyster mushrooms, stalks removed. If large, slice. If small, use 8
mushrooms
2 limes
1 stick lemongrass
3 kaffir lime leaves
2 tablespoons Thai fish sauce
6 sprigs coriander
2 red Thai chilli peppers
2 teaspoons nam prig pow

Boil the water in a pot. Cut the lemongrass into pieces three to four inches long. Pound the lemongrass with the back of the knife to release the flavour, tie it into a knot to make it easier to manage, drop it into the boiling water and let it boil for five minutes.

Put half a tablespoon of fish sauce and the juice of one lime into the bottom of each bowl in which the soup will be served.

Crush the chilli peppers with the flat of a knife and add one to each bowl.

Remove the stems from the kaffir lime leaves and add the leaves to the pot. Add the mushrooms. Add the pheasant breasts and boil until just cooked. Remove the breasts, allow them to cool to the point you can handle them, then shred the meat with your fingers and return to the pot. Add the nam prig pow (which is a paste made from shallots, garlic, shrimp paste, dried chilli, salt, sugar and tamarind – purchased at speciality oriental food shops). Bring the broth back to the boil. Serve immediately by scooping the pheasant breast meat, mushrooms and liquid into the serving bowls. As soon as you add the liquid to the serving bowls, the broth becomes cloudy because of the lime juice. Sprinkle with coriander leaves.

This soup is supposed to be hot and sour and intense. The different citrus flavours complement the pheasant and create a unique flavour. It should not taste bland. If it does then add more fish sauce and more lime juice.

CAPE MALAY PHEASANT CURRY

(Serves 4–6)

2 pheasants

2 large Spanish onions, chopped

1 red Romano pepper, deseeded and chopped

100 g dried apricots

50 g raisins

50 g sultanas

800 g chopped ripe tomatoes

1 tablespoon tomato puree

2 cloves garlic, grated

4 cm piece of fresh ginger, peeled and grated

20 ml white wine vinegar

150 ml white wine
150 ml chicken or game bird stock
250 ml crème fraîche
2 teaspoons Worcestershire sauce
4 tablespoons medium curry powder (or to taste)
2 tablespoons apricot chutney (preferably South African, i.e. Mrs Balls')
2 tablespoons vegetable oil
100 g fresh butter

Remove the breasts from the pheasants and joint the thighs and legs. Slice each breast into two or three pieces. Heat up the vegetable oil in a large pot and brown the pheasant pieces. Remove the pheasant. Reduce the heat slightly and add the butter, onions and Romano pepper. Fry until the onion is lightly golden and the pepper is soft. Add the curry powder and fry for one minute. Add the garlic and ginger and fry for a further minute. Add the vinegar and mix vigorously to form a rough paste. Add the apricot chutney, Worcestershire sauce, dried apricots, raisins and sultanas. Mix and fry for one minute. Add the white wine, mix and boil until the liquid is reduced by about one third. Add the stock. Return the pheasant to the pot and add the tomato puree and chopped tomatoes. Depending on how juicy the tomatoes are it may be necessary to add a little water at this stage to ensure that the pheasant pieces are more or less submerged. Cover the pot and simmer for about an hour, stirring occasionally. If time is not of the essence, then at this stage take the pot off the stove and let everything go cold. Once it is cool enough, put the pot in the refrigerator and leave it for two days.

If time is of the essence (or two days have passed) proceed as follows: bring everything to the boil again and reduce the liquid a little so the sauce concentrates and intensifies; then add the crème fraîche, which will further thicken the sauce as it heats through, and the curry is ready to serve. Serve it with Basmati rice, sliced *banana, peeled and chopped cucumber, sliced avocado, pickled limes and mango atchar.*

Take a mouthful of this curry and close your eyes. You will hear the warm waves of the Indian Ocean lapping the white beaches of Muisenberg while the cold Atlantic crashes into the rocks on the other side of Cape Point. In the background the frenetically cheerful rhythm of a Cape Malay banjo band sets a happy counterpoint to the lazy sunshine warming your back. Ah! Time for a cold beer.

Incidentally, it is true that you could cook your socks in this curry and they would be quite tasty. Pheasant is better though – and you could not ask for anything more exotic or further from most people's idea of a game meal.

PIKE

The idea of pike settles into the darker recesses of the mind where werewolves, vampires and other denizens of evil lurk in the half-light of the unconscious, even when experience teaches that it is not really so. Surely, a fish that looks like that must be dangerous? The glint in those blank, black eyes seems malevolent. That long, angular jaw, like the snout of an anorexic wolf filled with teeth like shards of broken glass, must be for dragging down sheep, horses and small, careless boys to a slimy end amongst the waving tendrils of waterweed. Well, if you are a dace or a minnow this attitude to pike is entirely understandable, but for humans it is just so much poetic licence. There are very, very few reports over the past 1000 years of pike attacking people and no attacks at all that were even close to fatal. The pike is simply a good, feisty angling fish that grows to forty pounds, but is usually between six and ten pounds, and they are great fun to catch, particularly on fly tackle. But once your pike is landed it is a surprisingly docile customer and you really have to try quite hard to get bitten, although one sure way is to stupidly attempt to take the hook out of its mouth with your bare hand instead of with a long-nosed hemostat.

The decline and fall of pike, as both a prestigious angling fish and as a desirable item on the menu, can be traced through both angling and cooking literature. This decline was particularly marked in Britain, but also in the rest of Europe, although there remain a few strongholds in Germany and Eastern Europe where pike still enjoys something of its former glory. The Romans ate pike with enthusiasm and even legislated that, in order to be considered edible, a River Tiber pike had to be caught 'between the two bridges'. This meant between the Tiber Isle and a point upstream of the confluence of the river and the main city sewage canal. They knew a thing or two those Romans. In fact much of Europe still gives the impression that things have gone downhill since the Romans left. In medieval times, a large pike was as likely to be the centrepiece at a banquet as was a swan or a peacock and it would have been presented in the same way too, with its uncooked skin sewn back on after the flesh had been roasted or poached. No sissy Roman-style health and safety regulations for our ancestors then. Why they did not all die of salmonella poisoning is a mystery. Still, no feudal lord or regal bishop would have dreamed of letting the peasantry anywhere near a prime eating pike and would have insisted that such lowly types limit themselves to dirt-common wild salmon, fresh-run and totally organic, or maybe a bucket of oysters.

The sporting magazines of circa 1825, apart from their complete obsession with horses and with coach drivers (who were like modern-day Formula One racing drivers – temperamental celebrities who wore out and discarded a pair of white kid gloves every ten miles or so and who had astronomical tailor's bills), make little mention of angling. But the angling they do mention occasionally, as being suitable for gentlemen, is angling for pike. It was not until the advent of fly fishing for salmon and trout, and the 'gentrification' of those pastimes in the late nineteenth century, that the decline of pike began in earnest; as trout and salmon became the only fish that a gentleman would consider angling for in fresh water, so too, by a peculiar application of culinary snobbery by association, they became the only freshwater fish that anyone with social aspirations (i.e. almost everyone) would consider eating. Which left the good old pike out in the cold, relegated to the category of a 'coarse' fish and firmly in the domain of the largely working class 'coarse angler'; a figure popularly, but inaccurately, conceived of as wearing a blue shirt and baggy overalls, slouched beside a scruffy stillwater slinging maggots out as groundbait and wrestling slimy garden worms onto brutal hooks.

Today, the only way to get hold of a pike in Britain is to go and catch it yourself, an activity I highly recommend. Once you have landed a decent one, you are in the position of a Lord of the Manor of old and can serve up an ancient delicacy to your family and friends in the fairly certain knowledge that they have never eaten it before. The following recipe is derived from the Westphalian[54] approach to cooking pike using sour cream and a full-flavoured cheese. In fact, most German recipes for pike involve sauces made from sour cream, often with the addition of veal gravy, which is a quirky, old-fashioned touch. The use of cheese is also unusual, because cheese and fish is often a poor combination. It works well with pike though.

PIKE AND CHEESE BAKE

1 fresh pike
Butter
Salt
Lemon juice
Onions, chopped
Flour
Sour cream
White pepper
Parmesan cheese, grated

---

54 Westphalia is an area of Northwestern Germany centred on Dortmund, Bielefeld, Münster and Arnsberg.

Behead, gut and skin your pike. Then separate the flesh from the bones. One of the biggest criticisms of pike as an eating fish is that it is full of bones. It does have a lot of bones, but avoiding them is about understanding the anatomy of a pike. It is not like an ordinary fish with a flat body constructed around a central spine that has mainly vertical bones protruding from it. A pike is more tubular in shape and is supported not only by vertical bones but also by a set of slanting spikes that radiate laterally from the spine through what would normally be the bone-free flesh of the main fillets. This means that instead of peeling a fillet away from the spine, you have to dig it out from between the bones using a sharp deboning knife. The result is long strips of flesh rather than the conventional fillet and consequently pike recipes usually call for 'goujons' rather than fillets. This is also the reason why any pike under six pounds is not really worth the trouble.

Cut the strips of flesh into goujons about two inches long. Sprinkle a little salt over the goujons and give them a good squeeze of lemon juice. Heat up some butter in an ovenproof casserole dish and fry up enough chopped onions to cover the bottom of the dish. Then add the fish pieces and fry for a few minutes. Remove the fish and keep warm. Fry a little flour in butter in a separate skillet and then add sour cream and stir until you have a smooth, thick sauce. Pour the sauce into the casserole and mix it up with the onions. Add freshly ground white pepper. Roll the pieces of fish in the grated Parmesan, generously covering them, and place them back in the casserole. They should be more or less submerged in the sauce. Cover with a generous layer of more grated Parmesan and bake in an oven at 200°C until golden brown. Serve this with fresh bread or boiled potatoes and a green salad. It is really quite special. Nothing is nicer with this dish than a bottle of cold Riesling from the Mosel Valley.

Pike is dense in texture and rich in flavour and the flavour is complemented by bacon. A very satisfying way to enjoy pike is to simply wrap goujons in good, very thinly sliced pancetta and then grill them until the bacon is crisp and the fish is cooked. Serve these with mushrooms (preferably wild field mushrooms) fried at a high temperature in a little butter. Although it is simple to prepare, this is by no means a flippant dish and the flavours are memorably intense. It is the sort of thing you should eat in front of a roaring fire on a dark autumn evening after a long day out tramping across the hills. A pint of ale and a couple of inches of single malt scotch would be fine accompaniments.

PIGEONS

As a sweeping generalistion covering Britain and Western Europe, there are only three types of pigeon worth eating: the wood pigeon, the rock pigeon (blue rock, rock dove) and the domestic pigeon. In fact, genetically speaking, there are only two because the domestic pigeon is apparently nothing other than a strain of rock pigeon, domesticated so long ago that any record of the event is lost. Probably, rock pigeons shared caves with our more hirsute ancestors and one thing led to another. There are other worthwhile pigeons in the world, but apart from a few African species that are very edible, I do not have experience of them. I know for example that the dodo was a type of pigeon and probably it was tasty because it got eaten into extinction during the nineteenth century.

Wood pigeons are the great stalwart of the ordinary British wing shooter. They occur in millions upon millions all over the British Isles, where they are regarded as a serious agricultural pest by farmers and may be shot all year round. Most shooters correctly regard them as a superb game bird, swift in flight and very sharp of eye. Wood pigeons rest easily on the conscience of the hunter in Britain because the more of them you shoot, the more of them there are. This seemingly ridiculous statement is true because wood pigeons breed like crazy – every six weeks or so – and establish themselves in vast numbers during the summer and autumn months when food is abundant. In fact, they breed up to the maximum number that the food supply can sustain. Come winter, however, the food supply becomes fixed because no more food is naturally produced either in the wild or on the farms until spring. But the horde of wood pigeons carries on eating as though there is no tomorrow, which for many of them there isn't. It is simple mathematics. If there is enough food for fifty wood pigeons to make it through the winter, but at the start of winter there are a hundred wood pigeons, then it follows that the one hundred wood pigeons will eat all the food by halfway through winter. Then there will be no food and all one hundred pigeons will die. If, however, fifty of the wood pigeons are shot in the autumn, then the remaining fifty make it through to the following spring. No shooting equals few pigeons, shooting equals many pigeons. Obviously, it is not quite as neat and linear as this, but it demonstrates the principle.

In the UK, wood pigeons roost in woodland and then go out each day in small flocks to forage amongst the crops and fields for grains, pulses and green shoots. Over the rest of their range they are quite scarce and are a protected species in much of Europe. The rock pigeon, on the other hand, is at its most abundant in Sub-Saharan Africa, particularly in South Africa. Originally a bird of remote coastal and mountain cliffs, the Southern African race of rock pigeon has taken to roosting and nesting on the concrete ledges and sills of skyscraper office blocks in all the major cities from where flocks go out each day to the agricultural areas to forage, sometimes flying thirty miles each way to do so. A combination of abundant nesting sites and plentiful crops has led to a population explosion in South Africa over the past fifty years, where rock pigeons are now regarded as an agricultural pest and, like the wood pigeon in Britain, may be shot all year round. This adaption to city living has not occurred anywhere else that I am aware of and they are an occasional species over the rest of their range. They are protected in Britain, where they only occur in Northern Scotland. The rock pigeon is at least the equal of the wood pigeon as a game bird and what it lacks in caution it more than makes up through its ability to jink and dive at incredible speeds in response to a shot.

The domestic pigeon is abundant everywhere, particularly in its feral form as the ubiquitous street pigeon. These street pigeons will interbreed with the rock pigeons where both occur, producing hybrids having mixed coloration, much to the distress of shooters who psychologically prefer 'pure-bred' birds and who illogically often refuse to eat the mixed ones. Various strains of domestic pigeon are also specifically farmed for the table, particularly in France. These tender, succulent farmed pigeons, covered with a layer of fat and with most of the gamey flavour bred out of them, are very good to eat indeed, whether roasted on a string revolving slowly in front of an open wood fire in a Provençal kitchen (where they would be called *pigeonneau*), or presented on a pristine white plate surrounded by a glistening sauce amid the glitter and flash of a top Manhattan restaurant (where they would be called 'squab').

The writers of cookbooks sometimes fail to understand the limitations of wild pigeon as a culinary experience. This results in a great unfairness because after subjecting the wild pigeon to various interesting and increasingly complex preparations, they are forced to conclude that it is not up to much. Then they more or less dismiss it entirely. They also have a tendency to compare it to the cosseted, corn-fed and very-young-when-slaughtered farmed domestic pigeon, which is like comparing a haunch of elderly wildebeest to the finest fillet of Kobe beef. What they often do not realise is that there are very few things you can successfully do with a wild pigeon (recipes below), but these things produce a really excellent result. Incidentally, the same goes for the wildebeest, but more of that elsewhere. Other recipes, particularly those designed for the domestic pigeon, are usually simply inappropriate. For all practical purposes, there is no culinary difference between a wood pigeon and a rock pigeon. The two species are very closely related and taste almost exactly the same. What does make a difference, though, is what the pigeon has been eating over the previous few weeks. For my money, the best is a South African rock pigeon crammed to bursting with ripe sunflower seeds, although an English wood pigeon feasting on beech mast (as the nuts of the beech tree are called) in the autumn is a close second. The best recipe of all is the simplest: pigeon salad. If ever there was a counter-intuitive combination of flavours, this is it. For years the earthy, dark flavour of wild pigeon led me along a sort of imagined medieval road involving root vegetables, herbs and strong red wine in various stews, pies and casseroles. They were not much good. One of the biggest problems is that if you stew a wild pigeon it becomes very tough –almost inedible. All you can then do is carry on cooking it until the flesh falls apart, whereupon what you have is a stringy mess suspended in gravy. Also the flavour is very strong, almost acrid, and you tend to try and sweeten the pot by adding things like red currant jelly or copious amounts of sweet Madeira, which even further complicates the flavour.

One Saturday morning I happened to shoot half a dozen wood pigeons instead of going shopping as instructed. Come lunchtime I was faced with a gaggle of hungry children and an irritated spouse and all there was in the house was the makings of a very ordinary green salad and the aforementioned freshly done-in wood pigeons. Well, expectations were not high to begin with, but every last morsel of this salad was eaten with great enthusiasm and it became the family's favourite game meal. Prepared this way the wood pigeon is tender and succulent and there is just something about the combination of the pigeon and the salad and the vinaigrette dressing that is delicious.

WOOD PIGEON SALAD

6 wood pigeons
5 tablespoons olive oil
100 ml white wine
A few twigs fresh thyme
½ an iceberg lettuce
4 ripe tomatoes
1 red onion, thinly sliced
1 teaspoon Dijon mustard
1 tablespoon red wine vinegar
½ teaspoon brown sugar
Salt and freshly ground black pepper

Remove the breasts from the wood pigeons. Slice each breast into three 'goujons' roughly the size of a finger and then marinate them for about half an hour in a mixture of one tablespoon of olive oil, the white wine, salt, pepper and a few twigs of fresh thyme. While the slices marinate, make a basic salad of the iceberg lettuce, torn by hand, the four tomatoes cut into wedges and the onion. Then make a basic vinaigrette dressing by combining the remaining olive oil, red wine vinegar, brown sugar, Dijon mustard and salt and pepper.

Remove the strips of pigeon breast from the marinade and dry with absorbent paper towel. Fry them briefly in a little olive oil in a very hot cast iron frying pan (and when I say briefly, I mean briefly – no more than two minutes on each side, depending on the size of the strips; what you are looking for is a browned exterior and a pink interior). Then simply toss the strips into the salad, cooking juices and all, pour over the vinaigrette dressing, mix it all up a bit and serve it with crusty bread and a glass of German weissbier.

For a more upmarket version on the same theme as wood pigeon salad, Simon Hopkins' recipe below, as published in his famous book *Roast Chicken and Other Stories,* is excellent with wild pigeon breasts, even though he states that his pigeon recipes are designed for farmed pigeon:

GRILLED PIGEON WITH SHALLOTS, SHERRY VINEGAR AND WALNUT OIL

Breasts of 2 wood pigeons
Salt and pepper
5 tablespoons walnut oil
4 shallots, peeled and finely chopped
2 tablespoons sherry vinegar
1 tablespoon chopped flat-leaf parsley

Baste the pigeon breasts with walnut oil and then grill them (ideally over a hot charcoal fire) for no more than two minutes on one side and one minute on the other, getting them nicely browned on the outside. Then put them on a plate or ovenproof dish and scatter the chopped shallots, more walnut oil, the sherry vinegar and the salt and pepper over them. Cover the plate or dish and put it in a preheated oven at 150°C for fifteen to twenty minutes. The breasts cook a little more and relax at the same time, while the shallot/oil/vinegar mixture combines with the pigeon juices to form an interesting 'vinaigrette' sauce. Slice each breast into three and sprinkle with the parsley just before serving with mashed potatoes and a green salad.

It is very good and is one of the few things outside of Spain that should be accompanied by chilled Palomino Fino.

There is one other great thing to do with wild pigeons. When you make pigeon breast dishes you are, of course, left with the rest of the carcass. Due to the strong flavour, these are not a successful addition to general game stock. It is far better to turn pigeon carcasses into a specifically pigeon-flavoured stock and use this in the following mushroom soup recipe:

MUSHROOM AND WILD PIGEON SOUP

500 g fresh mushrooms or 100 g dried mushrooms (soaked and drained), sliced
50 g butter
2 onions, finely chopped
1 litre pigeon stock (exactly the same as chicken stock only with the addition of pigeon carcasses)
125 ml white wine
2 potatoes, peeled and diced
2 cloves garlic, finely chopped
Small bunch fresh thyme
Small bunch flat-leaf parsley, leaves only and finely chopped
100 ml fresh cream
Salt and pepper

Melt the butter in a soup pot, add the onions and gently fry until they are light golden. Add the garlic and fry for one minute. Add the mushrooms, season with salt and pepper and fry for about five minutes. Pour in the wine and let it steam away for a few minutes then add the stock. Bring to a gentle boil and add the thyme and the potatoes. Reduce the heat, cover and simmer for half an hour or until the potato is cooked. Remove from the heat and extract the thyme. Blend the soup in the pot with a hand-held blender to create a smooth texture. Check the seasoning and add cream and parsley just before serving.

This soup works with any mushrooms, fresh or dried, but some are much better than others. Also, there is a balancing act to perform between the strength of the flavour of the mushrooms and the strength of the stock. For some mysterious reason, pigeon-

flavoured stock enhances the flavour of mushrooms, while the mushrooms tone down the flavour of pigeon. Consequently, bland shop-bought mushrooms are transformed by a strong stock. On the other hand, subtly delicious fresh ceps, morels or horn-of-plenty do not need much enhancement and so are better with a milder stock. Needless to say, this soup never tastes the same twice and lends itself to endless combinations and experiments.

PORCUPINE

The sound of angry indigenous voices approaching through the dark of an African night causes a chill to clutch at the heart of a white colonial, even a very young and innocent one. We were seated around the table in the large farm dining room and as the hubbub approached the external door of the adjacent kitchen, Mr Campbell hurriedly pushed back his chair and heaved himself to his feet. With a grim look he placed his hand comfortingly on the shoulder of his wide-eyed, grey-haired Dutch wife and then turned towards us:

'Pete, you and your friend get the pump guns. Go to the study windows and look out over the kitchen yard. Stay in the shadows and don't turn on the light, but if proper trouble starts and I say so or if they try to get into the house, start shooting. Try not to shoot me, hey!'

Like a shocked automaton, I scrambled after my friend as he leapt from his seat and made for the passageway leading to the bedrooms. As we went by, I saw Mr Campbell tuck a revolver into his waistband and head for the kitchen door.

The 'pump guns' referred to by my schoolfriend's father were short-barreled Mossberg pump action 'six-shot' shotguns (five cartridges in the magazine plus one in the chamber) loaded with SSG buckshot – a formidable weapon at close range and much favoured by farmers for home defence during those troubled times. Pete hurriedly opened the gun safe in his parents' bedroom, grabbed the shotguns, handed one to me and then we sprinted back to the study and peered cautiously out of the darkened windows. In front of the kitchen door in the harsh glare of a bright security light stood a ragged crowd of farm workers, many speaking loudly and gesticulating. Slumped in their midst and being supported on both sides was a large man with his shirt open. Mr Campbell was inspecting his bare torso and was speaking softly to him in his own language. At his feet a glistening pool spread slowly across the concrete.

So it turned out not to be the night of the long knives after all and was simply the consequence of an internecine brawl which had ended with one of the protagonists being stabbed several times in the chest and stomach. This necessitated a long drive over gravel roads to the nearest clinic where they were eventually able to patch the victim up. But what was the brawl about? What would cause such ructions, potentially kill a man and cause the perpetrator to flee for his life into the bush and probably over the border into Zambia? Money? A woman? Politics? No, a porcupine – or rather the crisply roasted carcass of a recently deceased porcupine whose provenance and consequent disposition became subject to dispute, followed by a potentially murderous altercation. In the African bush, when they say, 'I could kill for a slice of porcupine', they really mean it.

Because you see, porcupine is utterly, totally delicious and is universally regarded by those who have tried it as being the finest, sweetest, most flavoursome of all wild meats. Of course I am talking here of African porcupines,[55] of which there are two widespread species with somewhat overlapping ranges: the North African crested porcupine (*Hystrix cristata*) and the South African or Cape porcupine (*Hystrix africaeaustralis*).

---

55 Other porcupines elsewhere in the world are edible and are eaten, but do not seem much esteemed, although I wouldn't know personally.

These porcupines are very similar to one another, are roughly the same size and have virtually identical habits and so can easily be confused where both occur together. Both are spectacular to eat, so in a culinary sense it doesn't make much difference which one you have got your hands on. Personally, I have only sampled the South African variety and this came about more or less by chance. I was hunting on a very unusual mixed bushveld farm where the farmer was attempting to grow a diverse selection of crops in a cleared fifty-acre section of irrigated land entirely surrounded by more or less primordial and bone-dry bush. Of course, the crops acted like a magnet and sucked in game and birds of all sorts from the surrounding area in such numbers that neighbours had to reconsider the efficacy of their game fencing. It is amazing how determined creatures can be in getting through, over or under a fence if ripe melons, crunchy maize and savoury groundnuts are beckoning from the other side. The most numerous and destructive of these uninvited guests were porcupines and the farmer mentioned to me that they had become so bold they often abandoned their usual nocturnal habits to engage in daylight raids. He asked me to please shoot any 'porcupine bastards' (as he put it) that I might come across because he was well on his way to having no crops at all.

Some days later I was quietly sitting under cover on the side of a hill overlooking the cultivated land hoping for a shot at a bushbuck ram as evening approached, when I heard a strange snuffling, shuffling kind of noise coming from the hillside below me. I was really unsure about what creature could possibly be making such sounds and scanned the grass and thorn scrub below through my telescopic sight. It took a while, but finally I picked up a large porcupine making its way slowly along a contour some fifty yards below me. Most of the time the porcupine was obscured by long grass but occasionally there would be a gap and I would briefly see the stocky body and long back quills pass through. Remembering the farmer's request, I decided I would take a shot the next time an opportunity presented itself. Fortunately, in the next gap the porcupine stopped and I fired, hitting the animal cleanly in the head and killing it instantly. I went down to inspect the carcass, having never had the opportunity for a close examination of a porcupine before. They really do have the most aggressively uninviting external features and the numerous sharp quills along the back and rear made me hesitant to touch the animal, even though it was clearly completely dead. It was much bigger and heavier than I had previously appreciated and this one must have weighed about fifty pounds. I ended up gingerly dragging it down the hill front feet first so as to stay on the right side of those murderous-looking quills[56] and eventually made it to the road, fortuitously just in time to intercept the farmer who was making his rounds in a pickup truck. The half-dozen farm labourers on the back of the truck brightened up considerably at the sight of the porcupine, but were immediately disappointed by the farmer who quickly said:

'No, no, chaps. That one is for me.'

Later, I watched the kitchen staff as they prepared the porcupine for spit roasting. Carefully, all the quills were pulled out. Most came away easily with a gentle tug, but some, seemingly less mature ones, had to be extracted with pliers. Then the creature was plunged into a basin of boiling water for a minute or so and then thumped down on a wooden table

---

56 Porcupines do terrible damage to lions and dogs that mess with them. Some prides of lions specialise in hunting porcupines and learn to avoid the quills, although if they slip up and get stuck with a jawful of those dreadful spikes, it can be the end of the lion which subsequently dies of starvation or blood poisoning. Although African porcupine quills are not barbed, they can snap off in the wound and are then very difficult to remove by pawing at them. Dogs that attack porcupines usually do so only once and often have to be anaesthetised before the quills broken off in the mouth, jaw and chest can be removed with a combination of a scalpel and a pair of pliers.

where the hair was progressively scraped from the skin using metal scrapers such as are usually used when processing the carcass of a domestic pig. The reason for this process is the same as with the pig: so that the skin itself can be cooked and eaten as crackling. More boiling water was applied to the carcass as things progressed until it was completely denuded of all hair. The animal was then gutted, its head and feet removed and it was taken away to be placed on a spit over a large charcoal fire. I wish I had a record of how long it was cooked for and precisely how it was done, but at that juncture I was invited inside for a beer by the farmer and thus missed any further technical details of porcupine roasting. By the time we returned outside for dinner the creature was cooked and looked tremendously appetising, being a crispy golden brown all over, much like the look of a suckling pig but without the disturbing head. The farmer made gravy based on fried onions and homemade apple schnapps in a *skottel*[57] over the fire and then carved generous slices off the porcupine. These were served on a bed of rice with a side portion of South African-style coleslaw (sweet, with a lot of vinegar in the mayonnaise) and a large glass of that peculiarly South African wine, Pinotage[58]. Well, it was absolutely spectacular. Porcupine meat is unctuous, sweet and delicately perfumed. The skin turns into fabulous soft crackling that is far superior to any pork crackling I have ever had. The taste of both the meat and the crackling is unique, but at the same time carries hints of flavours found in other meats. At times it reminded me of mild lamb, then of duck, then perhaps a hint of outdoor-bred, rare-breed pork. I ate a prodigious amount and it is unquestionably my favourite wild meat.

There were only three of us at dinner that night and so regardless of the spontaneous gluttony there was a fair amount

---

57 An old plough disc used as a large frying pan.

58 A blend of Pinot Noir and Cinsaut (Cinsaut was formerly known as 'Hermitage' in South Africa).

of porcupine meat left over. I didn't give that a second thought until a couple of days later when sitting down to lunch after a happy morning stalking kudu unsuccessfully in the hills. Lunch was a potato salad, cold green beans and a dish of what at first glance I took to be a cold fish curry in the mild, sweet and fragrant vinegar-based South African style known as 'pickled fish'. After we had settled into our seats, the farmer turned to his wife and said:

'Ag, please, Marie, pass the pickled porcupine.'

QUAIL

I associate quail with America because of evocative writers like Hemingway and Ruark, who so convincingly captured the atmosphere surrounding shooting bob white quail in early twentieth-century rural America. It was all about frosty mornings, the smell of gun oil and coffee strong enough to require an age limit, making youngsters feel adult for the first time if granted the privilege of a cup. It was clear that in some parts of America bob white quail occupied iconic status as the principle indigenous game species pursued by shotgunners and their dogs and that they were (and still are) held in an affection not shared with other game birds. Landowners monitored and protected individual coveys and came to regard them as 'part of the family', to be nurtured and only very carefully shot at no more than once or twice a year. I suppose this protective, proprietary attitude comes from the fact that bob whites are naturally occurring and not generally a stocked species, or certainly they weren't back then. These days commercially bred bob whites can be purchased, but if you stock them I suppose you create the same sort of dichotomy that exists in so many trout streams between truly wild fish and stocked fish.

There are many different types of quail spread about all over the world – twenty-five species in the New World and seventeen species in the Old World. Old World quails are part of the pheasant family *Phasianidae*, along with partridges, but the New World quails are in their own family, *Odontophoridae*. In the Old World the common quail (*Coturnix coturnix*) holds culinary sway in most places as being the wild species most often shot and eaten. The common quail engages in massive and complex seasonal migrations across Africa and Eurasia, the Eurasian races overwintering in the Sahel[59] and India before returning across the Mediterranean to encompass almost all of Europe and much of Russia within their range, with the African races migrating within Africa between the Sahel and Southern Africa. It is hunted most frequently in the Mediterranean countries of Europe, particularly Spain, and in Russia where historically huge numbers of migrating quail support an abundant late summer slaughter with over a million birds being shot each year. These days numbers of quail are somewhat in decline and this has led to the supplementing of wild stocks in Mediterranean countries by releasing hybrid mixtures of common and Japanese quail just prior to the hunting season. Japanese quail, although taxonomically considered a separate species by some (*Coturnix japonica*), are actually the domesticated version of the Asiatic sub-species of common quail, domesticated around the eleventh century in Japan, initially as song birds and thereafter for meat and egg production. They are thus able to breed with wild European birds, and breeders do this to create a more manageable stock for release into the wild. Of course, this brings with it all sorts of concerns about what is termed 'genetic pollution' and the fear that an inferior, genetically watered-down version of the common quail will result.

Every single quail shot each year is destined for the pot and it is a very tasty game bird with flesh somewhat darker than

---

59   The Sahel is the ecoclimatic and biogeographic transitional zone between the Sahara to the north and the Sudanian Savanna to the south, i.e. where the Sahara starts to give way to the savannas of West and Central Africa.

that of partridges because its migratory habits cause it to fly a good deal more. There is thus a marked distinction between old and young birds and a very noticeable difference between wild birds and domestically raised ones. As with pigeons, domestic quail bred for consumption are slaughtered when very young and without their having flown so much as a single real wingbeat. This results in tender flesh but a vague flavour that is sort of gamey whilst not really being sufficiently fragrant for proper character. Wild quail, on the other hand, whilst given to toughness, are of excellent flavour but you overcook them at your peril. Overcooking destroys both the flavour and the texture. As appears in the recipe below, the secret is quick and very hot. There is another thing you should be aware of when it comes to eating wild quail, particularly in a Mediterranean country and that is 'coturnism' or quail poisoning. It is a rare thing, but it has been known since the fourth century BC[60] that quail are one of those creatures capable of eating something poisonous to humans without ill effect to themselves, accumulating the poison in their flesh and then in an instance of instant karmic retribution, poisoning the human that shoots and eats them. Symptoms include muscle tenderness, muscle cell breakdown and in severe cases, renal failure. It is not certain precisely what it is that the quail have been eating when they cause coturnism, but the possible culprits are thought to be hellebore or henbane (*Hyoscyamus niger*) or hemlock (*Conium maculatum*). The birds are known to sometimes eat parts of these plants during their migration out of Africa.

In the late 1980s some friends and I used to shoot birds of various sorts on grassland adjoining a large lake in North-West South Africa, near the border with Botswana. The grassland abutted a long range of low hills and in these hills we would occasionally notice ruins signifying habitation and mining

---

60 Coturnism was known to ancient Greek (and subsequently to Roman) naturalists, physicians and theologians.

in the distant past. The bird shooting was very good and the species present included partridges, guineafowl and the African sub-species of the common quail. The grass was thick and the birds sat tight, creating a situation in which birds, particularly the quail, would explode from beneath our feet in a sudden flush that would require a quick, reflexive shot. At the end of each traverse of an area of grassland we would find that amongst the casualties retrieved would be a number of small, quail lookalikes known as hemipodes, or button quail, which had been killed in the cross-fire, so to speak. Button quail are not related to true quail and are much smaller, but flush out of the grass in a very similar manner, flying for a short distance before plunging suddenly back into the grass, from which they will not flush again. A keyed-up shotgunner, particularly a less experienced one, on edge for a sudden flush would understandably blast away at the button quail, mistaking them for the real thing. As it only takes a hit from one pellet to bring down a button quail, a number of them would inevitably get shot. At the end of the first day we found ourselves in possession of over half a dozen tiny bodies and in an application of the principle of always eating whatever has been shot, these were prepared for barbecuing by spatchcocking them, covering them in rosemary and garlic-flavoured olive oil and then generously sprinkling them with salt and pepper. They were then grilled briefly over the coals of a hardwood fire and turned out to be fabulously good eating, much better than real quail. They have very white, sweet flesh that caramelises quickly on grilling to create a very appealing crisp and golden appearance, and with a squeeze of lemon juice and a glass of chilled champagne they became the gastronomic highlight of any trip to the area. They are now (and were then) a protected species and should not have been shot[61], but as they were accidentally dead anyway it would have been a pity to

---

61   Button quail are an abundant species and there is no concern about their preservation status.

waste them. It must be admitted, though, that on subsequent trips certain members of the party might actually have shot at the button quail on purpose, although I am by no means certain of this and will not name any names. What I do know is that no button quail ever made it into the freezer back home as they would always be enthusiastically eaten within hours of being shot.

When we first encountered button quail, I had no knowledge of the species and on looking them up in an identification guide, discovered that they were called the 'common, small or Kurrichane' button quail. I had encountered the word 'Kurrichane' before in the context of a species of thrush that is abundant in Zimbabwe, but was unable to discover the word's origins or what it meant. Of course, this was in the days before the internet and if you wanted to find out something you went to the local library to consult an encyclopedia and often failed to find out anything at all. As a result I spent nearly three decades not knowing even how to properly pronounce this word and imagined it might have Indian Raj origins (its spelling and appearance is not a million miles away from 'kedgeree' or 'mulligatawny' and other similar anglicised Indian words). On researching this book, however, I discovered that the word Kurrichane is a corruption of the Tswana word 'Kaditshwene', the name of an Iron Age settlement in the Tshwenyani hills, sixteen miles north-east of the present-day South African town of Zeerust. Kaditshwene was established in the late 1400s on the site of extensive iron and copper deposits and became probably the most important cultural and industrial centre for 1000 miles in any direction. It was the capital of the Bahurutshe people, one of the principal tribes of the Tswana, and was visited in 1820 by a missionary, one John Campbell. At the time of Campbell's visit Kaditshwene had a population of over 20,000 which exceeded that of Cape Town. It is Campbell who corrupted the word 'Kaditshwene' into 'Kurrichane' and the word was later used by the naturalist Andrew Smith who first described both the Kurrichane button quail and the Kurrichane thrush from there. Kaditshwene came to a sad end after 350 years of significant existence. In 1821, and as a result of the disruptions caused by the genocidal episode of war and displacement in Southern Africa known as the *mfecane*, Kaditshwene was attacked first by the Batlokwa people in 1821 and then again by the Bafonkeng people in 1823. The death and destruction were so profound that the settlement was abandoned and by the 1980s had become nothing but the wind-rippled grassland and empty hills where my friends and I first encountered the delicious button quail.

Almost all recipes for quail of any species, but particularly European or Middle-Eastern recipes, involve roasting the birds with a fruit-based stuffing or serving them with a fruit-based sauce or reduction. Typical fruits encountered with quail in recipes are prunes, figs, dates, grapes, pomegranates, redcurrants and cranberries, in other words, fruits that have intense flavours and are often delivered in a rich syrupy preparation. In Europe, quails are also often served with some form of fatty, salted and preserved pork, like bacon, pancetta or prosciutto, which complements the sweet fruit as well as the quail. The recipes are almost always very simple. This is an example:

ROAST QUAILS STUFFED WITH PRUNES IN ARMAGNAC

4 quail
1 tablespoon olive oil
100 g butter
10 minced shallots
Small bunch fresh thyme
2 garlic cloves, pureed
150 ml rich stock (duck, chicken, veal)
150 ml Armagnac

12 seedless grapes
12 pitted prunes marinated in Armagnac for 3 weeks, liquid
reserved
Salt and freshly ground black pepper

You have to prepare the prunes three weeks in advance, but otherwise it is simple. To make the sauce, melt the butter in a saucepan over medium heat. Add shallots, garlic and thyme and cook until the shallots wilt and turn lightly golden. Deglaze the pan with the Armagnac and scrape any bits from the bottom of the pan. Add stock and stir. Reduce the heat and cook for about one hour, until the liquid becomes syrupy. Strain the liquid and season with salt and pepper if necessary. Add the grapes and let them soften in the sauce.

To cook the quail, preheat the oven to 240°C. Baste the quail with a little of the reserved Armagnac/prune juice, then brush on a light covering of olive oil. Season the quail inside and out with salt and freshly ground black pepper. Stuff the quail with two or three prunes each and close the cavity with a toothpick. Place the quail in a baking pan and roast for twelve minutes. Baste again with Armagnac/prune juice and rest for three minutes. Serve with polenta and lamb's lettuce or watercress. A bottle of something rich, smoky and peppery works well with this dish – a rustic Cahors maybe or a Bandol.

RABBIT

Once upon a time, somewhere near Emperor Hadrian's massive civil engineering project in the north of England designed to keep the Scots and other troublesome types out and the peaceful country-villa-style existence of high-born Roman immigrants safe, a legionnaire was doing his best to do in a furry brown creature known to him as a *lepus*. The creature, being very fleet of foot, sharp of eye and long of ear, would not let the legionnaire anywhere near it and after a hot afternoon of frustration the legionnaire was heard to say, 'Damn it, this *lepus* is a bit *timidus*. What we need around here is a few stupid Italian *cuniculi*. If those were around we would soon have a stew boiling away in the pot.' Now before you go leaping to conclusions about the word *cuniculi* possibly referring to some exotic Italian sexual practice, let me explain that *cuniculus* is the colloquial Latin name for the common European rabbit (*lepus* is the latin name for a hare[62]). It is thought that the rabbit might not be a naturally occurring species in Britain and that it was introduced about 2000 years ago

---

62 *Lepus timidus* is the mountain or blue hare, indigenous to Scotland and possibly the north of England.

by Roman soldiers interested in a quick and easy meal[63].

However it got to Britain, the rabbit is now prolific and ubiquitous and countless thousands of them occupy every bank, hedgerow, meadow and woodland all over the entire island. In fact there are thought to be at least thirty million of them around each spring and although numbers are constantly reduced by predation and disease, there are almost always enough of them that one or two can be obtained for the pot quite easily. Although they have the normal acute senses typical in prey species, their abundance and the fact that they live in burrows makes them an easy target for the hunter who is prepared to sit and wait. They are creatures of habit and in benign weather will emerge in the late afternoon or evening out of the same burrow entrance day after day. If the hunter takes position thirty or forty yards downwind of the burrow entrance and then sits under cover or just remains motionless, he will usually get several chances before it becomes too dark to shoot. In Britain, most rabbits are hunted with very sophisticated, but low-power, air rifles. The law prescribes that a person in Britain may possess and use, without a licence of any sort, an air rifle generating less than twelve foot-pounds of energy at the muzzle. If you want a more powerful air rifle a firearms certificate is required, which is something of a performance because then you have to explain to the authorities why you need such a weapon and precisely when and where you propose to use it. The authorities also run checks on you to make sure you are not a potential mass murderer, which is quite right. People who just want to shoot a few rabbits on a nearby field are usually not prepared to go to all that trouble.

Twelve foot-pounds of energy is sufficient to propel a sixteen-grain .22 air rifle pellet at a velocity of about 600 feet per second and this is sufficient to kill a rabbit stone dead at

---

63 There is also a school of thought that suggests rabbits were introduced by the Normans in the twelfth century and that the Romans had nothing to do with it. Who knows?

forty yards, if you hit it in the head. Hitting the rabbit in the head is where the skill lies, but the modern precompressed pneumatic (PCP) rifles with regulated valves are so consistently accurate that you can literally shoot the head off a matchstick at forty yards if you fit a good telescopic sight. Nevertheless, these rifles and their use in rabbit hunting raise questions about appropriate weapons and shot placement that have relevance to hunting generally. In principle, I suppose that if the projectile is capable of lethally penetrating a vital organ like the brain in the creature being hunted, then theoretically it is an adequate weapon for the purpose. However, this approach discounts the skill of the hunter as a marksman in the field. Too often one finds a situation where the capabilities of the hunter do not match the theoretical capabilities of the rifle. What is most unfortunate about this is that the risks attendant upon failure in marksmanship are borne entirely by the animal being hunted because it is the animal that runs away wounded and then potentially dies a slow and agonising death. All the hunter has to deal with is a bruised ego. This has led, correctly in my view, to a 'use enough gun' philosophy amongst hunters in general because there is no doubt that the more powerful the weapon, the greater the margin for error. This is not to say that adequate marksmanship can be entirely replaced by weapon power. You can hit a deer in the backside with a .50-calibre round from an anti-aircraft gun and it will still run away, but when it comes to shots taken at the generally targeted heart/lung area then a shot with a powerful weapon that is a little off line is very much more effective than the same shot with a much lighter weapon. In the case of rabbits the 'use enough gun' philosophy is interfered with by the laws relating to air rifles. If unrestricted, I think almost all rabbit hunters would opt for a more powerful air rifle than one generating a mere twelve foot-pounds and would probably end up with one that generates thirty or forty foot-pounds. This would kill rabbits out to about eighty yards if hit almost anywhere in the top half of the body and would expand the target area and effective range considerably. This would not much endanger passers-by either because the light weight of the pellet would cause it to lose momentum very quickly, like a shotgun pellet.

I have a friend who lives in rural Wiltshire and basically subsists on rabbits, with the occasional pigeon, trout or pheasant thrown in for variety now and then. He is not compelled to do this for he is well off, but he does it as a kind of eccentric sport where he tries to spend as little cash as possible just to see if it can be done. He is a very skilled, very practised shot and can down a rabbit at sixty or even eighty yards with an ordinary PCP air rifle. He buys a few other supplies from local supermarkets, timing his purchases right at the end of the day when supermarkets heavily discount all food that has reached the end of its labelled 'best before' period and it is astonishing how well he eats for almost no cost at all[64]. According to him, you do not get sick of the flavour of wild rabbit quickly because it is a delicious meat derived from a creature that lives a happy, free existence with an abundant and varied food supply and lots of sex. The only drawback is that it can be tough and thus must be subjected to slow cooking if it is to be rendered palatable. My friend, who is Greek, makes an excellent stifado-style stew from wild rabbit which he cooks in a slow-cooker for about nine hours. Here is the recipe:

RABBIT STIFADO WITH CHORIZO

1 rabbit, jointed
150 g chorizo, sliced

---

64 This totally contradicts the suggestion that the poor in Britain are fat because they can only afford to eat cheap fast foods. It just is not so. See page 268 for more on this.

1 tin chopped tomatoes

250 g button mushrooms

3–4 tablespoons olive oil

Salt and pepper

1 teaspoon sugar

1 tablespoon balsamic vinegar

½ cinnamon stick

6 cloves

1 tablespoon tomato puree

300–400g shallots, peeled and left whole

1 small onion, chopped

3 cloves garlic, crushed or grated

2 bay leaves

250 ml water

1 teaspoon chilli flakes

Brown the rabbit pieces in olive oil and then remove from the pot. Add the onion and some more olive oil and sauté until light golden and soft. Return the rabbit pieces to the pot. Add all the other ingredients except the shallots and stir to mix the ingredients. Cook in the oven at 160°C for two hours, alternatively simmer in a slow-cooker for six to nine hours. If using the slow-cooker omit the water. Shortly before the end of the cooking time roast or fry the shallots until they are golden brown and slightly soft. Add the shallots to the pot shortly before serving. Serve with pasta, rice or thick-cut chunky chips.

In my experience, wild rabbit has a much better flavour than domestic rabbit. Domestic rabbit meat is far more popular on the Continent than it is in Britain and the following extremely simple Provençal recipe, designed for domestic rabbit, is exceptionally good with wild rabbit instead.

Do not be tempted to substitute wine for water in this recipe. It does not work nearly as well and makes the simple flavours unnecessarily complex. What is so appealing about this dish is that the flavour of each component blends harmoniously, even the high-quality salt, to create an honest, straightforward and delicious dish in which the highlight is the rabbit, which is as it should be.

LAPIN À LA MOUTARDE ET HERBES DE PROVENCE

1 wild rabbit, jointed and cut into convenient pieces
50 g bacon or pancetta, cut into small lardons
1 small onion, chopped
150 ml crème fraîche
4 tablespoons good Dijon mustard
2 tablespoons olive oil
1 tablespoon dried herbes de Provence
Small handful of fresh flat-leaf parsley, chopped
Fleur de sel salt and freshly ground black pepper
150–250 ml water

Preheat the oven to 160°C. Coat the rabbit pieces generously in Dijon mustard – if four tablespoons is not enough, use more. Heat the olive oil in a casserole dish, preferably one made from enamelled cast iron. Fry the bacon lardons until lightly browned, making sure they release all their fat. Remove the bacon and reserve. Brown the rabbit pieces in the oil and bacon fat. Some of the mustard will come off, start to caramelise and stick to the bottom of the pan. Turn the pieces and scrape the bottom to prevent anything burning. When the rabbit is lightly browned remove from the casserole. Add chopped onion and fry until soft. Add water slowly bit by bit to free up any caramelised mustard clinging to the dish and create a sauce that is the consistency of very thin gravy sufficient to cover the rabbit pieces. Add the herbes de Provence, fleur de sel and black pepper to taste. Return the rabbit and bacon lardons to the casserole. Bring the sauce to a boil and then cover the casserole and place in the oven for around two and a half hours. Check the liquid level after one and a half hours and if the dish is drying out, add more water and stir before returning to the oven for the remainder of the cooking time. After two and a half hours take the casserole out and check the rabbit pieces for tenderness. If they are still tough, return to the oven for a further hour. When the rabbit is tender, stir in the crème fraîche to thicken the sauce, check the seasoning and sprinkle with the chopped parsley. Serve with rice or a crusty fresh baguette, a green salad and a bottle of young red Burgundy, Saumur Champigny or a Provençal rosé.

REEDBUCK

Veal is a controversial meat which, according to my vegetarian family, strongly taints dairy farming and causes them to think twice about whether they should in fact become vegans. Vegans, of course, do not consume dairy products and adopting the vegan way would be a strong personal statement against the universal practice amongst dairy farmers of condemning all male calves (and excess female calves) to a very short, totally constrained and often entirely miserable life before being slaughtered to provide the essential ingredient in *Wiener schnitzel, saltimbocca, blanquette de veau* and so forth. I think they have a point, but fortunately for those who can get hold of it there is an antelope that produces meat from adult animals that is very similar to veal and when prepared, say, as a *Weiner schnitzel*, would fool most people. I am talking here about the meat from a prime mountain reedbuck (*Redunca fulvorufula*).

The mountain reedbuck is a small, common African antelope that weighs about sixty pounds. They inhabit ridges and hillsides in rocky areas and high mountain grasslands across most of Southern and Central Africa. There are three sub-species occupying three distinct geographical zones, but from both the hunting and the culinary point of view, all three are very similar. Mountain reedbuck are one of my favourite antelope to hunt, not least because the terrain where you find them usually boasts a spectacular view of the surrounding countryside. There is a trick to hunting them and that is at all costs to get above the antelope before you begin any approach or stalk. Mountain reedbuck hang about in groups of about six animals consisting of either an adult male and his harem or small bachelor herds made up of adolescent males. Either way, the group will always have at least one member with its head up, primarily surveying the downwind and downhill approaches to the group's position. Strangely, they very seldom look uphill and so uphill and downwind is where your best chance of an undetected approach lies. They are not alone in their negligence of the upward view. Other antelope seldom look up either. I have seen a large impala ram weighing at least 160 pounds killed by a caracal lynx that would have weighed less than forty pounds, but which was able to lie unseen on a branch overhanging a game trail and leap upon the impala from above. This angle of attack allowed the caracal to drop onto the impala's neck and get a grip on its windpipe before the impala could do anything about it. The result was the rapid asphyxiation and collapse of the impala. The caracal then opened a small hole in the impala's belly, ate some soft flesh and left the rest for the hyenas and jackals. However, I got there first and appropriated the very fresh carcass for purposes of Impala Chops Teriyaki.

You set off on a mountain reedbuck hunt by leaving very early in the morning and climbing straight up to the top of the highest part of the hill, ridge or mountain you have decided to hunt that day. This is an energetic start to say the least and by the time you get to the top, your rifle will feel like it weighs sixty pounds rather than six. Mountain reedbuck are not big and so fortunately can be hunted with smaller-calibre rifles sporting light stocks, a bonus if the weight of the rifle is an issue for you and your state of fitness. It is also preferable for the rifle to have the velocity to handle fairly long-range shots, usually angling downhill[65]. Once you reach the top, you walk along very slowly into the wind, keeping just below the horizon and stopping frequently to scan the hillsides below with binoculars. Eventually, you will find a group of mountain reedbuck and, doing everything you can to stay above them, will usually be able to stalk within range. At this point be very careful. Just walking in mountain terrain is very tiring, let alone stalking by crawling, climbing and creeping along bent over at the middle. Take a moment to catch your breath before lining up the shot. You really do not want to wound a mountain reedbuck and have to follow it up over cliffs and valleys and into the next mountain range. Like all African antelope, mountain reedbuck are very tough, and precise bullet placement is necessary if exhausting follow-ups are to be avoided. They have marvellous balance and can leap up steep, rocky hillsides at a very rapid pace. This allows them to cover in a few minutes terrain that will take you half a day to traverse.

I was once hunting mountain reedbuck with a friend who was armed with a .257 Roberts, a beautiful custom-fitted rifle with a heavy barrel for extra accuracy. We spotted a mountain reedbuck about 200 yards away, standing on a rock ledge looking away from us and down the valley. Taking plenty of time to settle himself, my friend took a seated position and rested his rifle on a convenient rock, cushioning the forestock with his jacket. Gently regulating his breathing and doing everything right, he took aim in a leisurely fashion, centring the cross-hairs on the animal's near-side shoulder. He fired and the shot echoed out across the valley. However, the mountain reedbuck

---

65   Thus appropriate calibres would be flat-shooting rifles propelling a bullet weighing around a hundred grains at about 3000 feet per second, which would include the .243 Winchester, the 6.5 mm Remington magnum, the .264 and the .257 Roberts, although I often successfully hunted mountain reedbuck with my standard bushveld .308 using bullets weighing 150 grains rather than the usual 180 grains.

remained standing, apparently unscathed and unalarmed. Quietly cursing what he assumed was his bad marksmanship, my friend reloaded and once more took aim in an unhurried manner. Again a loud crack reverberated around the hillsides, but the mountain reedbuck remained unmoved. Three further times my friend fired, becoming increasingly puzzled with each shot and only on the last shot did the animal sway a little and then topple over onto its side. Upon inspecting it we found that all five bullets had struck the near-side shoulder, the entry wounds being close enough together that you could have covered them with the lid of a large jam jar. The far side revealed a huge composite exit wound that had basically destroyed the far-side shoulder and the entire front half of the animal's torso was little more than jelly as a consequence of the massive dose of hydrostatic shock. Whether the animal remained standing after the first shot because mountain reedbuck are incredibly tough or whether this is an example of their inherent ability to balance is uncertain. I think that probably the first shot killed the animal within a few seconds of impact and before the animal could resolve to flee its precarious position on the ledge. It thus just remained standing and balanced on the ledge even though it was dead. Bullets from subsequent shots, striking very close to the first one and each other, would have encountered less and less resistance from the antelope's body as they passed through it by virtue of the damage caused by earlier shots and, much like a rifle bullet can pass through an empty can without moving it, were not able to topple the antelope until the last shot struck. Whatever the truth of the matter, this is the only occasion upon which I have seen this happen.

Recovering the carcass of a mountain reedbuck you have shot high up on some rocky ridge can be challenging. If you are young and strong you can carry it out over your shoulders, but the traditional approach is to use a horse. In the old days before hunting in Southern Africa had become formalised by commercial considerations and we simply hunted on the farm of a friend in return for a share of the meat and a bottle or two of Scotch, we would arrange for a farm labourer to follow along on horseback about a mile or so behind us, leading another horse upon which the carcasses could be loaded. If we shot an antelope we would immediately gut it and then mark the position of the carcass with a long strip of white toilet paper so the horse bloke could find it. We would then hunt on, for we always wanted more than one mountain reedbuck for the pot. These days recovery is usually by some sort of extreme off-road vehicle and a large team of employees, all dressed in identical khaki overalls emblazoned with the logo of the safari company. Also, today it is rare for the client to have anything to do with the processing of the animal after it has been shot and most clients would have no idea how to gut an antelope.

Prime mountain reedbuck meat, particularly from a young female, is a dead ringer for veal of the types known as red veal and rose veal. It is a noticeably pale meat in comparison to other venison and has a very mild herbal flavour which has virtually no gaminess to it at all. Any recipe calling for veal as its central ingredient will be suitable for mountain reedbuck. It is particularly suited to Italian dishes that call for sauces made from lemon juice or sweet wine. Roast saddle of young mountain reedbuck served with a Mediterranean-style sauce based on a game bird (or chicken) stock reduction with fresh herbs, wine, olive oil and capers is superb with crisp roast potatoes and green beans with fresh garlic. Mountain reedbuck is not one of those meats that you can easily buy, even in Africa, so you will have to go and hunt one yourself if you want to sample it. There is something about the aesthetic of the high, rocky grassland and the superb eating quality of the meat that makes the whole exercise seem particularly worthwhile.

If you are not from Africa then you may have thought to yourself, why is this mountain animal named after a type of grass usually encountered on the banks of a lowland lake or river? It is because the mountain reedbuck's larger and formerly more numerous close relation, the common or southern reedbuck, *Redunca arundinum*, is the species that got to define the nomenclature for the whole of the *Redunca* family through having been taxonomically named first. The southern reedbuck is a much larger antelope (females 110 pounds, males 150 pounds) that frequents grasslands and reed beds near water over most of Central Africa and down into the northeastern coastal region of South Africa. It is dependent on water and will not move far from its chosen supply, preferring to spend its days lying hidden in the rank cover to avoid the heat and only emerging into the open in the early morning and evening to graze on grass and herbs. When threatened, the southern reedbuck prefers to hide in the grass rather than immediately flee, with the result that if you walk up onto it, it will suddenly spring out of the grass right at your feet. All on its own this is a startling event, but if you are in lion country there is the added difficulty that southern reedbuck, with their tawny, grey-tinted coats, are exactly the same colour as a lion. Now believe me, if you are hunting in lion country and find yourself in the long grass where visibility is limited, you tend to be a little tense because lions also like to hunt in the long grass where the other animals cannot see them coming. Bumping into lions at very close range in long grass is extremely dangerous because the encounter can go either way. Everyone gets a huge fright and the tendency is to instantly shoot or charge as the case might be, with potential fatalities on both sides. You can imagine the effect of a lion-coloured blur erupting out of the grass at your feet under these circumstances. It can take a week to get your heartbeat back to normal.

Southern reedbuck are superb to eat. They live a comparatively sedentary existence and because they spend most of the day lying in the grass instead of charging about across some dusty plain, they have soft, fine-textured meat that is reminiscent of lamb. They are simple to hunt because they live alone or in pairs and have a very small home range of around 200 acres. Thus if you bump into one you can be sure of finding it again on another occasion in more or less the same vicinity. A quiet upwind walk through the area in the early morning or evening will usually bring the opportunity of a shot and any of the classic 'medium' rifles will be more than adequate[66]. Some people attempt to hunt these antelope with a shotgun and buckshot, relying on a snap shot as the antelope springs up out of the grass. This is not recommended. Reedbuck are too big to succumb easily to buckshot at anything but very close range and the risk of wounding is too high. It is a great shame to ruin such fine meat by wounding the animal. Although southern reedbuck remain common in conservation areas and game parks throughout its range, numbers have been significantly reduced through habitat loss and overhunting in other areas.

---

66 'Medium rifles' in my book span everything from the .270 Winchester and 7 mm rifles on the one hand to the .338 and 8.5 mm rifles on the other.

ROCK FISH

As I did with the term 'game fish', I use the term 'rock fish' as having a particular meaning which is not necessarily shared by everyone. By rock fish I mean sea fish of various sorts, usually but not universally members of the *Sparidae* family, that can be caught by anglers on rocky coastlines, either from the shore itself or from a boat in nearby inshore waters. These are the fish suggested by the 'rock' element in the expression 'rock and surf angling' and are almost always caught using bait. They vary in size from the 200-pound bulk of the enormous grouper on one hand to numerous small, hand-sized sea bream of many different species on the other, but all share common characteristics: they live amongst or near rocks and eat food that is generated in a rocky environment, which includes crustaceans, molluscs and seaweeds. They are invariably powerful fish, but they are not built for speed. Instead they have chunky, flat-sided bodies that enable them to negotiate the turbulence of wave-washed rocks and seek their food in the turmoil of heavily disturbed seabeds.

Big rock fish have always been a prime target for inshore and shore-based anglers, but the smaller varieties have tended to be relegated to the second league of angling and are sometimes not accorded the respect and esteem they deserve. This is usually a consequence of a mismatch between tackle and fish. If you arm yourself with a robust, fourteen-foot-long bait casting rod coupled to a large multiplying reel loaded with forty-pound breaking strain line and go seeking sixty-pound musselcrackers on some savage, wave-torn shore, then when you hook a three-pound bream it hardly registers at all on such tackle and is unceremoniously hauled in to be treated as something of a disappointment and nuisance. Catch the same three-pound fish on a willowy ten-foot spinning rod with a fixed spool reel and ten-pound breaking strain line and it is suddenly transformed into a serious angling challenge as it darts amongst the jagged rocks. You feel justifiably proud when you manage to land it. It took me many years to realise that ignoring the big ones and concentrating on the smaller varieties with appropriate tackle generally produces a much more active and satisfying angling experience. Perhaps back in the old days when there were more large inshore fish around, pursuing the big ones was a more viable strategy. But sadly, today the big fish are largely gone from almost everywhere and although you might get lucky, you will spend many long, fishless days grimly staring into the distance pretending to yourself that your heavy tackle is somehow more macho.

Of course, the quality of the fishing for rock fish is not the same everywhere. On one of my first visits to a taverna on a Greek island we were invited into the kitchen to inspect the dishes being prepared prior to ordering dinner, in the charming and these days old-fashioned Greek way. In pride of place amongst that evening's offerings and displayed in splendid isolation on a tray of crushed ice was a very fresh gilt-head bream (*Sparus aurata*) of about two pounds. The fish was pointed out to us with great reverence, and in hushed tones we were advised that it could be grilled for us at a cost only slightly less than the daily rate for a luxury hotel room in the area. We were astounded. We had recently lived on the Cape coast where rock fish of that size could be had any time by anyone who simply took the trouble to go down to the rocks and fish for half an hour. In fact, fish that size we usually tossed back, preferring somewhat larger ones for filleting and frying. We came to realise that the cobalt clarity of the Mediterranean was actually indicative of it being an oceanic desert, relatively speaking, where a two-pound gilt-head bream was a prize of some significance, particularly anywhere near a Greek island where dynamite fishing might once have taken place. By comparison, the opaque richness of the Indian Ocean is a bonanza for marine life and its vast marine ecosystems burgeon with interdependent life that, relative to the Mediterranean anyway, are much less impacted by human interference. Incidentally, and in the interests of being fair, I must point out that gilt-head bream are probably the most delicious of all breams and possibly the most delicious of all rock fish, although it has serious competition from rock cod in the Indian Ocean and snappers of various sorts that hang around rocks in tropical seas.

During the brief few years that I lived on the Cape coast, I had the pleasure of fishing off nearby rocks on almost every day that conditions were propitious. I consequently caught many rock fish of various sizes and had the opportunity of experimenting with various ways of both catching them and cooking them. The most significant thing about how to catch rock fish is to remember that they hang about right next to the rocks, often in water so turbulent it is hard to believe anything could survive, let alone function happily and effectively in such a maelstrom of heaving white water. But they do. Some species in fact sweep up the face of ragged and barnacle-strewn rocks actually in the breaking wave and sometimes covered by just a few inches of water. It is thus no use casting off the rocks into the distant deep water if it is rock fish you are after. The rock fish will be right at your feet or right up against adjacent rocks, so often the very short cast is the way to go. It is also a good idea if the bait is highly mobile in the water and is anchored, if at all, by the lightest of sinkers. Food in the white water moves about violently and is grabbed instantly by any fish that comes across it. Bait that is anchored to the bottom with a heavy weight does not move naturally and will not appeal to anything other than tiddlers intent on nibbling it out of existence in tiny mouthfuls. Using no weight at all (other than the bait itself) and allowing it to drift freely can seem very strange and uncontrolled to an angler used to fishing off a beach or boat with weighted tackle, but if it can be done, as when fishing off high rocks, it is deadly. There is no need to worry about striking the fish. Rock fish that take an unweighted bait invariably swallow it and you will soon enough get a heavy pull as it tries to swim off.

As for cooking rock fish, if the fish is big enough, say more than two pounds, it can be worthwhile just filleting it, dusting the fillets in seasoned flour and frying in hot clarified butter. This is often difficult to beat with a very fresh fish because it allows the untrammelled flavour of the fish to dominate and that is usually most excellent. However, it often fell to me to barbecue a fish, either because I felt like some lunch while out on some distant rocks somewhere or because the barbecue was a social event calling for a measure of culinary drama in the preparation of the food over an open fire. Here is how you do it:

HOW TO BARBECUE A FISH

There are three basic approaches to cooking a fish over an open fire and which one you use is best determined by the type and size of the fish being cooked. All three methods benefit from the use of a sandwich grid to securely enmesh the fish and facilitate turning on the fire, although the third method was initially developed in order to avoid turning the fish over at all. In the case of the second method, appropriate for thin-skinned, soft-bellied fish, a sandwich grid is almost essential.

1. The Whole Fish Method

This is the method used in Greek tavernas and in virtually every other beachfront restaurant in the world. It is particularly suited to smallish fish of a pound or less in weight and is also suitable for any fish you feel needs pepping up through the addition of a stuffing of some sort in the body cavity. In this method the fish is cleaned in the conventional way by being scaled and then slit open at the belly to remove the entrails. The head is almost always left on, but the gills are removed. Two or three diagonal cuts are then made in the flesh on each side of the fish. A stuffing of some sort, even if it is only a few slices of lemon and a dab or two of butter, is almost always placed in the body cavity. The fish is then clasped in an oiled sandwich grid and grilled over the coals. The fish is often basted with melted butter or flavoured oil during cooking. The result should be a well-cooked fish with a crisp and slightly charred skin that is served whole on the plate and is eaten very carefully in order to avoid creating a tangled mess of bones and flesh. It is important to know that if you overcook a fish (regardless of the method of cooking) then the bones detach very easily and go floating off into the flesh with the lightest encouragement from a clumsy diner. This can quickly render a fish more or less inedible and avoiding this consequence is one of the strongest reasons why people often prefer to fillet a fish, even if it is quite small.

2. The Fillets of Fish Method

A method that is exactly what it says on the tin and which is suitable for larger fish weighing more than four pounds. Scale and clean the fish in the usual way and then fillet it, taking care to remove the pin and other bones that might traverse the fillet, so it is entirely bone-free. Leave the skin on. Place the fillets in an oiled sandwich grid, which piece of equipment comes into its own when the fish must be turned. There is a great debate in fish cooking as to whether fish should be cooked skin side first or flesh side first. The skin-side-first camp is interested in getting the skin crispy whilst at the same time protecting the delicate flesh from overcooking. To achieve this you have to cook skin side down for about eighty percent of the cooking time. On the other hand, the flesh-side-down school point to the fact that if you start with the skin side, the skin contracts and causes the fillet to curl and buckle, which makes cooking the flesh side difficult. There is no clear answer and much depends on what you are trying to achieve and what type of fish you are cooking. What is certain though is that if you are cooking a soft-fleshed fish with thin, delicate skin and are not using a sandwich grid it is best to start flesh side down because the skin will be what holds the fillet together as it cooks. If the skin is cooked first it will tend to disintegrate and become weaker. Then, even if you are using a sandwich grid, the fillet might fall apart and pieces drop through the mesh into the fire. It is usual when employing this method to frequently baste the fillets on both the flesh and the skin sides so that they do not dry out.

3.   The Butterfly Method

The fish is prepared differently for this method and it is particularly suited to any fish that stores quantities of fat in its belly flesh. It is not essential to scale the fish, but I usually do. Remove the head just behind the gills. Do not open the belly as one usually would. The belly is left intact and the innards are removed after the flesh has been separated from the spine. Taking a sharp filleting knife and starting at the tail end of the fish, slice along the backbone first on one side and then on the other, carefully separating the fillets from the bone. On fish with relatively thin belly flesh, slice down through the rib bones to separate from the spine and leave them in the belly flesh. If the fish has thick belly flesh and strong skin, it is possible to avoid slicing through the ribcage and instead continue filleting around the ribs so that they remain attached to the spine and can be removed together with it. The spine (and ribs, if applicable) should come free of the flesh entirely and be left attached at the tail only. Using kitchen scissors snip through the spine at the tail and remove. You should be left with the two fillets joined together by the belly flesh in roughly the shape of a butterfly.

It is not essential to use a sandwich grid, but if you have one it is better safe than sorry. Baste the flesh with clarified butter or flavoured oil. Place the butterflied fish flesh side down on an oiled grid over the coals AND DO NOT TURN IT OVER at any stage. The fish cooks progressively upwards through the flesh until the skin is reached and it becomes possible to peel the skin away from the flesh. You will know it is cooked when you can push a fork through the skin side and into the flesh easily, but it does take some judgement on your part. The entire grid is then taken off the fire, the skin is peeled away and the butterfly is removed in one movement using a spatula or egg flipper. Only then is the fish turned over to reveal a deliciously caramelised flesh surface with soft cooked fish beneath. I always worry that the fish will overcook when using this method, but it works very well and you avoid the catastrophe of the fish falling apart when being turned during cooking. This method, with an interesting twist, is invariably used when cooking galjoen (**Dichistius capensis**, also known as black bream), an endemic South African species and South Africa's national fish. Before placing the fish over the coals, the flesh side is covered with a mixture of crushed salt and vinegar or tomato ketchup-flavoured potato crisps (or a mixture of both), very finely chopped tomato and onion, a squeeze of lemon juice and a dash of oil or melted butter to bind the mixture, which is then pressed into the flesh (there are many variations to this theme along the Cape coast). The fish is then carefully lowered flesh side down onto an oiled grid and because the fish is not turned at any stage during cooking the mixture adheres to the flesh and turns into a robust and very tasty crust that somehow complements the unique flavour of the black-veined flesh of the galjoen. I have tried it with other fish and it works, but with galjoen it is great.

SALMON AND SEA TROUT

There are just over 140 salmon rivers in Scotland[67]. There are also just over 140 Scotch whisky distilleries. I strongly suspect a connection. Salmon fishing, particularly with a fly, requires that the angler be either drunk or slightly mad, or perhaps both. This is because the whole concept of angling for Atlantic salmon in fresh water is entirely preposterous. Salmon are marine fish that breed in freshwater rivers and they *do not eat at all* while in fresh water. Yet salmon fishing proposes that the angler will attempt to catch a non-eating fish by presenting to it a bundle of feathers artfully attached to a hook, or a shiny metal lure festooned with treble hooks, or a wriggling earthworm drifting quietly down a low-water run, all these things being conceived of as representing food of some sort. Unsurprisingly, most of the time this does not work, but incredibly, sometimes it does. Thus the remarkable thing about salmon fishing is not that it is difficult to catch salmon, but that any salmon are caught at all. It is a little easier to understand if the salmon being caught are

---

67   In fact, if you count every brook and burn that might hold a few salmon in a good year, then there are more than 140 salmon rivers in Scotland. There are ninety-four *major* salmon rivers. The figure 140 is thus a little dramatic licence on my part.

freshly run in from the sea with the mechanism that inhibits feeding recently and perhaps incompletely engaged. But it is also possible to catch a salmon that has been in the river for months and has had literally hundreds of flies and spinners presented to it. Sometimes such a fish will suddenly take a fly or lure on the forty-seventh or one thousand and forty-seventh time one swims past its nose. Nobody knows why. This phenomenon makes salmon fishing a great leveller. On any particular day a novice with shoddy tackle and little skill might be the one to place the final fatal fly and maybe hook and land the fish while the seasoned expert looks on in carefully disguised dismay. Sure, over time the expert will catch more fish, not least because he or she casts so many times, but on the day anything can happen and all men and women are equal. This is not true in any other type of angling.

The extraordinary unpredictability of salmon fishing imbues it with a mystical atmosphere that encourages elderly gentlemen to write ponderous and lengthy tomes examining every aspect of the sport in excruciating detail, when in fact there is little more to be said about it than is said in the paragraph above. Every attempt to formulate a rule or tenet is necessarily accompanied by so many qualifications and exceptions that the exercise is essentially pointless. However, this does not stop the elderly gentlemen from waxing lyrical at length. At the risk of including myself amongst their number, I will add that what they are trying to communicate is an allure that is virtually impossible to put into words. In part it derives from the spectacle of outrageously large and beautiful sea fish lurking within the confines of what would otherwise be a trout stream. Such disproportionality is both exciting and unnerving. It also derives from the artistry of casting with a fly rod, particularly a double-handed fly rod, and the absorbing quest of trying to cover the lies both thoroughly and accurately, with the fly swimming through the current in a convincing way, at least to the angler. This is equally true for those who fish with spinner or bait. Some of it is a nebulous atmosphere of archaic tradition combined these days with exciting space-age technology producing feather-light rods, splendid reels and in the context of fly fishing, exceptionally effective plastic fly lines that make the process of fly fishing for salmon more pleasurable than perhaps it was in the past. And then, of course, there is the heart-stopping excitement of actually hooking one of these almost mythical fish. So far I have fished for salmon for a total of twenty-four days and on twenty-three of those days the only thing that happened was a single fish 'bulging' at the fly as it swung past. That single insignificant event was the total return for over 130 hours of casting effort. But on one day (the twenty-fourth, but not chronologically) I caught five fresh-run salmon in just under two hours, almost on consecutive casts out of five contiguous lies, the smallest weighing in at eleven pounds and the largest at seventeen. I cannot express the excitement I felt. I was incoherent with joy and the fish gave a tremendous account of themselves, leaping and rushing all over the place and running long lengths of backing off the reel. It was beyond thrilling and the many empty days that had preceded, and indeed succeeded, it gave it greater significance and depth of pleasure. That is the secret, of course. Salmon fishing is tantric angling.

Angling for sea trout on the other hand, is to go over to the dark side. Like salmon, sea trout migrate out of the rivers of their birth to the sea where they spend some years feeding in the relative abundance of the inshore waters before returning to their home river to spawn. They are not a separate species but are normal brown trout (*Salmo trutta*) that just take to a marine life, driven by some mysterious genetic imperative or perhaps by something as mundane as a shortage of food in the river. The best way to catch them is to fly fish for them after dark, for they are extremely shy during daylight hours and behave very differently to their resident brethren, being sort of like small, extra-paranoid salmon. Night fishing is a strange experience that is not for everyone. Some people find it quite unnerving. They imagine all manner of spooks and goblins in the shadows and persistently feel something is creeping up on them from behind. You might imagine that fly casting in the dark would be challenging, but it is surprisingly simple for an experienced caster who does most things by feel anyway. You also use a short, stout leader which makes the process much easier. Unlike salmon, sea trout do feed in fresh water occasionally, particularly the smaller ones and in situations where there is an abundance of food available. Although some authors have cast doubt on this, I have personally watched sea trout taking mayflies and have cleaned sea trout that had definitely been eating a variety of insects, but granted not in great numbers.

The fly fishing technique used to catch sea trout is similar to that used for salmon, where a cast quartering downstream is employed to swing the fly through the lies at a pace the angler imagines is attractive. You cannot see the fly or the line in the dark so the whole process is achieved by feel and you learn by experience the particular tension on the line that results in strikes from fish. Although it is difficult to be precise, I suspect the fly is moved more quickly for sea trout than it is for salmon, although sometimes salmon are caught by sea trout anglers. Like salmon, sea trout are effectively sea fish and so are about five times as strong as a river brown trout. They run and jump prodigiously, crashing about in the darkness and once your aching arm eases the fish into the landing net you are surprised by how small it is. Sea trout can grow to over twenty pounds, but most weigh somewhere between two and six pounds, depending on how long they have been at sea.

I have grouped Atlantic salmon and sea trout together not only because the techniques used to catch them are similar, but because they also have similar flesh. These days the flesh of a prime wild salmon or sea trout is considered a luxury item and has a price tag to match. This was not always the case and it did not enter the pantheon of gourmet foods in Britain until the late nineteenth century when Eastern European immigrants living in London's East End introduced the concept of delicately smoked salmon to London restaurants. They used fresh Scottish salmon purchased at Billingsgate market to do this and although the Scots had smoked salmon before this time, the style was heavy, like kippers or bloaters, with the smoke doing much to conceal the flavour of the fish and its level of freshness. By contrast, Eastern European-style smoked salmon at its best produces a light, fresh and exceptionally delicious dish that is particularly suitable as a starter in a gourmet meal. The increasing popularity of salmon, both smoked and fresh, escalated during the twentieth century to the point that wild stocks were severely threatened by extensive commercial netting both out at sea and in the rivers, a situation that has not yet been properly controlled. I feel sure that salmon would now be more or less extinct were it not for the advent of extensive salmon fish farming, starting in the 1970s and continuing to expand to this day. The high price of salmon and its luxurious connotations attracted investment into fish farming and over time produced such a vast supply that farmed salmon is now abundantly available in every supermarket at a very reasonable price. Like many so-called commercial success stories though, salmon farming produces a number of serious negative externalities that are visited upon the environment without proper control. Amongst these are high levels of chemical pollution of various sorts arising out of the use of cages that are open to the flow of the ocean and a proliferation of both diseases and parasites that impact adversely on what remains of wild fish stocks.

Farmed salmon and wild salmon are not the same thing at all from a culinary point of view. Farmed salmon is inferior in my view and is three times as rich in fat, which is to be expected in a captive fish that does relatively little exercise and is fed high-nutrient commercial fish feed to speed along growth. This does not improve its flavour or texture. Farmed salmon flesh is also very much richer in undesirable chemicals, mainly pesticides used to control parasite infestations in the farm cages. This is such a problem that some organisations concerned with food safety recommend that farmed salmon should not be consumed more than once per month. This hardly boosts confidence in the product. These negative elements can, to an extent, be concealed by smoking the salmon, although at its worst that process becomes a travesty of the original concept, with the farmed fish being rapidly wet-cured in a mixture of salt, sugar and water, then subjected to an infusion of artificial liquid smoke. The result is glutinous, damp and strongly flavoured and can only benefit from a substantial drenching in lemon juice (putting lemon juice on decent smoked salmon is anathema to smoked salmon aficionados). The wild fish, on the other hand, is truly delicious, with sushi-grade wild salmon being one of the most popular and expensive of all fish. It is absolutely great raw in sushi or sashimi, and as a steak or cutlet can be quite spectacular when either fried or grilled. The skin in particular has a very appealing flavour when cooked to a crisp finish, and crisp salmon skin (without the meat attached) is a well-known Japanese delicacy, often included in maki rolls or served on its own with wasabi mayonnaise.

Wild sea trout is, if anything, better to eat than wild salmon, particularly fried or grilled, with a similar but more delicate flavour. It is also superb cured and smoked just like salmon. These days there are also commercially farmed sea trout available and regrettably they suffer from the same disadvantages as farmed salmon.

If you catch a big salmon or sea trout it is possible that you will find yourself with an excess of fresh fish that you and your family and friends simply cannot eat immediately. As an alternative to freezing this excess you might consider making your own gravlax instead. Gravlax is a Nordic dish in which salmon (or sea trout) is cured for a few days in a dry cure of salt, sugar and dill and is usually then served on rye bread with a mustard and dill sauce. In the Middle Ages Nordic fishermen made the original gravlax by lightly salting salmon and then fermenting it by burying it in the sand above the high tide line. These days we leave out the fermenting bit and rely simply on the dry cure which draws moisture out of the fish and creates a concentrated brine as a by-product that can be used in making the sauce, but which I find too strong for that purpose. Thinly sliced gravlax is really good to eat as a snack or starter and rivals smoked salmon in my book. Here is a simple gravlax recipe that will work with any fatty fish, including ordinary trout.

GRAVLAX

2–3 kg fresh salmon, sea trout or other fatty fish, in two matching
boneless fillets
250 g coarse flaky sea salt (like Maldon)
250 g golden caster sugar
2 tablespoons freshly ground white pepper
Bunch fresh dill
50 ml akvavit (or schnapps, or gin, or vodka)

Sprinkle the akvavit over the flesh side of the fish. Mix the salt, sugar and pepper to make a dry cure mix. Place a sheet of cling film in a large dish that will fit in the refrigerator. Make a bed of cure mix on the cling film in the dish and place one of the fish fillets skin side down on top of it. Cover the flesh side of the fillet with sprigs of dill and then with cure mix and then again with more dill. Place the other fillet on top, flesh side down. Cover the skin side of the second fillet with the remaining cure mix. The idea is to 'bury' the fish in the cure mix. Then wrap the two fillets up in the cling film so that they are firmly pressed together and the cure mix is also pressed into the fish. Put a weight on top of the fish (tin cans, heavy bottles, bricks, anything) so that it is compressed slightly. Leave in the refrigerator for a minimum of twenty-four hours. Do not mess with it or pour off the liquid that will form around the fish until at least this time has passed. You can cure the fish for longer than twenty-four hours if you prefer a more concentrated flavour and dryer texture. When you are ready to serve the gravlax, remove it from the cling film and wipe off thoroughly with sheets of paper towel to remove all remaining cure mix, the dill and any brine. Slice thinly and serve with a sweet mustard sauce and rye bread. Vodka or Scandinavian akvavit served very cold is excellent with gravlax and certainly gets the dinner party off to a rapidly relaxed start.

SARDINES

Everything that lives in the sea eats sardines, or 'pilchards' as the ones longer than six inches are sometimes known. Seriously, I have caught rock fish that allegedly only eat seaweed on a thin strip of sardine tightly wrapped in elastic thread and mullet that allegedly only eat plankton on a tiny flap of sardine attached to a size 16 hook. I have also hooked large game fish and even larger sharks on a single six-inch sardine and have had tiny fish smaller than the hook itself impale themselves in an effort to engulf sardine bait three times their size. It is unquestionably the most versatile and probably the most successful bait of all. Many fishermen all over the world thus primarily experience sardine in bait form, which is usually far from fresh and is powerfully and distinctively pungent. Non-fishermen usually experience sardine as something that comes in a tin, often smothered in rich tomato or mustard sauce and which is also fairly strongly flavoured, although in a less putrid way. Few people, globally speaking, get to sample fresh sardine, which, *when very fresh*, has delightfully savoury and surprisingly light-textured flesh.

You cannot go out and catch your own sardines, generally speaking. They are pelagic plankton feeders of various species in the *Sardinella* family that are only caught by net from ocean-going fishing boats. An exception is the 'sardine run' that occurs along the South African coast during the winter months when shoals of migrating sardines are occasionally forced up onto the beach by encircling battalions of predators. Then you can get some with a light throw net or even with a bucket as the helpless fish thrash about in a few inches of water. But most of the time the sardine you buy in the fish market or supermarket is at least forty-eight hours dead, probably more. In common with many very oily fish they start to deteriorate within a couple of hours of death and, even if carefully packed in ice, will not taste quite as clean and light when purchased by you two or three days later. Nevertheless, as long as the eye is clear and the gills are deep ruby red when you buy it, a fresh sardine will still be worth eating. Frozen sardines are only suitable for bait. The freezing process is unkind to sardine flesh which becomes unattractively mushy when defrosted and seems to go off very rapidly.

Sardines as a resource are easily overexploited. The Cornish sardine fishery collapsed through overfishing in the mid-nineteenth century, setting a precedent for fishery collapses all over the world during the twentieth century. Currently, the Japanese, South American, South African and Californian sardine fisheries are all in a parlous state, with fishing either banned or severely curtailed. Overexploiting a natural resource upon which you depend for your livelihood has always struck me as a particularly self-destructive way forward, but in an essentially lawless, globalised world with huge international fishing fleets prowling the oceans paying scant regard to minor inconveniences like territorial limits, a contemporary 'tragedy of the commons[68]' is all but inevitable. The overexploitation

---

68 The tragedy of the commons is an economic theory of a situation within a shared-resource system where individual users acting independently according to their own self-interest behave contrary to the common good of all users by depleting that resource through their collective action. In plain language, the more sardines you catch the more money you make and you may as well catch them all because if you don't, someone else will.

follows a familiar pattern. As the total catch begins to decrease the usual response is to decrease the size of the mesh used in the nets so that ever smaller fish are captured. In this way all restraint is abandoned incrementally until the fish stock is damaged beyond its short-term recovery capability. The fishery then collapses with much loss of capital and jobs. It is not easy for bystanders to intervene. Things happening in the sea are not readily discernable by people on land and fishermen facing declining catches and the prospect of unemployment tend to misinform in an effort to keep things going for as long as possible. All is not necessarily permanently lost, but recovery can take a long time. The Cornish sardine fishery at its peak in the mid-nineteenth century yielded around 40,000 hogsheads[69] of sardines (roughly 122 million fish) per annum. In modern terms that is around 12,000 tons. Today the fishery has recovered, but a mere twenty-six small boats fish for Cornish sardines within six miles of the Cornish coast and catch less than ten percent of the nineteenth-century catch. This is considered the sustainable level of catch, which gives some idea of how unsustainable the nineteenth-century catch actually was.

Surprisingly, given the history, Cornish sardines are really cheap to buy. They appear in supermarkets from time to time throughout Britain and generally cost less than £3 per kilogram (at time of writing in 2017), which would be about 30p each. When I saw them for sale in my local supermarket the other day I was reminded of a television show I saw recently in which a famous and clearly earnest celebrity chef was bewailing the fact that people on low incomes in Britain tend to eat fast food and become fat because they are too poor to eat properly. This

---

69 A hogshead was a wooden cask usually used for transporting or storing liquids like ale, wine or cider but was also used for some solid goods like tobacco or fish. A hogshead of liquid weighed 300 kilograms, fish something similar, but tobacco weighed 1000 pounds (453.6 kilograms) presumably because it could be compressed.

proposition has become received wisdom over the past few years and the chef was merely restating an apparently well-established fact. As I was in the supermarket anyway and a well-known burger chain beckoned from across the street, I thought I would do a little research. This proved very interesting. I will not burden you with the details but I can confidently state that a very healthy meal of grilled fresh sardines with a large portion of chips and a good green salad made from lettuce, tomatoes, avocado, onion and a generous dressing of olive oil and lemon juice comes in at under £2.50 per person. By contrast a typical fast food meal consisting of a medium burger with medium fries and a medium soda simply cannot be purchased for a comparable sum unless there is some extreme and temporary promotion on the go. So much for received wisdom.

The best way to cook fresh sardines is to grill or barbecue them with olive oil and rock salt in the Mediterranean and North African manner. This is very simple. Clean and scale the sardines. If grilling, place them on a bed of coarse rock salt, sprinkle with a little olive oil and lemon juice and grill for a few minutes, turning once, until the fish is browned and cooked. The bed of rock salt prevents the fish from sticking to the grill pan and enhances the flavour. If barbecuing, use a sandwich grid and whilst the one side is cooking, sprinkle the other side with olive oil and rock salt. Sprinkle a bit more on just before serving. Serve with lemon wedges. Sardines absorb the smoky flavour of the barbecue and are exceptionally delicious prepared this way.

SNAILS

I was recently on holiday in Western Crete where, to my surprise, I saw snails on the menu of a beachfront taverna. Until that moment I had ineluctably associated snails with French cuisine and had not appreciated that others might eat them too. I tried to discuss this with the waiter, but neither my Greek nor his English was up to the task. Nevertheless, I immediately ordered some and sat back, ouzo in hand, to await the arrival of the Greek version of this iconic dish. Well, what a surprise. Instead of the expected dozen or so standard-sized snails, what arrived was a vast pile of small, green-striped snails that had been fried in olive oil with salt and rosemary and then doused in a light wine vinegar. Later on, further conversation with the taverna owner revealed that these snails were indigenous to Western Crete and were 'hunted' in the mountains in spring and early summer, particularly after rain. Thereafter, the snails are kept in captivity for a month or two being purged on a diet of pasta and water before being served up as an endemic Cretan delicacy. At least these days they are considered a delicacy. In the past mountain snails were firmly in the category of peasant food and apparently were only eaten by those on the edge of starvation. Perhaps the fact that traditionally the snails were simply boiled and then served on top of whatever starchy food was available might have had something to do with that. I wish I could now write that I proceeded to eat these snails with a high level of pleasure, but I did not. There was altogether far too much snail involved in the dish and both the flavour and the rubbery texture of the flesh became tiresome when served in such generous quantity. It was then that I realised that I do not enjoy snails for themselves so much as I enjoy them as one of the more or less equally important ingredients that flavour the melted butter sauce in the classic French rendition of *escargots à la bourguignonne*, the other material ingredients being, of course, garlic and parsley. What I truly enjoy is soaking up that melted butter with a slice of fine white bread, sponging out the snail shells and the depressions in the purpose-made snail dish that *escargots* are served in all over France. That one has to chew on a dozen or so actual snails to earn that privilege seems a small price to pay.

I have no doubt that many molluscs, whether on land or in water, have been eaten by humans and by human progenitors for a very long time. Archaeologists working in Cova de la Barriada, Spain, have found large and concentrated amounts of snail shells among stone tools and other animal remains in pits that were used for cooking during the early Gravettian era – 32,000 to 26,000 years ago. As I mentioned in the context of mussels, you need no equipment at all to cook molluscs, including land snails, because you can simply pop them directly onto the coals and in a few minutes the contents of the shell are cooked and can be wheedled out with a sharp stick. Also, snails are full of protein, but can be captured with the absolute minimum of effort, making them a good idea ergonomically speaking. The most famous snail species from a gastronomic perspective is *Helix pomatia*, the Burgundy, Roman or edible snail. Very popular in Roman times and ever since, this snail is indigenous to Europe and is found throughout the whole of the continent and in Southern England, where it was introduced by

Roman colonists around 2000 years ago and is now a protected species. It is extremely difficult to cultivate this snail and so it is rarely farmed and is usually collected in the wild. This is the snail that will be served to you in a good restaurant in Dijon or Paris and it is renowned for its juicy plumpness. Elsewhere in the world what might happen is that you will be served the European garden snail, *Helix (Cornu) aspersa,* placed into a Burgundy snail shell. Garden snails are commercially farmed and vast numbers of them are processed and canned annually. As you can readily buy cleaned and dried Burgundy snail shells, the temptation to open a tin of garden snails and dress them up as Burgundy snails in the classic *à la bourguignonne* style overcomes many restaurateurs in places where the customers might not be as discerning in matters of snail eating as those in Dijon or Paris. In any event, the garden snail is considered good eating in its own right and is known as *petit-gris* in France. The French also regularly eat two other species: *Helix lucorum,* another widely cultivated European snail native to the east and south, but introduced into France, and the *escargot de Quimper, Elona quimperiana,* a large snail widespread in Brittany and in Spain.

As for Spanish snails, most people are unaware that snails are an ingredient in the Valencian version of paella, which is the original version (and Valencians say, only genuine version). Non-Spaniards regard paella as Spain's national dish[70], but Spaniards tend to regard it as a regional Valencian dish that has sprouted copies in a few other regions. Paella seems to have begun its development into its modern form in the eighteenth century on the shores of Lake Albufera where fishermen and peasants cooking outdoors over open fires prepared a rice dish that boasted water vole meat, eel and butter beans as its principal ingredients. As living standards improved in the

---

70 Spain's actual national dish is probably *tortilla española,* or Spanish omelette, widely consumed all over Spain.

nineteenth century, the water vole and eel were replaced by other meats and the seasoning took on a more adventurous and expensive aspect with the introduction of paprika and saffron by more affluent people enjoying outings and gatherings in the countryside. The dish became exceptionally famous during the mid-nineteenth century and has remained so to the present time. Other versions in other regions are copies, sometimes using different ingredients including various types of seafood and the spicy chorizo sausage. If anything the 'mixed' or seafood paella has become more widespread and popular than the original, particularly internationally. Valencians insist, however, that authentic paella can consist only of short grain white rice and some or all of the following ingredients: chicken, rabbit, duck, snails, butter beans, great northern beans, runner beans, artichoke (as a substitute for beans in the winter), tomatoes, fresh rosemary, sweet paprika, saffron, garlic, salt, olive oil and water. Interestingly, there is a version that relies on snails alone as the meat component.

On my home continent of Africa lurks the largest of all edible snails, the giant African land snail, *Achatina fulica*, a molluscan behemoth of dubious benefit to mankind that has a shell more than seven inches long and two and a half inches high when fully grown. Originally a native of East Africa, this snail has been introduced all over the world by the pet trade and as a potential food source. Unfortunately, it is also a supremely invasive and destructive pest that is a vector for plant pathogens causing severe damage to crops and native plants. It also competes with native snails and just to top it off, spreads human disease. Although it abounds with protein and might seem like one of those really good ideas on paper, absolutely everyone who has been invaded by these snails deeply regrets the introduction. When I first moved to Britain my sons were little more than toddlers and I recall the enthusiasm with which the prospect of some small tank-dwelling pet was received.

Amongst the frogs, newts, lizards and spiders were these giant African snails and they were actually considered briefly as a candidate by my youngest son. The idea of a snail or some other small and creepy creature as a pet seemed really strange to me, but our circumstances at the time did not permit consideration of a puppy or kitten. The desire to have *something* as a pet was very strong in the boys, however, and in the end we became the proud owners of a very ferocious-looking tarantula called Bob, a most successful and trouble-free pet for young boys intent on impressing the hell out of all their little mates. Thus I did not get to experience giant African snails first hand, so to speak. I believe they are very messy and quite difficult to prepare for the table, but must be cooked very thoroughly at all costs. One of the possible consequences of eating undercooked giant snails is exposure to the parasitic nematode worm, *Angiostrongylus cantonensis*, which can cause very serious meningitis in humans. That might not be a chance you would be willing to take.

SNAKES

I lay on the bunk in the thatched bedroom hut dressed only in a scraggly pair of old underpants. My then lean and nut-brown body was covered in sweat and I could feel droplets trickling down my scalp and dropping onto the pillow. Being in the bushveld in summer is a poor idea and in the middle of the day the temperature can be over 40°C. As the sun reaches its zenith in the pale sky all creatures seek shade and sleep so that early afternoon in the bush is much like the early hours of the morning in the suburbs – still and quiet and vaguely haunted. Even the insects are too hot to buzz and the only sound is the ticking of the galvanised metal roof fittings as they bake in the direct rays of the sun. I had drifted into a state of uncomfortable semi-consciousness when the echoing crash of a shotgun blast from nearby shocked me into wakefulness and sent me leaping to my feet to peer cautiously out of the hut door. Another shot boomed out followed by a long stream of heartfelt invective, apparently coming from the long-drop toilet[71] some distance behind the bedroom huts. From this small thatched-wall and tin-roofed

---

71 A long-drop toilet is an outdoor lavatory consisting of a wooden box with a hole in it (sometimes also a toilet seat) placed over a shaft dug into the ground to a depth of around eight or ten feet. Given the depth, the name is self-explanatory.

facility there emerged an indignant-looking individual holding a shotgun in one hand and a dead black mamba fully eight feet long in the other.

'Bugger nearly got me!' said the red-faced member of the safari company's staff. 'Caught him with a couple of pellets just below the head. Very lucky. Would have got me if I'd missed.'

The second shot had been just to make sure and had shattered the snake's head entirely. Black mambas, one of Africa's most dangerous venomous snakes, have a predilection for long-drop toilets for some reason. Maybe they are after the rats and mice that hunt the insects that are attracted to the somewhat unsavoury quality of all long-drops, notwithstanding the practice of dumping quantities of chloride of lime down the hole from time to time. Usually a retiring snake that will avoid humans if possible, black mambas can become extremely aggressive if they feel trapped or pressurised in any way. Naturally, if a mamba is exploring the dank confines of a long-drop and a human suddenly bursts in, it will feel under attack and in those circumstances has a 'strike first, flee afterwards' philosophy. As it is able to lift forty percent of its length off the ground, it is able to strike both high and long and with the blinding speed common to most snakes. This is a huge problem for the blundering human who then might receive multiple bites high on the body where treatment is extremely difficult. Not that it matters a great deal where on the body you are bitten by a black mamba. Mambas have extremely potent neurotoxic venom that causes rapid onset of symptoms and is, for practical purposes out in the bush, one hundred percent fatal (a tiny handful of people have survived, all in exceptional circumstances)[72]. Thus it is the practice in the

---

72 Modern antivenin snakebite serum is effective for black mamba bites if: a) it is instantly available on the spot; b) it has been stored properly, i.e. refrigerated; c) it is not too old; d) it is administered correctly; and e) it does not kill the victim anyway through anaphylactic shock arising from allergic reaction.

bush to enter a long-drop with a high level of caution, preferably pushing open the door with the barrels of a shotgun loaded with birdshot. Birdshot is immensely effective on all snakes, including black mambas. If a shotgun is not available, then a long stick would be better than nothing.

The fate of the headless mamba carcass is interesting. In many parts of Africa the indigenous folk have a great phobia about snakes that underpins a total taboo on eating them. This taboo can even extend to fish, which are seen as an underwater extension of the concept of a snake, presumably because they both have scales. Additionally, the eating of reptiles is prohibited by Islam, the faith of many inhabitants of North and East Africa. Thus it fell to those of European origin to decide to eat this particular snake, an unusual event driven by one particular individual, because usually everyone in Africa simply throws a dead snake away. I watched the snake being prepared. First it was skinned, a relatively simple process where the skin is slit open and is then progressively stripped back off the carcass. The creature was then gutted, also simple because once the belly is slit open the innards could simply be pulled out of the belly cavity in one long continuously attached package. The flesh was a translucent white, not dissimilar to fish. In fact a headless, skinned and gutted snake looks somewhat like a skinned eel. Memorably, though, the flesh smells very different to any fish and has its own unique aroma which I suppose is correctly described as 'reptilian'. The snake was then cut into pieces of a manageable length of about five inches and these were simply tossed onto the barbecue like sausages without further ceremony.

Well, it turns out that black mamba is alright to eat in a tough and exceptionally chewy sort of way. The outer flesh did not caramelise much over the coals as one might have hoped, aesthetically speaking, and looked somewhat like skinless and overcooked chicken breast, but it was a perfectly acceptable snack as an accompaniment to several beers whilst sitting around the fire, particularly if dipped into hot chilli sauce. One thing about a snake, though, is that there are a very large number of delicate rib bones along most of its length, excluding only the last eighteen inches or so of true tail. The tail has only a spinal column running through the centre, but has by far the toughest flesh. Casual snake eating is thus something necessarily done with the fingers because much of the meat has to be separated from the ribs, either with the fingers or the teeth. There is a reasonable strip of flesh running along each side of the spine (what would be called the loin or back-strap on a deer or antelope), but this too is only effectively removed with the fingers. The flesh was also dry, but I suspect this was because it was somewhat overcooked. It is fun to say you have bitten a black mamba rather than the other way around, but I would not go to any trouble at all to repeat the experience.

In Asia the eating of snakes is popular, particularly in Thailand, Vietnam and parts of China. In these places the process often takes on either a medicinal or a theatrical tone depending on whether you are a local attempting to remedy a physical complaint or a tourist after a thrill and a good story to tell back home in Des Moines or Basingstoke. Naturally, snakes are also eaten all over the continent by people who are simply hungry. As a source of medicine, snakes have been relied upon in China for a very long time. Legend has it that during the Tang Dynasty, around the late 700s, a peasant suffering from a terrible skin disease that covered his body with lesions and boils for many years suddenly showed a remarkable improvement, culminating in the condition disappearing entirely. When asked how this had happened, the peasant was unable to point to anything different in his life apart from the fact that he had taken to drinking rice wine from a particular vat. The vat was examined and was found to contain a large, dead and decomposing snake. From this incident, it is said, doctors came to realise that skin diseases of various sorts could be treated with extracts from snakes, a traditional remedy that has persisted into the twenty-first century. Indeed, snakes preserved in bottles of spirit or wine can be found for sale all over Asia, as can potions, pills and packets of powder all made from dried or processed snake. 'Snake-wine', a snake-infused liquor with high alcoholic content, is a popular drink in bars and restaurants and many men are said to take one now and then as an alleged enhancement to manly performance in the bedroom. Poisonous snakes are particularly popular for this because the venom is denatured and rendered harmless by the alcohol but is thought to contribute meaningfully to the essence of snake dissolved into the drink.

A dramatic tourist-oriented rigmarole has developed around drinking snake blood in both Thai and Vietnamese restaurants. A live and ostensibly dangerous poisonous snake is brought wriggling to the table where first it is decapitated to the shrieks and grimaces of the happy tourist diners. The blood that pumps from the wound is caught in an appropriate vessel for later transfer to small glasses from which the diners will drink it, usually mixed with rice wine and various herbs. The snake's still-beating heart is also removed and placed into a shot of strong spirit, whereupon one of the party quickly downs it, to cries of thrilled horror from many onlookers. Apparently, if you swallow it quickly enough you can still feel the heart beating down in your stomach, which must be an unusual sensation indeed. The rest of the snake is then converted into a selection of stir-fried and steamed delicacies which are incorporated into the meal.

Although you are very unlikely to ever want to catch and eat a snake yourself, you should note that all snakes are edible, even the very toxic ones. All you have to do is remove the head, which contains all the toxins. Beware, however, of the fact that a snake's head can remain 'alive' for quite some time after it is severed from the body. Several chefs have died from poisonous snake bites received from severed snake heads – an extraordinary way to go.

SPRINGBOK

The 1890s were profoundly tragic when it came to the fate of three of the most numerous aggregations of creatures the planet has ever seen. Two of these aggregations, the bison and the passenger pigeon, occurred in North America and are well known. The third, the springbok migration in Southern Africa, few have heard of and now that there is nobody left alive who witnessed it, seems destined to remain a quaint footnote in out-of-print history books.

The bison population of North America in the early 1800s exceeded sixty million animals. The plains-dwelling Native American people relied heavily on the bison for meat and skins and it was essential to their way of life. European immigrants took to hunting bison in a big way, for meat and skins, but also seemingly for socio-political reasons aimed at getting rid of Native Americans, one way or another[73]. By 1850 the bison population had been reduced by half, to around thirty million

---

73 Using the population level prior to contact with Europeans as a yardstick, by 1900 the Native American population of North America had been reduced by around ninety-seven percent, not only as a consequence of the demise of the great bison herds, but following upon disease and various effectively genocidal activities on the part of government agencies. There are no words to adequately convey such tragedy.

animals, but over the next fifty years, and culminating with ferocious intensity during the 1890s, bison were effectively exterminated. In 1900 there were a few hundred animals left, all in small, privately owned herds or in Wild West shows. From these few animals the species has recovered, under heavy legal protection, to around 400,000 individuals today, many in private hands but some wandering wild in national parks.

The situation with the passenger pigeon was even more extreme. Originally probably the most numerous birds ever to have existed, with a naturally fluctuating population of between *three and five billion* individuals, passenger pigeons literally blocked out the sun with huge flocks that would pass in dense, wheeling formations many miles long, like waves rippling across the North American sky. In his 1831 *Ornithological Biography*, American naturalist and artist John Audubon described a migration he observed in 1813:

'*I dismounted, seated myself on an eminence, and began to mark with my pencil, making a dot for every flock that passed. In a short time finding the task which I had undertaken impracticable, as the birds poured in in countless multitudes, I rose and, counting the dots then put down, found that 163 had been made in twenty-one minutes. I travelled on, and still met more the farther I proceeded. The air was literally filled with pigeons; the light of noon-day was obscured as by an eclipse; the dung fell in spots, not unlike melting flakes of snow, and the continued buzz of wings had a tendency to lull my senses to repose...*

I cannot describe to you the extreme beauty of their aerial evolutions when a hawk chanced to press upon the rear of the flock. At once, like a torrent, and with a noise like thunder, they rushed into a compact mass, pressing upon each other towards the centre. In these almost solid masses, they darted forward in undulating and angular lines, descended and swept close over the earth with inconceivable velocity, mounted perpendicularly so as to resemble a vast column, and, when high, were seen wheeling and twisting within their continued lines, which then resembled the coils of a gigantic serpent...

Before sunset I reached Louisville, distant from Hardensburgh fifty-five miles. The pigeons were still passing in undiminished numbers and continued to do so for three days in succession.'

Extraordinarily, the passenger pigeon was exterminated through overhunting and habitat loss during the nineteenth century. The last wild bird was shot in 1900 and the last captive member of the species died in Cincinnati Zoo in 1914 – surely one of the most extreme and senseless exterminations ever perpetrated by humans.

Falling numerically somewhere between the sixty million bison and the billions of passenger pigeons was the Southern African springbok population in the nineteenth century. The springbok (*Antidorcas marsupialis*) is a delicate-looking, long-legged gazelle that weighs between sixty and ninety pounds. It is the national animal of South Africa and is the emblem of the South African national rugby team. Over two million of them survive within its range from the dry scrubland of the southern Karoo across the immense grassland savanna (or what was once grassland savanna) of North-West South Africa and the Kalahari to the Namib Desert. Although two million is plenty of animals and the springbok is in no danger from the conservation point of view, this is a remnant population that is possibly only one percent of the population that existed during the nineteenth century. In the early nineteenth century the springbok's range was very sparsely populated by humans. Small groups of San hunters roamed the interior, but apart from them the country was empty. Clustered around Cape Town and in the Southern Cape coastal region lived 40,000 people, white settlers with their slaves and servants. The Nguni migration from the north, involving probably some tens of thousands at this point, avoided the western reaches and clung to the central plateau and the east coast. The principal reason for this was water. North-West South Africa and the Kalahari of Botswana have very little surface water. The Namib Desert has none at all. Springbok do not have to drink water but get their modest moisture requirements from the foliage they eat. Springbok were thus able to live a virtually undisturbed existence in an area roughly the size of Western Europe. Every so often the springbok would aggregate into massive herds and would then migrate from one area to another, always travelling from north to south, probably driven by a shortage of food *in situ* and the promise of fresh, new foliage following rain in the southern or southwestern Karoo. This phenomenon was never scientifically studied, but its occasional impact on the 'trekboers', the then wandering Afrikaans sheep and cattle pastoralists of the Karoo, was sufficiently vivid for a lasting folk memory to be implanted into Afrikaans culture. There are very few eye-witness accounts of the *trekbokke*, as the migrating springbok were known in Afrikaans. The most graphic was recorded by the South African writer Lawrence Green following an interview with a trekboer who had experienced one of the last migrations at a time when numbers had already been reduced considerably:

'At first there was a faint drumming coming from an enormous cloud of dust and only the front rank of the springbok, running faster than galloping horses, could be seen. This front line was at least three miles long. Hares and jackals and other small animals were racing past the hill and taking no notice of the human beings. Snakes were out in the open, too, moving fast and seeking cover under the rocks on the hill...

The first solid groups of buck swept past on both sides of the hill. After that the streams of springbok were continuous, making for the river and the open country beyond. Then the buck became more crowded. No longer was it possible for them to swerve aside when they reached the fires and the wagon. Some crashed into it and were jammed in the wheels, and trampled upon. The wagon became the centre of a mass of dead and dying buck...

At the height of the rush, the noise was overwhelming. Countless hooves powdered the surface to fine dust, it became hard to breathe. Within an hour the main body of springbok had passed, but that was not the end of the spectacle. Until long after sunset, hundreds upon hundreds of stragglers followed the great herd. Some were exhausted, some crippled, some bleeding...

The trees were reduced to gaunt stumps and bare branches. Every donga leading into the river was filled with buck. It seemed that the first buck had paused on the brink, considering the prospects of leaping across. Before they could decide, the ruthless mass was upon them. Buck after buck was pushed into the donga, until the hollow was filled and the irresistible horde went on over the bodies. Small animals were lying dead everywhere – tortoises crushed almost to pulp, fragments of fur that had been hares. A tree, pointing in the direction of the advancing buck, had become a deadly spike on which two springbok were impaled...[74]

It is clear that observers struggled to estimate the numbers of animals involved in these migrations, being overwhelmed by incredulity at the result of their own calculations. The plains and hillsides for miles in all directions would become covered with animals packed together as closely as sheep in a fold and this relentless mass could then take several days to pass a particular spot. This resulted in estimates of up to 200 million animals, which even the estimators themselves found difficult to credit. However, given the vast extent of the territory from which smaller herds of springbok could have been drawn into the one huge migrating herd, such extreme numbers might in fact be possible. Certainly the migrations would have involved tens of millions at the very least. By way of comparison, the annual wildebeest migration on the Serengeti in Kenya, a currently famous tourist attraction, involves only around 1.2 million animals.

Although the migrating springbok were as devastating as any swarm of locusts in stripping bare the county through

---

74   *Karoo* by Lawrence Green, published in 1955.

which they passed, they also created a fine opportunity to lay in some biltong for the leaner times. People would apparently start off by shooting animals from horseback, riding in amongst the herd and firing at close range, but they soon realised that this was a waste of ammunition and it was possible to approach on foot and simply bludgeon springbok to death with clubs. Vast quantities of meat could be obtained this way by those on the spot and the only restraint was that they would eventually run out of salt. For years thereafter springbok biltong would be in abundant supply and would constitute the main element in the cuisine of the area. Fortunately, springbok meat makes very fine biltong and indeed might well be the finest venison of all, resembling in many ways delicately textured baby beef. It has virtually no gaminess at all and is my personal favourite.

Nobody seems to have recorded where and how these migrations ended. The impression was that the springbok simply dispersed overnight and the huge herd effectively disappeared. Nobody knows whether the springbok ever returned from whence they came or even if they just all marched into the sea and died. It is remarkable to think that only 150 years ago the world was such an empty place that millions of animals could march from one place to another and nobody would be there to record what became of them. The migrations petered out and then ceased entirely in the 1890s. By then the Great Karoo had been effectively enclosed by thousands of sheep farms able to exist by drawing water from artisanal wells, boreholes and little dams on the mountain streams. Local populations of springbok were eradicated to make way for the sheep. Although the western reaches of their range remained unaffected by this rapid development due to lack of accessible water, springbok populations in the fastness of the Kalahari also reduced significantly and no longer attempted to migrate. Perhaps the species required both the vast expanses of the north-west and the herbaceous abundance of the pre-agricultural Karoo to sustain the huge numbers involved in the migrations. With the loss of the Karoo to sheep farming the entire system collapsed and numbers reduced to a fractional remnant that could be permanently and statically sustained in the uninhabited north-west.

Today springbok have been reintroduced into much of the Karoo where they form the backbone of the area's sport hunting and venison industries. When I lived in South Africa I would shoot half a dozen prime springbok each year and use the meat as a complete substitute for all domestic lamb and beef. The entire family thrived on the stuff and I am certain it was a much healthier option. Springbok, in the modern context of small herds wandering free on large, but enclosed, areas of land, are either very simple to hunt or very difficult, depending upon the approach adopted. If you attempt to 'walk and stalk' springbok then you are in for a very challenging time. Like all antelope, springbok have acute senses and have little difficulty spotting an approaching hunter, given the flat, scrub-covered plains where they normally live. Getting within range thus requires a great deal of crawling and using the shallow contours of the land for concealment. In principle this is much like deer stalking in the Highlands of Scotland, with the significant difference that the ground undulates much less and there are few hills interrupting the flat expanses stretching between the mountain ranges. A donga or dry riverbed is a godsend, but springbok seem to know this and somehow are never in range of such an easy approach. Even using a very flat-shooting rifle suitable for long-range shots it is very hard work and you count yourself fortunate if you shoot a single springbok in a day. Approached like this, springbok become one of the most difficult African antelope to bag and the hunter is justifiably proud of his achievement when he gets one. Unfortunately, most proprietors of private hunting reserves do not see it that way. They charge a 'trophy fee' for each animal shot and because springbok are small and numerous, they do not demand a high price. For things to make commercial sense the proprietors prefer that many springbok get shot and there are two ways of achieving this. The first does not qualify as sport hunting at all and is more in the nature of a culling exercise. The paying client climbs onto the back of a pickup truck where he sits on a padded seat with his rifle resting on a padded bench bolted to the roof of the cab. He is then driven around the property and up to herds of springbok where he fires away, often killing or wounding dozens of animals. All of these are then recovered by a backup and carcass recovery team while the client is whisked away to enjoy a large gin and tonic and a barbecue. Personally, I find this distasteful, but some people much enjoy it and are prepared to pay thousands for the privilege. I have heard of some clients who arrange to shoot hundreds of springbok over a period of just a few days and become completely immersed in the slaughter. This is not hunting – it is just killing.

The second approach is to organise what amounts to a gentle drive, similar in principle to some driven game shoots in Europe and elsewhere. The client is positioned behind an anthill or some such cover alongside a path that springbok are known to use when moving from one area to another. A rider on horseback is then dispatched to very quietly and subtly disturb the springbok so that they move off along the path and into range of the waiting client. The idea is to ensure the antelope move in the right direction, but do not panic or run. This takes both skill and experience to achieve. The client for his part has the nerve-wracking experience of watching the herd approach into range and then selects and shoots an animal. Often the herd will not bolt after the first shot and as long as the hunter remains still, a second or even third shot is possible. Two or three of these drives can be undertaken in a day and the hunter is unfortunate if he does not bag at least one springbok on each drive.

Springbok have such wonderful meat that almost the entire animal is palatable in some form or another right down to the shanks, which make a delicious stew surpassing lamb shanks in my view. The meat also lends itself to roasting. A leg or shoulder of springbok is succulent and tender if not overcooked and is at its best if prepared using a kettle barbecue which produces a moist and delicate result. The loin of a young springbok should be reserved for steak which, when grilled to medium-rare, rivals any beefsteak I have ever eaten. The fillet is so tender that it makes excellent steak tartare, the very low fat content being an enhancement to this raw meat dish. In fact, springbok can be substituted for lamb or beef in any recipe whatsoever with good results. The culinary merit of springbok has been discovered by the rest of the world and it is now extremely popular in Germany where it can be found for sale in supermarkets and butchers' all over the place. It is available in Britain, particularly from speciality South African shops, and I recommend you try it if you come across it. It is, however, a touch on the expensive side. In Surrey, where I live, two kilograms of springbok steak costs the same as the entire animal in Beaufort West, a middling town in the Karoo. I cannot bring myself to pay, so limit my springbok consumption to times when I am visiting South Africa.

SQUIRRELS

One of the most endearing characters I have ever known is a springer spaniel. His name is Rosco and he is an alleged gundog. He is also a friend and a fully fledged member of my family. Wherever he goes his kindly face and cheerful manner wins him admirers, to the point that he now knows far more people locally than I do and it is not unusual for passers-by to greet him fondly whilst more or less ignoring me. If he had a Facebook page he might take over the world.

Rosco's nemesis is squirrels. To be precise, North American grey squirrels which abound in the woodland about my house and which long ago drove the indigenous red squirrels into local extinction. When Rosco was still very young and was just starting out on his very chequered career as a gundog, he happened upon a squirrel lurking about in the meadow grass some distance from the trees. At this stage he was accustomed to flushing rabbits occasionally (and then charging after them like a crazed lunatic, deaf to whistles and shouted injunctions) and he clearly saw the squirrel as some sort of long-tailed rabbit. Off went the squirrel like a grey streak towards the trees with Rosco a short distance behind. Rosco was gaining when, to his utter astonishment, the long-tailed rabbit suddenly leapt onto the trunk of a tree and scrambled upwards into the foliage. Rosco was completely incensed. Tree-climbing rabbits! An outrage! He stood with his front legs on the trunk staring upwards into the leafy heights and barked like a coonhound, a most un-spaniel and uncharacteristic behaviour. Puffing somewhat, I arrived on the scene and Rosco's clear desire was that I immediately blast the arboreal aberration out of the lofty shelter to which it had retreated. This proved difficult because squirrels are intelligent creatures and this one was nowhere to be seen. If an attacker is on one side of the tree, squirrels generally hide on the other side and will keep going round the tree so as to keep the tree between them and the perceived threat until it goes away. Clearly, we were not going to get anywhere by stomping around the tree and barking up into the branches, so I pulled Rosco away and settled him down some distance into the woodland. Although he absolutely refuses to sit next to me when we are waiting for game, he will sit as still as a statue some thirty yards away. He developed this peculiarity when first exposed to pigeon shooting and I think it is because the loud report of the shotgun hurts his ears. His practical solution is to sit some distance away, yet be completely responsive to any commands. It is not regulation, but it works for us. It took about twenty minutes for the squirrel to reappear on our side of the tree. If you just sit quietly, squirrels will eventually forget about you and become active again. Rosco saw him before I did and began trembling with eagerness for action, although he did not break cover or give our position away. The squirrel frolicked about for a while jumping from branch to branch and then inevitably presented me with an opportunity for a shot. I fired and the birdshot exploded into the leaves all around the squirrel, which hesitated on the branch for an instant and then toppled over and plunged to the ground. Rosco was there under the tree waiting for it, having charged forward as the shot was fired[75]. He instantly grabbed the squirrel in his jaws, but to his horror and considerable surprise the squirrel grabbed him back, repeatedly sinking its teeth into the tender flesh of his muzzle a couple of inches behind the nose. Brave dog that he is, Rosco did not relinquish his hold but simply set up a dreadful yelping howl as he brought the squirrel to me in the straightest and fastest retrieve he has ever performed. This put me in a quandary. What do you do with an irate squirrel that is biting chunks out of your dog and which seems perfectly capable of biting you too? Do you grab it? Do you run away? Do you tell the dog to drop it and undo months of training? How will you tell the members of the local shoot that your dog got eaten by a squirrel? Before I could overcome my uncertainty the squirrel solved the problem by wriggling free, dropping to the ground and rushing off back up into the trees before either Rosco or I could react. Rosco and I looked at each other in dismay, blood dripping from multiple wounds around poor Rosco's mouth. Although we waited for a long time we never saw this squirrel again and it hopefully recovered from the experience and went on to found a dynasty of ferocious kung-fu squirrels savaging dogs and cats in some distant neighbourhood. For his part, Rosco remains furious with all squirrels and shows boundless enthusiasm for their destruction whenever we encounter them. However, he is now very careful to check that the squirrel is dead before he picks it up.

Grey squirrels are delicious to eat, having dark, sweet flesh

---

75 This is also not regulation and charging forward when the shot is fired is a serious technical fault which would lose you a field trial if you were into that sort of thing. In practice many gundogs do this because it is almost impossible for them to resist the sight of the quarry tumbling down to the ground. It is only a matter of form, however, and makes no practical difference. It might in fact improve the dog's chances of a successful retrieve.

that hints at the hazelnuts they eat in the autumn. They are very popular throughout North America, where they are regarded as a delicacy. This esteem is not shared in Britain, not because grey squirrels taste inferior in the British Isles, but because most British people seem to regard grey squirrels either as some sort of dirty, furry-tailed rat or else have a romantic vision of squirrels induced by a childhood immersed in the saccharine anthropomorphisms of Beatrix Potter. In the more robust era of centuries past when squirrel eating might have been expected to develop in Britain, the grey squirrel had not yet been introduced and the indigenous red squirrel is apparently far less palatable. For those concerned about the hygienic qualities of grey squirrels, I can testify that they are very clean animals, are usually free of fleas and other parasites and are always well groomed. They have very thick skins, compared to, say, a rabbit, and have luxuriant hair. This influences how they should be hunted. A body shot with a standard air rifle is out, unless at very close range. The skin and hair reduces penetration to an unacceptable extent. A head shot is fine at ranges to around forty yards. With a shotgun nothing less than number six shot should be used and number four would be better. A shotgun is not an ideal weapon for squirrel hunting because of meat damage from multiple pellet hits and the ideal weapon in my view would be the .22 long rifle. This is not an option in Britain because of the density of habitations surrounding every woodland and because the .22 long rifle can be lethal to humans at a range of over a mile. It would be a potentially life-ruining event to land a .22 bullet in the playground of the local infant school. In the vast emptiness of a North American wilderness area, however, the .22 would be a good option.

There is a very fancy bit of marksmanship that can be executed when hunting squirrels called a 'barking shot'. This is when, instead of hitting the squirrel, the hunter aims for the branch upon which the squirrel is sitting. When the bullet strikes the branch, the branch transfers the shock of the impact to the squirrel, often shattering the bark in the process, hence the name, and this can be fatal to the squirrel. Apparently the practice developed in the muzzleloader era, when hunters out after deer found at the end of an unsuccessful day that a couple of squirrels for the pot would be a really good idea. The problem was that if you hit a squirrel with a one-ounce lead ball there was not much squirrel left[76]. Killing the squirrel with shock waves transmitted through the branch was the solution. In fact the shock waves sometimes only knock the squirrel out, but of course it then plunges to the ground and can be despatched forthwith. Fail to despatch it and it might revive, much to your detriment if you are carrying it on your person somewhere – ask Rosco.

The most popular recipe for squirrel in North America is a slow-cooked concoction called Brunswick stew. There are a number of competing contenders for the identity of the meat in an authentic Brunswick stew, some claiming the original contained either opossum or rabbit, but most believe that squirrel has the better claim. Brunswick stew is a pleasant tomato-based ragout of Southern origin and contains lima or butter beans, corn, okra and other seasonal vegetables. It much resembles a very thick vegetable soup with pieces of meat in it and it is an excellent supper on a cold night with a hunk of crusty bread and a glass of good beer. As you can buy squirrels ready prepared in some village butchers in England or because you might one day lose patience with the little grey bandits bark-stripping the fruit trees in your back garden and let fly at them with your shotgun, here is a recipe for Brunswick stew:

---

76 Modern deer hunters armed with modern high-velocity rifles face the same problem if they are camping out in the wilderness and have not managed to bag a deer or something else substantial to eat. A 'barking shot' works just as well with a modern firearm apparently.

BRUNSWICK STEW

Back legs from 4 squirrels
1 tablespoon all-purpose flour
1 teaspoon cayenne pepper
4 tablespoons vegetable oil
1 medium onion, chopped
1 medium green pepper, chopped
100 g fresh okra, sliced
2 garlic cloves, finely chopped
2 bay leaves
1 litre chicken stock
400 g can chopped tomatoes
Pips from 2 sweetcorn cobs, boiled and then removed from the cob
400 g can of butter beans

In a large pot, cover the squirrel legs with the chicken stock and bring to the boil. When boiling, reduce the temperature and simmer for thirty minutes. Remove the squirrel legs from the pot, and reserve the chicken stock. When they have cooled slightly remove the meat from the squirrel legs and reserve. Discard the bones.

Heat the oil in a pot. Add the onion, green pepper, okra, garlic, salt and pepper and cook over a medium heat until the vegetables are softened. You can add any other appropriate sliced or chopped seasonable vegetables at this stage, but then add more flour and stock in the following stages to compensate for the increased volume.

Add flour and cayenne pepper and stir to prevent lumps forming. Then add 500 ml chicken stock and stir until the liquid thickens slightly.

Add the bay leaf, tomatoes and squirrel meat and simmer, covered, for about an hour.

Stir in sweetcorn and butter beans and simmer uncovered for a further fifteen minutes.

Serve with fresh corn bread, a shot of bourbon and a glass of decent American craft beer.

STRAWBERRIES

I discovered wild strawberries through the intervention of a vole. On a sunny day in late June, one of the dozen or so such days we get on average each summer in sunny Surrey, I took Rosco for a walk across nearby fields. It was hot and spaniels soon tire in temperatures much above 25°C, so coming to a flat and inviting stretch of meadow covered with brilliant green ground cover, I decided that a rest was in order, for the sake of the dog, you understand. I flung myself to the ground and suggested to Rosco that he should do the same. He said he would, but first needed to explore the adjoining hedgerow just in case some silly pheasant or reckless rabbit might lurk amongst the tangled undergrowth. *Stupid dog*, I thought, and eased myself back into a comfortable position looking out over the valley below the house. Southern England on a bright day in summer is probably the most reassuringly beautiful place on earth – an exquisitely crafted countryside with endless varieties of green scattered across fields, ancient hedgerows and woodland patches, all under a comfortable blue sky. The meadows are speckled with wild flowers growing in profusion amongst the grasses and here and there the startling scarlet of tall poppies distracts the eye. It is entirely man-made and somehow, without formal arrangement or material reward, generations of farmers have nurtured and improved upon the landscape to create a timeless scene of organised natural abundance. It is an incalculably valuable asset which thankfully almost everybody agrees is worthy of the most stringent protection.

After basking in the glorious warmth and enjoying the view for a while, I noticed a small, brown rodent about four inches long scuttle out of the undergrowth, dash across in front of me, snuffle about under the bright green leaves carpeting the ground all around me and then emerge with a tiny ruby-red fruit between its teeth. This it hurriedly carried off back into the undergrowth. Curious, I leaned forward to inspect the ground cover more closely and discovered, to my delight, that I was lying on a bed of fine-leaved wild strawberry plants and that nestled among and beneath the leaves were hundreds of tiny wild strawberries in various stages of ripeness.

About the size of a nonpareil caper (or an AAA buckshot pellet, if you prefer a more virile comparison), the European wild or wood strawberry, *Fragaria vesca,* packs a huge punch of fundamental strawberry flavour, notwithstanding its small size. When you taste one for the first time, with its tart burst of distinctive perfume and intense background notes of sweet fruit, you realise that commercially grown domestic strawberries[77] have simply expanded the flesh, the sugar and the water content of each berry without much increasing the flavour, which finds itself diluted into a mild and probably more approachable state. Wild strawberries are nothing if not powerful. They are accordingly a great addition to anything made with domestic

---

77 The wild European strawberry was the first to be grown commercially during the seventeenth century and was subjected to selective propagation to increase the fruit size and succulence – a process of domestication. In more recent times many other strawberry varieties from around the world have been crossed with one another to produce modern strawberry cultivars. The wild strawberry I am talking about here is the original undomesticated wild plant which still grows all over the Northern Hemisphere.

strawberries if you want to increase the 'strawberryness' of the dish. In particular, I like to use them to make a jus for serving with steak. I simply take a few domestic strawberries, slice them, add a small handful of ripe wild strawberries and fry them in butter in a small pot, adding a little sugar, some black pepper and a dash of balsamic vinegar or splash of red wine. The wild strawberries break down into a jus very quickly upon being heated but the domestic strawberries retain their structural integrity for longer and add a better texture to the sauce. This sauce is really very good with red deer rump steak.

I also use wild strawberries to make an English version of carpaccio, where I try to substitute totally English ingredients for the usual Italian ones. This came about through trying to make a very low-food-mile[78] meal upon coming into possession of a choice loin of roe deer shot in my local woodland. To make this dish you proceed exactly as suggested in the traditional carpaccio recipe on page 72 in the preparation of the meat. However, the meat is then dressed with different ingredients, namely: fine drops of English hazelnut oil, shavings of aged cheddar cheese, a scattering of fresh wild strawberries, a restrained dusting of grated fresh horseradish, a very thin drizzle of local woodland honey and fine droplets of cider vinegar. The dish is completed with a scattering of individual watercress leaves, sea salt and freshly ground black pepper. Remember that fresh horseradish is very powerful stuff and it gets hotter and more pungent as the sinigrin oil in the root is exposed by grating and reacts with the air. The strong flavour of this oil dissipates after about thirty minutes, but you can stop the reaction and stabilise the flavour with vinegar if you like. Personally, I find it more exciting to grate the horseradish onto the dish at the very last moment and with some restraint. It is quite challenging to get the wild

---

78 A 'food mile' is a mile over which a food item is transported during the journey from producer to consumer, as a unit of measurement of the fuel used to transport it.

strawberries, a fruit of the summer, and the fresh horseradish, a root of the autumn, together at the same time. The wild strawberries cannot be frozen because they defrost into a mush, but the horseradish can. Just wrap it in cling film and put it in the freezer and it will more or less retain its flavour and texture for up to a year. It is also possible to buy out-of-season horseradish grown in somebody else's autumn. This dish combines really interesting flavours that people find quite memorable and the strawberries scattered over the plate are visually very appealing. The dish should be accompanied by a good English sparkling wine or a dry vintage cider.

TERMITES

Even lions eat termites. As ridiculous as it may seem to watch the great cats prancing about and snuffling in the grass trying to stuff themselves with these little insects, they do it sometimes when they are hungry and huge swarms of flying termites leave the nest in the early evening or in anticipation of a savanna rain storm. In fact, almost everything else also eats flying termites – birds, lizards, frogs, snakes, bats, moles, mice, rats, shrews, mongooses, jackals, foxes, other cats, baboons, monkeys, beetles, flies, wasps, every single fish that swims in fresh water and human beings. This is because termites are delicious and also extremely nutritious. Of course, some creatures like the aardvark, the anteaters and the aardwolf subsist more or less entirely on termites, but they are specialised feeders who dig non-flying termites out of the nest. Everyone else is simply an opportunist who happens to be in the right place at the right time when clouds of potential kings and queens emerge from the nest and flutter into the air in the hope of propagating another colony.

Termites are really interesting creatures. Specialised forms, or 'castes' as they are sometimes called, are produced by a single queen, the matriarch of the colony, who mates for life with a single king. By means of ordinary sexual reproduction, workers of both genders, various sorts of soldier and winged potential kings and queens are born from prodigious quantities of eggs laid by the queen. In addition, some queens have the ability to switch from sexual to asexual reproduction and parthenogenically produce more queens without fertilisation by the king. That these different types of offspring should emanate from a single organism is extraordinary – the equivalent of your golden retriever bitch producing Yorkshire terriers, Dobermans, pit bull terriers and Great Danes in the same litter and then later generating more golden retriever bitches by way of virgin birth. Each caste has a specialised function within the colony and each individual works away at its allocated task without respite or sleep for the duration of its life. Some species build termitariums, as their nests are called, of spectacular complexity, containing networks of underground tunnels, a queen's chamber, thermoregulatory veins, air-conditioning vents, protective structures, fungus gardens, brood chambers, tower-like superstructures and deep wells accessing underground water, all made of mud, termite spit and faeces. This is very advanced engineering and the puzzling question is where are the blueprints kept? There is undoubtedly some form of intelligence at work here that organises the individuals into a functional collective in much the same way that the cells and microbes in a human body create a symphony of individual functions that, in concert, produce a physically functioning human. With humans we point to the brain as the organising element. But what do we point to in the case of termites?[79]

The first person to seriously study this conundrum was the South African intellectual and polymath Eugene Marais. A strikingly eccentric and lonely figure, part scientist, part poet, part morphine addict, Marais studied termites in the field over a period of ten years in the early twentieth century and then published his observations and conclusions in a number of

---

79   Or bees, ants and other collectives found in the insect world.

Afrikaans newspaper and magazine articles and then in a book entitled *Die Siel van die Mier*, usually translated into English as *The Soul of the White Ant*. The book is extremely evocative and well written and contains some extraordinary insights, bearing in mind that Marais was working as a pioneer in the then non-existent field of ethology, as the scientific study of animal behaviour is now termed. Most prescient amongst these insights was the conclusion that the entire termite colony ought to be considered a single organism, a type of composite animal, and that behaviour of an individual element, such as a worker or a soldier, bore the same relationship to the whole as a cell or cluster of specialised cells (like an organ) does to the whole human body. This is a concept that has been pursued and elaborated upon by famous modern scientists such as Robert Ardrey and Richard Dawkins, who both acknowledge Marais as the originator of the idea. In his own time Marais was less fortunate and his work was extensively plagiarised by the Nobel laureate Maurice Maeterlinck, who copied lengthy tracts from Marais's work verbatim and without acknowledgement in his book *The Life of Termites*, thereby stealing the recognition and critical acclaim rightly due to Marais. It speaks volumes about the scientific establishment of the time that, notwithstanding abundant proof of Maeterlinck's intellectual and literary dishonesty, they continued to fete and acknowledge Maeterlinck whilst piling scorn and derision upon the 'unknown boer worker' as Marais termed himself in correspondence. It is a pity that Marais, who committed suicide in 1936, doubtless partially as a consequence of this unconscionable theft of intellectual property, did not live to see the opprobrium and distaste that history has heaped upon Maeterlinck.

Marais's solution to the organising element in a termitarium was to postulate that the queen functioned as the brain of the composite organism. His insights and speculations as to how the queen might achieve communication with the disparate and distant parts of the organism through scent and vibration were nothing short of inspired, bearing in mind that he was working in an era when chemical mediums of exchange and stimulation such as hormones had only just been discovered. But he also suggested that, in common with all living things, a termitarium was imbued with a mysterious collectivising force that fundamentally motivated its separate parts in their functions in creating the whole, preserved its integrity and established its parameters as a defined living creature. In other words, that a termitarium has a soul. Although modern science has invalidated some of Marais's conclusions, his work is still studied and the question of precisely what the organising force is that governs the complexity of a termite nest continues to challenge modern science. The idea that a single termite might control the construction and operation of the nest no longer finds support. It is believed that the concentration of so much information into an individual insect and the challenges posed by communication with millions of subservient insects simultaneously render the concept implausible. Similarly, theories postulating that each insect contains within it a blueprint or recipe for the construction of the nest are considered inappropriate, more particularly because the nests are adaptive (for example, in response to damage, food locations and brood sizes) and storage requirements for such an immense blueprint make it unrealistic. Currently it is believed that the termite nest is a product of self-organisation. Each worker responds to local stimuli from the structure being created to guide its building behaviour through a process known as stigmergy[80]. The individual termite does not need to have any concept of the consequences of an individual action in terms of the structure, only that a particular action

---

80 Stigmergy is a mechanism of indirect coordination, through the environment, between agents or actions. The principle is that the trace left in the environment by an action stimulates the performance of a next action, by the same or a different agent.

agrees with its behavioural rules. The concept of stigmergy underpins recent thinking on what is now termed 'swarm intelligence' and its consideration very quickly turns into a process that is orgasmic for mathematicians and bewildering for everybody else. Suffice it to say that it is just a theory at this stage and personally I find it unconvincing as an explanation for a structure with thermoregulation, air conditioning and chambers with specific, organised and integrated purposes. However, I am no mathematician so perhaps I simply do not understand.

After such intriguing revelations it seems particularly unenlightened to speak of termites simply as food, but they are genuinely good to eat. I first sampled them when I was little more than a toddler and given to wandering into the small compound occupied by the domestic servants adjacent to our house in what was then colonial Southern Rhodesia (now Zimbabwe). On one of these occasions the servants, off duty in the late afternoon, had made the most of an abundant emergence of flying termites following the usual sub-tropical afternoon rain shower. About 1000 termites had been collected and were now struggling in a dense mass contained in a large, water-filled tin bowl. A frying pan was heated on the fire and one of the women fried handfuls of termites in a little oil, having first made sure that each insect had shed its wings completely. I was given a taste of fried termites wrapped in a small ball of stiff maize porridge colloquially known as *sadza*. It was good and tasted something like a combination of peanut butter and mashed carrots, mixed with the mealy flavour of the *sadza*. I sampled this dish on several occasions whilst growing up and always found the process of collecting the termites to be great fun, sweeping the insects out of the air with an old tennis racket and picking them up off the ground near the nest entrance where they crawled out in glistening thousands preparatory to attempting to fly away. They usually shed their wings quite readily when you picked them up and stuffed them into the paper bags we used to collect them before transfer to the water-filled bowl. The young black kids we did this with would also eat the termites there and then by simply popping every third one or so into the mouth and chewing, much like one does with blackberries here in England. My brothers and I could never bring ourselves to do this, however, so I regrettably cannot report on how raw termite tastes from personal experience.

There are probably around 4000 distinct species of termite (of which 2600 are taxonomically known) but there are huge differences in diet and behaviour between the different species. Some gather food and use it to feed fungi in their nests. Some eat soil, somehow gaining enough food value from organic remains. There is a huge range of species that use wood, from small colonies in single pieces of house frame to rainforest species that live in rotted timber you could wring out like a sponge. They are literally everywhere in the temperate, sub-tropical and tropical world and might represent a massive source of food for humans. As you sit there in your comfortable circumstances reading this book it might seem bizarre to contemplate that you personally might ever be reliant on termites for a square meal, but we are all just one decent asteroid strike away from such possibilities.

TILAPIA

All six boys on the back of the pickup truck wore identical clothing: khaki shirt, khaki shorts and plastic sandals known colloquially as 'slip-slops'. There was not much difference in the hue of our skins. The four 'white' boys were burned mahogany by the sub-tropical sun. The two 'black' boys were the more translucent brown of a thousand generations of genetic adaptation. All were friends and 'brothers', united in the excitement of a shared purpose, although the strictures and discriminations of the adult world had begun to encroach upon the simplicity of youth. We were heading for the river and the river was most easily reached by going straight through the tribal area. The pickup shuddered and bucked along the gravel road, heading downhill through a patchwork of bare earth, pale grass and the squat resilience of acacia thickets. Thick dust roared from beneath the back tyres and billowed out behind in a luxurious vapour trail, spreading to turn the world into an old sepia photograph. Ahead, voracious goats had climbed trees to eat the last of the hard, spiny leaves. Ragged sheep, filthy wool hanging in tatters, resolutely trotted into our way. In an African tribal area it is virtually impossible to hit the goats and virtually impossible to miss the sheep. Cattle stood about in the heat, all ribs and flies.

Soon we reached the narrow belt of green riverine forest and turned to follow its twisting course for an hour or so, in search of our destination – Dutchman's Pool. Who Dutchman was and why the pool had been named after him is information lost in the tumult of even so short a history as that of Zimbabwe. But what a great pool! Moss-green river water flowed sedately into a rotund basin lined with dusky green fig trees. The pale roots of these trees twisted around the dark rocks lining the bank and disappeared into the water. The branches danced with hundreds of birds and a large troop of monkeys swung out at our approach and made off into the surrounding bush. We set ourselves up in the cool shade along the bank, threading the thin nylon lines through the eyes of our rods and impaling earthworms on hooks suspended below home-made cork floats. I flicked mine out into the dappled water and began the fascinating meditation that is float fishing, where all of creation is focused into a tiny point that might quiver at any time. Around me the other boys fell silent as their own concentration began. A cough now and then, the whine of a mosquito, the rasp of fingernails on skin; these were the only sounds.

The cork moved – I could have sworn it did! I leaned forward and watched closely. It was motionless on the surface again. Then it bobbed and slipped determinedly under the green water. I struck! The weight of the fish was instant, tugging this way and that in short, hard runs. The rod bent almost double and I cranked the reel, wrestling the fish up through the water where it thudded about just beneath the surface for a few seconds before being lifted onto the bank in flapping glory. It was a bream, as tilapia are called in Zimbabwe, weighing about a pound and with the green-blue scales of its flanks glistening and its red fins erect. This is what we were after – the best eating fish in all of inland Africa. That first bite heralded something of a run and soon all the rods were bent. A great and joyous chatter arose as fish after fish was heaved struggling from the water. The day brought us several dozen fish, not all of them big enough to eat, but enough to hold our attention until the sun dwindled into a dusty sunset.

We made camp some hundred yards back from the pool under towering musasa trees, black branches flat across the fading ochre sky. Any closer to the water would have much increased the volume of mosquitoes, which were bad enough anyway. The supervising adult with us, a great-uncle with a dour temperament, instructed the black boys to collect firewood and make a fire whilst the white boys unloaded sleeping bags, two tarpaulins and various cool boxes from the back of the truck. The uncle also unloaded two short, thick fishing rods with roller line guides and large multiplying reels, such as might be suitable for subduing a tuna or sailfish. These he took down to the edge of the pool where he knotted large silver hooks to the thick nylon line. He then baited the one with a large block of blue carbolic soap[81], massaged and squeezed into a sausage around the line with the vicious hook protruding from the bottom. On the other he impaled a small dead chicken which he removed from a plastic bag with a powerful waft of putrefaction. The target for these preparations, he informed us, was vundu, a very powerful catfish that lurks within the depths of some African rivers and grows to a weight of over 120 pounds. Of course, it was not possible to cast these huge baits out using the short rods, so line was stripped from the reels and the baits were slung out by hand into the deep green water in the centre of the pool. The rods were then laid on the ground some twenty yards from the water, the drags on the reels were screwed as tight as possible

---

81 Carbolic soap is effective bait for catfish in Africa and in Asia too, I believe. European fish of all species seem not to like it at all and it is used by scoundrels to mess up fishing in particular swims to which they do not have access so as to augment the supply of fish in other swims to which they do. It is thus not a good idea to try it in Europe for fear your intentions might be misunderstood.

and two long, thin ropes were attached to the reel seat on each of the rods. The ropes were then unwound all the way back to the camp where they were tied to the bumper of the truck, on the back of which my great-uncle intended to sleep. He then produced two shiny silver dinner bells which he had clearly 'borrowed' from my great aunt's silver dinner service and tied these onto the ropes with string. The idea was that if a fish took the bait in the night, the line would tighten to the reel, the rod would jerk forward against the rope, which would tighten and ring the bell.

Camping in the African bush is a special experience which is somehow viscerally more satisfying than camping anywhere else. The hardwood fire draws a warm circle on the dusty earth and you are surrounded by a darkness made more profound by the crackling flames. Soon after sunset myriad night noises begin and near a river these can range from the strange rasping cough of a passing leopard, repeated like the sawing of a rough log, to the songs of dozens of different frogs, chirping and booming away in a quest for matrimonial bliss. The keening yap of jackals carries for miles across the floodplain and the ghostly whoop of hunting hyenas causes you to shift a little closer to the fire. We made an excellent supper from some of the fish, impaling them on sticks and grilling them over the fire, the flesh roasting in its own fat. Abundant other food had been provided in the cool boxes, so something of a feast took place, my great-uncle enjoying large draughts of Cape brandy mixed with Coca-Cola to wash everything down. This made him far more loquacious and after supper he regaled us with stories, sitting up close to the fire on a fold-out deck chair while we boys sat on the ground in a circle. Adult men can seldom resist the temptation of telling scary stories to young boys around a fire at night. I can no longer recall the stories after such a span of time, but remember feeling quite nervous as the time to sleep arrived. Although the two black boys had fished with us and eaten with us around the fire, there was now a strange sleeping apartheid imposed by my great-uncle. He instructed the black boys to take the smaller of the two tarpaulins and lay it out on the ground some thirty yards away from the larger tarpaulin upon which we white boys would sleep. This was well into the darkness beyond the ring of firelight and the two black boys went off looking apprehensive, grasping a thin blanket apiece. We spread our sleeping bags out in a line on the tarpaulin, fashioned makeshift pillows out of clothing and towels and were soon comfortably dozing off. My great-uncle, who had brought along an actual mattress, climbed onto the back of the pickup truck and lay there in the eerie glow of a bedtime cigarette.

There were disturbances in the night. The first was a great crashing in the nearby bush, probably caused by some large antelope coming down to the river and then suddenly scenting us somewhere nearby in the dark. Humans can cause panic when we are accidentally encountered at close range. This ruckus was loud enough and close enough to wake me and the next thing I saw two small figures come hurtling out of the darkness, blankets trailing like cloaks. Quickly the two black boys wriggled themselves into the middle of the line of sleeping white boys, covered themselves entirely with their blankets and then lay dead still. I instantly worried that my uncle would object, but an amused chuckle emanated from the back of the truck and we all just went back to sleep.

The second disturbance was when one of the silver dinner bells set off a brief tinkling and then went quiet again. This woke me, but I was tired and by then it was cold, so there was no way I was going to get up. My uncle heaved himself up and trudged down to the river. A short while later he returned, climbed back into his bed and did not stir again until morning. The next day he told us that he had reeled in the line baited with the chicken, only to find that the bait was missing. Something had bitten it off the hook and in the circumstances that something could only be a crocodile.

'No chance of a vundu if there is a croc around,' he said. 'You kids better sit a bit back from the water's edge today. Don't want you to take any risks and for God's sake don't go in the water for any reason.'

The possible presence of a crocodile did not put the tilapia off in any way though and we had a very successful morning, catching enough fish to almost fill one of the cool boxes. Once again, some of these we cooked over the fire and ate them for lunch. The rest we took home to be turned into the universally popular:

ZIMBABWEAN PERI-PERI FRIED FISH

4 tilapia fillets
8 tablespoons fine-ground semolina
1 tablespoon paprika
1 tablespoon crushed dried chillies
1 tablespoon chilli powder (preferably South African peri-peri chilli powder)
½ tablespoon freshly crushed black pepper
½ tablespoon flaky sea salt
zest of ½ a lime, finely grated
zest of ½ a lemon, finely grated
4 tablespoons groundnut oil
75 g unsalted butter
4 cloves fresh garlic, peeled and crushed
1 egg, beaten
Juice of ½ a lemon
100 ml white wine

Combine the semolina, paprika, crushed chillies, black pepper, salt, lime zest, lemon zest and half the chilli powder in a large plastic bag. Shake vigorously to mix. Dip each tilapia fillet in the beaten egg and then, one at a time, place in the plastic bag and shake to coat with the mixture. Heat the oil to a good hot temperature in a non-stick frying pan and fry the fillets briskly for a few minutes on each side. The coating should be crisp and slightly caramelised and the flesh cooked through. Although I prefer to avoid overcooking any fish, this dish is good even if the fish becomes a little dry. Once the fish is cooked and has been removed from the pan, add the wine and deglaze to incorporate any bits of fish or coating into the sauce. Reduce the wine by half or so. Add the butter, lemon juice, garlic and remaining half a tablespoon of chilli powder. Reduce the heat so that the butter does not separate. Remove the garlic after a few minutes. Add a little salt and pepper if needed and pour the sauce over the fish just before serving. Serve with rice or boiled potatoes and a green salad.

This recipe is how a Zimbabwean, born and raised with Southern African peri-peri, would do it using ingredients you can get hold of in Britain. It is a very spicy dish, as exciting to the initiated as hot Madras curry is to a British person. If you are not used to it, tone down the quantities of chilli somewhat. It will still be delicious. And speaking of curry, tilapia is also one of the very best fish to use in a Thai curry. Although it is essentially a white, flaky-type fish it is also firm fleshed and so holds together well if fried briefly and then dropped into the curry sauce just before serving.

Of course if you have not yet tried tilapia, none of this talk about spiciness should lead you to conclude that this fish is in any way inferior if simply fried in butter and served with a squeeze of lemon. It has one of the great flavours of Africa. It is available in supermarkets and fishmongers all over Britain and although many come from Asia, some of these imported fish actually come from Zimbabwe where these days they are commercially farmed.

TROUT

My introduction to fly fishing for trout was so enveloped by ignorance that it could almost serve as a scientific experiment. When I was a boy my parents arranged a holiday at a lakeside cottage in a remote and beautiful mountainous region. The lake was stocked with rainbow trout imported from America and hearing of our impending visit, a friend more or less forced a couple of fly rods and a bag of tackle on us. No one in the family knew the slightest thing about fly fishing, but we packed the rods and tackle nonetheless and headed into the hills. Both the cottage and the lake turned out to be exactly what you would hope for in such things: stone walls, big fireplace, wooden-framed bay windows; deep, cool, clear water nestled into a bowl surrounded by pine forests and banks of aromatic heather. I was captivated from the start. On the first morning I went for a walk along the lake bank and soon encountered a fly fisherman sweeping his line back and forth through the air before depositing it onto the water in front of him. *Aha!* I thought. *So that's what you do.* Hugging these first revelations to my chest and bursting with eagerness to tackle up and get going, I hurtled off back to the cottage as fast as my skinny legs could take me.

It turns out that assembling and using fly tackle is not remotely intuitive. I fitted the reel incorrectly, took quite a while to figure out that the line was not supposed to go through the hook-keeper before being threaded through the bottom eye on the rod and most material of all, attached the leader back-to-front so that the fly was secured to the loop on the thick end whilst the thin end was knotted to the end of the fly line. For some reason, this seemed logical. Thus armed I went forth to do battle with the trout and needless to say, in a week of intense effort I caught nothing. My nascent casting skills did not allow me to project more than about ten yards of line out onto the water and even recently stocked rainbows are not going to take a fly attached to a thick leader loop. Yet I enjoyed every minute of it. All around me other anglers caught fish now and then and this did serve as an inspiration, but that is not what kept me at it from early morning until sunset. It was something else, something quite mysterious that seems to imbue all types of trout fishing. Many writers have tried to identify what this infinitely alluring element might be. Some point to the considerable complexities engendered by the minutiae of the sport, equating complexity with enjoyment, but I have not noticed that the angler who limits himself to a handful of fly patterns and a single rod and line enjoys himself less than the streamside entomologist with his thousands of patterns or the techno-buff with his nth-generation graphite rods and space-age accoutrements. Other writers emphasise the environment in which trout fishing takes place, stressing that it is almost always both natural and beautiful, but you can take a walk through the most exquisite countryside and not experience a tenth of the exhilaration enjoyed during a day fly fishing on a chalk stream. A few adopt a philosophical approach, suggesting that in approaching fly fishing with deadly seriousness, but also with the knowledge that such seriousness is entirely misplaced, a person enjoys a sense of freedom in pursuing a goal with intense concentration and anticipation, but with little concern for the outcome. In the wider scheme of life where most of us no longer fish for survival, it matters not a jot whether you catch a trout or not. Disappointment in the quest is superficial and fleeting. Yet success can be profound. There are captains of industry who manipulate billions, hold the fate of thousands in their hands and daily struggle with the creation or retention of empires, but who nevertheless count the capture of a five-pound trout on a fly in some wild river as one of the crowning achievements of life. Trout fishing somehow encompasses an aesthetic that is fundamentally appealing to the sensitivities of the participants no matter who they are. This is true whether the trout fishing in question is for stocked fish in some small, commercial stew pond or is for huge and spooky wild fish in a crystal spring creek. It is the angler who decides where in the spectrum he, his budget and his skills level will fit in, but wherever that is, the aesthetic will apply.

Although the pleasures of trout fishing seem largely immune to the vicissitudes of modern commercialisation, the same cannot be said for the trout themselves. Like many trout fishermen, I have spent most of my life pursuing and catching trout that have been artificially introduced into the water in some way. In Africa, where trout do not occur naturally,[82] the fish I caught were either introduced into the river as fingerlings in the hope of a result as natural as possible or were stocked at a good size to ensure the thrill of a significant-seeming capture at the expense of authenticity. Either way, and especially if they were stocked at a large size and had been in the water for some time, they performed poorly as fighters. At the time I put this down to the fact that they were alien fish occupying a non-existent niche in the tumbling mountain streams where we fished for them. Then later in life I had the opportunity to fish in rivers where trout occurred naturally, but where environmental and angling pressure was such that wild stocks were substantially supplemented, or indeed virtually replaced,

---

82 Brown trout do in fact occur naturally in the Atlas Mountains of North Africa – but nowhere else on the continent.

by stocked fish. Often it was the same story: the stocked fish put up a flabby performance upon being hooked that matched their somewhat flaccid and flat-flanked appearance. Hooking them in the first place was a pleasure because they rose to the fly with most of the circumspection and dedication to detail displayed by genuinely wild fish, but the disappointing performance in the fight prevented full satisfaction.

Then one day I had the opportunity to fish for trout that are entirely wild in water that has never been stocked, ever. This was in the far north of Scotland where dozens of lochans, small natural lakes, abound in an upland fastness of rolling moors, spongy sphagnum moss and ferocious biting midges. This place is unchanged since the end of the last Ice Age and has received absolutely minimum interference from mankind. Nobody is interested in fishing for these trout except for a few dedicated fly fishermen who wrap themselves up in midge-proof kit and stride for hours across the hills. For around £20 per week I had the freedom to wander about at will and fish in little waters that might not have seen an angler for dozens of years or indeed might never have been fished by anyone ever before. I found the experience fascinating. Not every lochan holds trout. Some of the smaller ones are entirely barren or contain little stunted fish. However, anything bigger than the average municipal swimming pool might hold really good fish and there is infinite mystery in waiting to see what the peat-stained water might surrender. The technique is simple, for these are not sophisticated fish. A large, fluffy dry fly is cast out onto the water and then you wait, trying to remember to breathe now and then. Within a few minutes, if there are fish in that particular lochan, one will have a go at the fly which will disappear in a noisy splash. A spectacular battle then follows. The first one I hooked ran the entire fly line and twenty yards of backing off the reel. It stopped at twenty yards because it ran out of lochan, not energy. This fish was arm-achingly solid in the water, like a sea trout, and it was capable of multiple runs, the last of which culminated in a tail-walk across the shallow water along the far bank. This gave me a first sight of the fish which seemed remarkably small. I never found out how big it actually was because after the tail-walk it retired to the deep water in the middle of the lochan where it shook its head like a bull terrier playing with a rope and snapped the four-pound breaking strain tippet. I sat down on the bank in a state of shock. Wow! I mean really, wow! What a fish! With unsteady hands I replaced the tippet with one having a breaking strain of six pounds, tied on another Yellow Stimulator[83] and cast out again. This time a take came in less than a minute and once more I was locked into battle with an absolute tiger of a fish that ran about all over the place to the continuous screeching of the reel. This fish I managed to land and was astounded that it only weighed a pound and a half. It was a brown trout with a dark speckled back and bright butter-yellow belly, but it was unlike any trout I had ever encountered. It instantly reminded me of a tuna, a stocky, streamlined bullet of pure muscle. *Well, now I see what all the fuss is about*, I thought to myself. *If all trout once looked and fought like that, then it would definitely have been the perfect fly-fishing fish.* I spent the next several days fishing for these trout and can say without hesitation that on the light fly tackle I was using they presented one of the greatest challenges of a long angling career that includes catching all manner of marine fish. There was no room for error at all with these fish – any mistake and they just snapped you off. The biggest I managed to land weighed a mere two and a half pounds and provided a titanic struggle that has yet to be equalled by any other trout I have ever caught and that would include a twelve-pound stocked rainbow.

It turns out that not all wild trout are like those Scottish ones. Since the time of my adventures in the distant Scottish

---

83   The Yellow Stimulator is a large, multi-hackled dry fly originally designed by American Jim Slattery as a stonefly imitation. It is one of the finest 'attractor' dry fly patterns and works on all kinds of trout all over the world.

hills, I have had the pleasure of fishing for wild brown trout in Wiltshire and Hampshire where, on some very special chalk streams, wild fish have been nurtured back into predominance through careful river management, a catch and release philosophy and a no-stocking policy. Like the inhabitants of some of the lovely homes that dot the chalk valleys and cluster around the picturesque villages, these wild fish are elegant, privileged and languidly charming. At a natural prime fighting weight of around a pound and a half, they are like muscular schoolboy rugby players from some advantaged private school, capable of a jolly good scrap old boy, but no match at all for their northern brethren who are like the revellers in a Glasgow pub on a Saturday night – short, stocky and viciously tough. That these disparate wild fish have different fighting abilities now seems to me to be entirely appropriate to their different habitats. In the case of the chalk stream fish, the comparatively lethargic fight is compensated for by the exquisite technicality of being obliged to fool them with an imitation of the natural flies they are feeding on at the time. This is an enhancement to the aesthetic if you are attracted by such things and have, or are interested in developing, the angling skills necessary to deal with it. On the other hand, the occupant of the lochan may be innocent in matters of feathered deception, but makes up for it in simple brutality. Both are wonderful to experience.

Trout are also an esteemed eating fish. I am tempted to say at this point that I am not entirely sure why, but I do recall a handful of trout out of the hundreds I have eaten that were exceptionally delicious. These exceptional fish share certain common features: they were caught by me, they were of good size, they came from pristine mountain water, they were grilled over wood coals within minutes of being landed and I was pretty hungry at the time. Of these common features I suspect that the extreme freshness might have been the material one. Certainly, no self-respecting Austrian would dream of eating a trout that had been dead for more than five minutes. Austrian fly fishermen traditionally drag a perforated wooden barrel behind them as they wade up the beautiful Alpine rivers that abound in Austria[84]. This barrel serves the same purpose as a live-well in a boat, keeping fish destined for the table alive until they can be transferred into the spring-water wells (or sometimes glass tanks) that waterside restaurants and inns maintain solely for the purpose of ensuring any fish served is as fresh as is possible. I have eaten trout in an Austrian mountain restaurant and they whacked the poor creature on the head literally a few minutes before it was served up to me. It was good, but not a patch on the zander (*Sander lucioperca*, also known as pike perch) that was also whacked on the head and served up at the same time. In Britain it is no longer a common practice to keep live fish in tanks in restaurants so you will not easily be able to experiment with extremely fresh trout unless you go out and catch one yourself and cook it then and there on the bank. The fishery management are unlikely to approve of this so you are probably stuck with just keeping a dead fish in a bag for a few hours before you can get it home and cook it. It might then be more palatable if prepared as part of a more exotic preparation, my favourite being the French classic:

TROUT AMANDINE

4 boneless trout fillets
250 g unsalted butter
1 tablespoon red wine vinegar
2 teaspoons fresh lemon juice
2 tablespoons groundnut oil, for frying
150 g all-purpose flour
Salt and freshly ground black pepper

---

84   Today most Austrian rivers are strictly catch and release, so anglers no longer drag the barrel.

250 g sliced almonds, blanched and toasted
Chopped flat-leaf parsley and lemon wedges to serve

Heat the butter in a frying pan over medium heat, stirring constantly until it turns golden brown. This takes about twenty minutes. Remove from the heat. Whisk in the vinegar and lemon juice. Pour out of the pan and set the sauce aside.

Return the pan to the heat and add the groundnut oil. Dredge the trout fillets in flour and then fry in the groundnut oil until cooked, around three to five minutes each side depending on the thickness of the fillets. Remove the fillets from the pan.

Return the sauce to the pan together with the almonds. Season the sauce with salt and pepper to taste. When the sauce is heated through, pour over the trout fillets, sprinkle with chopped parsley and garnish with lemon wedges. Serve with a good Italian Pinot Grigio or a Mosel Riesling.

It does not matter in the preparation of trout amandine because it is a boneless dish, but it pays to remember in other recipes that trout of all fish are the most susceptible to having the bones come loose in the flesh if the fish is overcooked. Good-quality trout can be eaten raw as sushi or sashimi, so there is no need to fear undercooking it a touch, just to the point where the flesh begins to flake from the bones. Stop cooking and serve it immediately. By the time it gets to the table it will be perfect. Delay and it will continue cooking in the retained heat until the cartilage that holds the bones in place melts and releases the bones into the flesh. This ruins the dish.

In my view cold-smoked trout, prepared in identical fashion to delicate, high-quality smoked salmon, is by far the best way to enjoy this fish. It is almost as good as smoked wild salmon. Unfortunately, it is not really something you can do at home unless you have invested in the substantial equipment necessary for cold smoking. Commercial smoking outfits, although happy to smoke your trout for you if you like, are few and far between and are far too expensive to be workable for dealing with a couple of stocked fish at the end of a casual day's angling. Hot-smoked trout is also very pleasant as a cold dish with good rye bread and a salad on a summer's day. This you can do yourself simply by purchasing a small hot-smoker about the size of a biscuit tin. In fact, you can use an actual biscuit tin if you can find a cake grid small enough to fit inside. I successfully used a biscuit tin for years, spreading the sawdust on the bottom of the tin, placing the trout on the cake grid just above the sawdust, closing the lid and then heating up the base of the tin by placing two methylated spirit burners made from a couple of small tin-foil pie dishes under it. It worked a treat. Hot-smoked trout is excellent with creamed horseradish sauce and a glass of Provençal rosé or New Zealand Sauvignon Blanc.

WARTHOG

The warthog is the most ferocious-looking of all pigs. If you live in America or Europe and you put a shoulder-mounted warthog trophy up on the wall alongside a European wild boar, everyone will assume that the warthog was by far the more hazardous acquisition. It's heavy, flat snout, scarred by bristles and facial wattles, appears malevolent, and the magnificent curving tusks protruding from the upper jaw seem designed to disembowel anyone or anything that takes liberties. However, this perception is entirely wrong. Outside of certain very specific circumstances, warthogs are not dangerous at all, even when wounded, and invariably prefer to flee at high speed rather than face any threat. It is only when a sow has young piglets in tow and feels that the usual option of running away is not available that there is a possibility of attack. Such an attack is then dangerous because the lower tusks, although much shorter than the flamboyant upper ones, are razor-sharp and are capable of inflicting very serious injury. I have only once had the experience of being charged by a warthog sow. After an exciting and stressful morning hunting antelope, I decided to take the afternoon off from pursuing mighty beasts and instead enjoy a little solitary bird shooting with my gundog of that time, a fiery and somewhat out-of-control springer spaniel by the name of Titus. One of Titus' many faults[85] was an enthusiasm for chasing warthogs whenever we encountered them. This regrettable tendency had established itself on his very first time out in the bush when he came upon a sounder of warthogs whilst quartering a patch of riverine grass. To Titus' considerable astonishment the pigs ran away from him. All training instantly vanished and he gave chase, overwhelmed by a sense of power that went straight to his puppyish head. From then on whenever we came upon warthogs off Titus would go, deaf to all admonishments and whistles and the pigs would run away. On this occasion it was different. We had walked about half a mile away from camp and Titus was busy searching out the tangled heaps of brush that accumulate around termite mounds in the hope of flushing some of the small (but delicious) crested francolin (*Dendroperdix sephaena*) that live in the thorny labyrinths. I was armed with a light twenty-bore shotgun loaded with birdshot and was hopeful of securing enough francolin for a *potje*. Titus was invisible somewhere in the bush in front of me when I heard the tell-tale alarm grunts and rattling hooves of a sounder of warthogs rapidly on the move. *Damn!* I thought. *Now it will take me half an hour to get that bloody dog back.* I moved away from the thicket just in front of me to look down a grassy corridor on my left in an effort to see what was going on. To my surprise, dashing towards me up the corridor at full speed was Titus. A short way behind him was a large warthog sow. Clearly, Titus had offended in his usual way, but this time there must have been piglets because the sow seemed very determined to get him. Now here is an interesting thing. I was just standing there innocent of any provocation whatsoever, but the instant that pig set eyes on me it appeared to conclude that I was the true source of the trouble and abandoned Titus to focus entirely

---

85 Gundogs seldom have faults that can be ascribed purely to the dog. Usually the fault is that of the trainer. I was nowhere near good enough as a trainer to handle a dog as difficult as Titus or to bring out the best of his considerable talents.

on me. Changing direction and accelerating, the pig charged, clearly determined to do me great harm.

If you are charged by a wild animal it is important to have given that possibility some thought beforehand. As I have emphasised earlier, wild animal charges happen at tremendous speed and although the surge of adrenaline you will unquestionably experience makes it feel as though things have slowed down somewhat (actually, what happens is you speed up), there is no time for cognitive thought during the charge. Thus, rule one is to have a plan already formulated which your brain can latch onto in the stress of the moment. Fortunately for me I had been charged by wild creatures before and thus had in place a plan to use when charged by something 'thin-skinned' whilst armed with a shotgun. Simply put, that plan was to wait until the relevant creature was about ten feet away and then blow its head off. This you can do with a shotgun, even a twenty-bore, because at ten feet even small birdshot has not spread out more than a couple of inches and the pellet load operates effectively as a single and very lethal head-shattering projectile. Of course, this does not work on anything 'thick-skinned' (elephant, rhino, hippo, buffalo, and in this context also lion, tiger, grizzly bear and polar bear[86]) because those creatures have size, hide, musculature and bone structure that can resist blasts of pellets from shotguns. Thick-skinned creatures require a deep-penetrating, heavy-calibre rifle bullet or possibly a rifled slug from a shotgun and if you have not got such a rifle or slug with you, then your emergency plan is limited to simply running like hell (although see footnote 86 below). Of

---

86 You might get lucky with lion, tiger, grizzly bear or polar bear because it is remotely possible to kill one of those with a blast of birdshot if the range is very close, but the odds are much against it. However, there is no benefit in running away from any of these predators because it triggers a pursuit reflex and they will definitely catch you and kill you, so you may as well stand your ground and have a go. The point is that in country inhabited by this league of predator you should really be carrying an appropriate rifle.

course, warthogs are thin-skinned and so I waited for the warthog to get closer, tracking its movement through the grass with the gun until it got to about ten feet. Just as I was about to fire, the pig accelerated again and in so doing managed to get beneath the line-of-sight of the barrels. A terrible micro-second of indecision followed. Would I be able to drop the barrels quickly enough to get off an accurate shot or was it too late? Should I jump rather than fire? I hesitated and then somehow and in some confusion, I managed to do both, leaping into the air and to the side whilst simultaneously pulling the trigger. The warthog literally passed beneath my feet just as the close-packed swarm of pellets missed its head (and my left foot) by inches. Rule two: stick with the plan. Fortunately, the warthog did not immediately turn and savage me as a truly dangerous animal would have, but simply crashed away through the grass, hopefully to be reunited with its piglets within minutes. Titus, author of all the trouble, reappeared looking sheepish, but without genuine remorse. He continued to chase warthogs for the rest of his life.

Warthogs are the easiest African game animal to hunt. This is primarily because they have poor vision. This makes them easy to stalk compared to antelope. They also have small home ranges, usually no more than forty or fifty acres, and as they are grazers, they occupy a particular type of savanna-style habitat usually consisting of grassland interspersed with thickets and termite mounds. This habitat is most easily recognised in bushveld terrain where it contrasts with the rest of the bush and is often found along rivers or near permanent sources of water. Also, the small home range means that the signs of warthog habitation – spoor, droppings, pathways and so on – are concentrated into a definite area and so warthogs become easy to find. They are not so easy to kill, however, being tough customers standing between twenty-five and thirty-three inches at the shoulder and weighing somewhere between 100 and 300 pounds. This is an animal that must be taken seriously and a properly powerful rifle in the .30-calibre bracket, firing a bullet of at least 150 grains, should be used. If you wound a warthog it runs off and then goes to ground in one or other burrow as soon as it can find one. They are then a terrific problem to extract, requiring to be literally dug out of the iron-hard soil. This is a sweaty, exhausting and terribly traumatic experience involving dust, blood, dirt and screaming warthog. You will not want to do it twice and I know people who hunt warthogs with rifles more suited to elephants in an effort to avoid going through it ever again.

People hunt warthogs because they are really good to eat, even when fully grown and several years old. They have the palest flesh of all pigs, some of it almost white when cooked, and they make the very best hog roast of all. Cooking a whole warthog on a spit over a large open fire is one of the most memorable culinary spectacles employed by lodge owners to impress foreign visitors to game-viewing lodges throughout Central and Southern Africa. It is an extraordinary experience to visit one of the very upmarket lodges, even if you were born and raised in the bush. There is just something exceptionally appealing about the combination of serious luxury and rugged, dusty bush. It is thrilling to sit at one of the linen-covered dinner tables placed strategically around the blazing central fire in a proper boma[87] and watch the warthog turn on the spit whilst sampling fine wine in glittering crystal glasses. It is one of the major attractions of what has become a premiere tourist activity.

---

87 A boma is a high-walled enclosure usually constructed from a combination of local tree trunks, thatch and reeds, within which food is prepared and meals served around a large central fire. Originally bomas were constructed as protection against lions, but they are very atmospheric places on a dark African night regardless of whether or not there are actual lions around. They are a central feature of many game-viewing and hunting lodges.

Unlike domestic pigs, warthogs do not have a pronounced layer of subcutaneous fat, nor is the gnarled, grey skin in any way appetising. Thus warthogs are skinned in the same way as all other game and as pigs go, warthogs have lean meat. It is, however, not lean enough to make biltong, and warthog biltong goes off before it dries. Warthog can be successfully made into very palatable salami or be used as part of the mixture in a traditional Polish-style smoked and dried cabanossi sausage by someone who knows what they are doing. Warthog is also excellent in the full range of Asian-style spiced pork dishes and sweet and sour warthog is memorable. Warthog is something that you can only experience out in the bush because it is a compulsory zero-food-miles meat. Warthogs carry swine fever, a contagious, often fatal, disease of pigs sometimes called pig cholera. It is illegal to transport warthog meat by any means whatsoever throughout Central and Southern Africa and the authorities are serious about this. If you find yourself staring down the barrel of an AK47 at one of the roadblocks that seem to have proliferated throughout Africa over recent years, you will be really sorry you have that cooler box full of warthog in the boot. You have been warned.

WILDEBEEST

The ease with which the farmer crawled forward to the edge of the shallow bluff belied his rotund and short-legged stature. I made a much more clumsy effort, scraping my knees through the reddish dust and scratching my forearms on the *voeljiekanniesitnie* bushes[88] as I pushed the rifle forward in front of me. Coming to the edge and sinking down onto my stomach, I looked down over the dust wallow some forty feet below us. Eighty yards away on the other side of the wallow stood a herd of thirty or so black wildebeest[89] cows. A single bull stood a little apart from the cows, looking more massive and heavily set. Something in the distance across the flat Karoo plain had caught the wildebeests' attention and they were all looking away. We were downwind so they had no idea at all that we were there.

'Ag man, do me a favour and shoot that bull,' whispered the farmer to me in Afrikaans. This request came as a considerable surprise. I thought we were hunting springbok and at the time black wildebeest was one of the most endangered antelope

---

88 *Voeltjiekanniesitnie* translates from Afrikaans into English as 'birdy cannot sit' and is the colloquial name for a Karoo bush so festooned with thorns in all directions that a bird literally cannot find a thorn-free patch to land on.

89 Black wildebeest (*Connochaetes gnou*) are also known as white-tailed gnu.

species in the world, with less than 5000 in existence. Although they had been extensively overhunted during the nineteenth century, the true reason for the dramatic reduction in black wildebeest numbers was simply lack of suitable habitat. They are endemic to South Africa and in the past occurred in the highveld temperate grasslands during the dry winter season and in the arid Karoo region during the rains, migrating between the two areas as the seasons dictated. By the early twentieth century both those areas had been extensively fenced and turned over to agriculture and stock-farming and so there was simply nowhere left for the black wildebeest to roam. Numbers had reduced to about 600 individuals, all in small, privately owned herds on private land, and that is about as close to extinction as you can come without actually going extinct. With the advent of commercially run private hunting reserves starting in the late 1970s, reintroductions began to take place in the Karoo and the species was also introduced into Namibia, beyond its historical range, and numbers had steadily improved.[90] Nevertheless, taking a shot at such a rare species was not on my agenda.

'Listen, man, that bull has got to go,' urged the farmer. 'He's too old now for breeding, but he is keeping the young bulls away from the cows. I've been meaning to shoot him for months now. Just shoot him, man. You can have the meat. No charge.' Persuaded, I carefully slid along on my belly until I was behind a waist-high bush growing right on the edge of the cliff a few yards to my left. Slowly, I manoeuvred myself into a sitting position and then gently pushed aside a branch with my foot so as to have a clear space through which to aim the rifle. Resting my elbows on my knees for stability, I found the bull in the 4X scope. He was facing at an angle away from me, leaving only a sliver of shoulder visible. This is a poor shot to take – a

---

90   Black wildebeest populations have been trending upwards for some time and there are now around 18,000 individuals – still mostly in private hands. They are no longer considered endangered.

couple of inches to one side and the animal is gut-shot and a couple of inches to the other side and you miss entirely or create a non-fatal glancing wound to the animal's shoulder. Realising my predicament the farmer let out a short, piercing whistle and the bull instantly shifted position to look our way, presenting a perfect broadside view. I squeezed the trigger and the .308 bucked, sending the 180-grain soft-point bullet thumping low into the bull's shoulder. The cows stampeded off in a herd and the bull seemed to want to follow, but although he vigorously galloped with the distinctive rocking-horse motion employed by wildebeests, he did so on-the-spot and without any real forward momentum. Thirty seconds later he dropped onto his front knees in the classic fighting pose of the wildebeest bull and then both his haunches and his heavy head sank slowly to the ground. The time from the shot to the bull's death could not have been more than a minute.

Seeing that the bull was elderly and probably exceptionally tough, I took the decision to have all the meat minced rather than going for the usual mix of various cuts for different types of recipes. This proved to be enormously fortuitous because it turns out that black wildebeest mince is the most fragrantly delicious mince I have ever encountered. It is excellent in hamburgers, lasagne, other pasta dishes, in fact in any recipe calling for mince of any sort, but it is completely outstanding in bobotie, a traditional favourite in South Africa. It is so good that one can only suspect that bobotie might have had something to do with why black wildebeest were overhunted in the first place. Bobotie is a mild curry dish made from minced meat and dried fruits moistened with milk-soaked bread, topped with chopped nuts and an egg and milk custard. The first recipe for bobotie appeared in a Dutch cookbook in 1609, some forty years before the colonisation of the Cape by Dutch settlers, so it is originally a Dutch dish. Its origins are undoubtedly Malayan, but precisely which Malayan recipe historically founded the Dutch adaption called bobotie is unclear. Doubtless further adaptions by the Malay and Afrikaans populations of the Cape took place in South Africa and it has been regarded as a quintessentially South African dish for at least 200 years. I served black wildebeest bobotie in lavish quantities at several dinner parties and on each occasion the guests kept eating until all the bobotie was gone, some returning for third or even fourth helpings. That is the sign of a great dish and it much warms the heart of the cook. Although it is extremely unlikely you will ever get hold of black wildebeest mince, I have included a standard recipe for bobotie below because it is nevertheless a very worthwhile and unusual experience when made with beef, lamb, a mixture of lamb and pork or with any venison.

BOBOTIE

1 kg minced meat
2 medium onions, thinly sliced
30 ml groundnut oil
2 tablespoons curry powder
2 tablespoons turmeric
2 tablespoons red wine vinegar
1 tablespoon brown sugar
1 slice white bread
250 ml full cream milk
2 large eggs
50 g seedless raisins
50 g yellow sultanas
4 tablespoons apricot chutney
Grated rind of 1 lemon
50 g sliced almonds
6 bay leaves
Salt and pepper

Soak the bread in the milk, then squeeze dry. Set the milk aside.

Boil the onions in just enough water to cover them until the onions are opaque. Drain the onions and reserve the onion water. Chop the onions and fry in the oil until golden. Add curry powder and turmeric and fry for a few minutes, stirring constantly. Add the vinegar, sugar, salt and pepper and fry for a further minute. Remove from the heat.

Crumble the mince into a pan with the onion water, topping up with boiling water if necessary to just cover the mince. Cook for five minutes.

Next, lightly mix the meat, soaked bread, onion mixture, one egg, raisins, sultanas, chutney and lemon rind. Pack into a greased casserole dish, cover and bake in the oven at 180°C for one and a half hours.

Remove from the oven and scatter the almonds over the meat. Twist the bay leaves into little cones and stick into the meat. Whip up the remaining egg with the reserved milk, adding a little more milk to make up a full 250 ml, then carefully pour onto the meat over the back of a spoon to create a smooth layer.

Return the casserole to the oven, reduce the temperature to 150°C and bake uncovered until the custard has set, about thirty minutes.

Serve with basmati rice, apricot chutney, chopped cucumbers, chopped apples, chopped tomatoes and sliced red onion.

The black wildebeest's more common cousin, the blue wildebeest, *Connochaetes taurinus,* also known as the brindled gnu, is much easier to get hold of, but is nowhere near as good to eat. The blue wildebeest is the one you will have seen charging across the Serengeti in large migrating herds in BBC nature documentaries, crossing rivers and getting eaten by 1500-pound crocodiles. Those crocs are really something, which you fully realise when you see them successfully execute a mid-body bite on a 500-pound animal and then drag it under as though it was a rabbit. That animal is almost always a blue wildebeest, although sometimes a zebra gets unlucky. Blue wildebeest are abundant across most of Southern and Central Africa and there are over 1.5 million of them, 1.3 million in the Serengeti National Park[91]. They are a common sight in every game reserve and national park where they often hang about on the open plains in the company of herds of zebra. They are a popular quarry species for hunters in many private hunting preserves, where the bulls present a fairly easy prospect and the cows are one of the most difficult antelope of all to hunt. This is because bulls are strictly territorial and are easy to find in more or less the same place day after day. They also have a macho 'I don't run from anybody' attitude to life. The cows on the other hand hang about in herds, have very refined senses and are exceptionally paranoid, making them excruciatingly difficult to approach because normally every conceivable angle of approach will be under observation by at least one member of the herd. The bulls are an example of an ancient strategy being rendered ineffective by modern weapons. Take humans and their guns/arrows/spears out of the equation and the only things a wildebeest bull has to worry about are lions. Lions, however, are not that keen to take on wildebeest bulls. It is not that lions cannot kill wildebeest bulls, but wildebeest bulls are very strong and fierce and the chance of a lion being injured is reasonably high. Being injured is often fatal for a lion in the medium term and so they tend to look for much softer targets if possible, like yearling females or newly born wildebeest calves. This explains the attitude of the female herds. The bulls on the other hand have the luxury of staying put in one place where they are not much bothered.

---

91 Sharp-eyed readers will have noted that earlier in the section on springbok I state that the wildebeest migration on the Serengeti involves 1.2 million animals, whereas here I state that there are 1.3 million. The apparent contradiction is resolved by the fact that 100,000 Serengeti wildebeest stay where they are and do not migrate.

Tenderloin of blue wildebeest is really excellent served as a tournados (*filet mignon*) fried in butter with a little garlic and served with a Dijon mustard or sweet wine sauce. A standard recipe for Tournados Rossini produces a very good result. The rest of the wildebeest is generally too tough in my experience to really be of much appeal. You can mince it up and use it in mincemeat dishes, but it lacks the delicious herbal notes found in black wildebeest mince and so suffers by comparison. It makes very good biltong, however, and is one of the best meats to use for the South African snack called *droëwors* (dried sausage). Droëwors is basically biltong in sausage form. It is made from thin sausages filled with lean minced meat mixed with a little beef or mutton fat and biltong flavourings such as crushed coriander seeds, salt and black pepper. These sausages are then dried quickly in warm, very dry conditions exactly like those suitable for making biltong. Droëwors is thus distinct from salami-type sausages that dry slowly in relatively cold and humid conditions and rely on a curing process involving specialised fungal moulds. If you get fungal mould on your droëwors then you have not dried it quickly enough and it has gone off. There is no way back from this so you should just throw it away. Although it is an acquired taste and does not rank as highly as biltong in the South African snack hierarchy, droëwors is very pleasant with a cold beer or a glass of Sauvignon Blanc.

WOODCOCK

It is best not to tell your guests how you cooked the woodcock until after they have eaten it. This will give them an opportunity to be totally blown away by one of the greatest combinations of flavours that exists without being prejudiced against the experience in advance. For traditionally, and uniquely in my experience, woodcock are cooked undrawn, by which is meant with the guts still inside, and the guts, somewhat modified with other ingredients, are served on toast together with the roasted bird. The head and long beak are also left on the body while roasting and are served alongside the bird, sliced lengthways into two, so that the brains can be eaten by the diner as though from a teaspoon. People are understandably put off by the concept of these things and might then decline to try the dish. However, once they have sampled the greatest of all game dishes it is remarkable how the method of preparation ceases to be a matter of horrified shock and instead becomes an interesting curiosity that the diner is prepared to defend to the last breath in any subsequent culinary argument.

The reason woodcock are cooked undrawn is twofold. Firstly, woodcock entirely evacuate their bowels on taking off and as the only way of securing a woodcock is to shoot it immediately after take-off, there is never any faeces present inside a woodcock.

Secondly and more significantly, the steam emanating from the innards of the woodcock imbue the flesh with a pleasant taste when the bird is briefly roasted at a high temperature. Why this should be is interesting because the innards contain the usual organs found in any bird, plus a length of intestine that will invariably contain a quantity of partially digested earthworm, earthworms being the woodcock's principal food. Woodcocks also eat beetles, spiders, caterpillars, fly larvae and small snails, but not in great quantity. Thus it must be the effect of steamed earthworm, perhaps leavened by a few assorted bugs, that contributes so definitively to the flavour of roast woodcock – an unusual thought to say the least. A comprehensive recipe for roast woodcock appears later in this section.

Woodcock are plump, wading-type birds with very long beaks and exceptional camouflage. The species abandoned the mud flats in favour of the woodland at some point in the distant primordial past and now frequent scrub-like forest and hedgerows across much of the Northern Hemisphere. They use their long beaks to probe the soil for earthworms and other soil-dwelling creatures and live a solitary, wraith-like existence, in wooded cover during the day and out on the earthworm-laden fields and meadows during the night. One can never be certain that woodcock will be present even if they were there yesterday because they move around within a particular area frequently and many also migrate from harsh weather areas to warmer climes on a seasonal basis. Having said this, woodcock will be found over and over again in the same patch of cover, it is just that you cannot know on a particular day whether a woodcock will be in the patch of cover or not. This gives them a reputation for elusiveness that is enhanced by the fact that in many areas they disappear without trace during the summer months, having migrated elsewhere. The mysterious atmosphere that surrounds woodcock has led to some peculiar myths. The strangest of these was the belief that woodcock migrated to the moon in summer. This had its origins in the work of Charles Morton, a seventeenth-century naturalist who wrote a well-reasoned but obviously totally inaccurate treatise claiming that many species of bird migrated to the moon and back every year. Morton was even aware of the distances involved in such an extraordinary claim, calculating that the trip would involve flying non-stop for some 179,000 miles (not a bad estimate for the times, the actual distance to the moon is between 226,000 and 252,000 miles, depending on where the moon is in its elliptical orbit). He calculated that birds would take around sixty days to complete the trip flying at the remarkable speed of 125 miles per hour. As whacky as it sounds to us today, Morton was being completely serious and in the context of those times, his treatise constituted the first substantive attempt to tackle the mystery of bird migration through the application of proper scientific principles. Some species, including woodcock, really did seem to disappear entirely and if that premise was accepted, the only logical conclusion was that they set off into space. 'Now, whither should these creatures go, unless it were to the moon?' is how Morton put it. Specifically as concerns woodcock, Morton's hypothesis found support in the report of sailors who claimed that a woodcock flew in to land on their ship not from the horizon, but 'right down from above' as though returning to our planet from space. Morton's claim was rapidly disproved by ongoing research and the discovery of the actual migration paths and destinations of migrating birds, but the association between woodcock and the moon initiated by Morton's work found a peculiar durability. In particular, many still believe that woodcock migrate on the first full moon in November, using the light of the moon to navigate. Woodcock do migrate around early November, but no link to the phase or light of the moon has been scientifically established.

One facet of woodcock behaviour long thought to be a myth by mainstream ornithology, but which turns out to be true, is that woodcock are able to move their chicks by grasping them between their thighs or in their claws and then flying off, carrying the chick beneath them. This seems so unlikely that for centuries it was considered nothing but an 'old gamekeeper's tale' and was met with the same level of incredulity that attends upon sightings of UFOs, but an accumulation of eye-witness testimony from respectable and reliable witnesses eventually encouraged a proper observational study that apparently established the facts beyond doubt. However, some people still do not believe, mainly because, as far as I can ascertain, the phenomenon has never been filmed and we live in an era where a YouTube clip is an essential prerequisite to credibility. It also does not help that in centuries past the goldcrest (*Regulus regulus*), Britain's smallest bird, was called the 'woodcock pilot' consequent upon the belief that this tiny bird managed to migrate from Scandinavia to Britain in the autumn by hitching a lift in the feathers of a migrating woodcock. People simply could not credit that so small a bird with such a tiny wingspan was capable of crossing the North Sea unaided, which is indeed what some of them do each autumn.

Woodcock are superb game birds. They sit tight in cover and usually allow the shooter to approach very close before flushing, often rising behind the shooter once he has walked past for some reason. A dog is a great asset when hunting woodcock, particularly a spaniel that thoroughly works the heavy cover close in and gets the bird to flush in front of the shooter. The enthusiastic body language of a dog that has picked up a woodcock's scent is the only warning you will ever get that a woodcock is about to flush because their camouflage is so good that they are, for all practical purposes, invisible on the ground. A dog is also invaluable in retrieving fallen birds which can be very challenging to find. The cocker spaniel is the breed of dog originally bred to hunt woodcock, but unfortunately this breed has become both complicated and compromised by the requirements of the show dog community. When flushed a woodcock rises quickly to about head-height and then flies off rapidly, often zigzagging between the trees if flushed in woodland. This is a very challenging shot and also extremely dangerous if taken during the course of a driven shoot where guns often lose their composure and fire at the jinking target without regard to the fact that the pellets will be whistling along at a potentially lethal level for beaters. Woodcock have indirectly contributed to the death of quite a few beaters in this way and if a woodcock rises in front of them, the universal practice amongst beaters is to shout 'cock' and then fling themselves to the ground. (I often feel like shouting 'cock' and flinging myself to the ground, but we cannot get into that here.)

Some people like to hang the woodcock for a few days before roasting, but frankly I find this an unnecessary refinement. Woodcock have fine-grained flesh and a unique flavour and I find a fresh woodcock just as delectable as one that has hung for three or four days. Here is a traditional recipe for roast woodcock that is my favourite game dish of all – the ultimate in luxurious indulgence.

ROAST WOODCOCK WITH FOIE GRAS AND TRUFFLES

2 woodcocks
2 thin slices of pork back fat
50 g clarified butter
50 g unsalted butter
20 g black truffle, finely chopped
50 g foie gras, in two slices
15 ml Cognac
50 ml Bual Madeira
200 ml rich chicken stock
50 ml red wine

2 slices of white bread, crusts removed
Salt and freshly ground white pepper

Pluck the woodcocks, including the heads. Remove the eyes. Remove the feet, but leave the shanks. Truss the bird – traditionally, the long bill is used as a skewer by twisting the head around and pushing the bill through the thighs, but you can use elastic thread if you prefer. Tie the pork back fat slices over the breasts and cover the legs with foil to prevent burning. Season with salt and pepper.

Heat 25 g of clarified butter in a roasting pan. Briefly brown the woodcocks on all sides over a high heat. Turn the birds onto one leg and then transfer the roasting pan to a preheated oven at 240°C. Roast for four minutes and then turn the birds onto the other leg and roast for a further four minutes. Finally turn the birds onto their backs, remove the pork fat from the breasts and foil from the legs and roast for five minutes. Remove the woodcock from the roasting tray and rest in a warm place for ten minutes.

Carefully carve off the breasts and legs from the birds and keep warm together with the heads. Remove the entrails. Discard the gizzard. Chop up the innards into a rough dice. Heat 25 g of unsalted butter in a small pan and add the chopped entrails and the truffle. Fry briefly, then add Cognac. Flame the Cognac immediately and then add the Madeira. Reduce until almost all the liquid is gone and the mixture has taken on a slightly sticky, granular aspect.

Heat the remaining clarified butter in a frying pan. Fry the slices of bread until golden. Place a thin slice of foie gras on the fried bread and then spread the entrails mixture on top.

Chop up the carcasses, return them to the roasting pan and lightly brown. Pour in the red wine to deglaze and then reduce until almost gone. Pour in the chicken stock and reduce until only about 80 ml remains. Strain the sauce through a fine strainer and then gradually add the remaining 25 g of unsalted butter. Check the seasoning of the sauce and adjust if necessary.

Heat the woodcock and the fried bread in the oven for one minute. Place a slice of bread on each plate and then lay the breasts and legs on top. Pour the sauce around. Slice the heads in two lengthways and balance against the breasts like teaspoons. Serve with a small pinch of watercress and nothing else.

This dish is very difficult to pair with a wine and anyway, it is so delicious that it can just stand on its own. I like to drink good champagne as an aperitif before this dish is served, nothing but sparkling water with the dish and then another bottle of champagne afterwards, perhaps with some ripe Camembert or Brie cheese just to round off this mind-blowing flavour experience in good style.

ZEBRA

As we began, so we end, with a reference to an animal that is not really considered a food animal, but which conveniently has a name that begins with the letter Z, thus satisfying all manner of obsessive-compulsive instincts on the part of the author, his editors and publishers. Zebras are in fact hunted frequently by sport hunters for their magnificent and exotically striped skins. Zebra meat is thus often available, including globally through exotic meat retailers, and in the absence of more emotionally palatable alternatives, makes a reasonably popular substitute for other types of venison. It is of mild flavour and has a particularly red colour. It is the most filling meat I have encountered and a little goes a long way. In the end though it is horse meat, for zebras are wild horses, and British people in particular have a culturally reinforced aversion to the concept of horse meat, even though they have unknowingly been sold it in hamburgers and lasagnes for decades by unscrupulous purveyors of ready-made meals. This aversion is not shared by Continental persons who have relished horse meat since the Middle Ages and continue to do so, although apparently in diminishing numbers.

There are three species of zebra endemic to Sub-Saharan Africa: the plains zebra, Grévy's zebra and the mountain zebra. The plains zebra is a common sight in many national parks and is the one you might get to eat. The other two are endangered species and are rarely hunted except by trophy hunters paying top dollar. All three species have the familiar black and white striped skin although there is a difference in the basic pattern between species and each individual zebra has its own unique set of stripes within the parameters of the species pattern. Stripes essentially define the zebra. For many years no one was able to work out precisely what function the stripes serve. Various theories were advanced: some postulated that it was simply a manifestation of God's infinitely artistic hand; others suggested they functioned as a means of sexual discrimination and selection; several theories based on camouflage found favour for a while, including that the blurring of lines caused by the stripes when seen in the context of a fleeing herd caused predators to misjudge distances and miss the target. All these theories seemed to stretch plausibility somewhat. More recent research has suggested that stripes discourage the attentions of biting flies and if you have ever been on the receiving end of an attack by tsetse flies you will immediately appreciate how a striped pelt might be a serious advantage, likely to find favour within the machinations of natural selection.

Of course it might be that the ancient San legend about how the zebra got its stripes is the one we should note most carefully. According to San oral tradition, in old times the animals could talk to each other like you and I do today. It was a time of plenty and all animals had as much to eat and drink as they liked. The antelope were sleek and the wildebeest frolicked on the plain in the company of a pure white wild horse known as a zebra. Then one day the baboon got it into his head that he should be in charge of the water and that other animals should only drink when and if baboon permitted it. Full of self- importance the baboon stormed down to the waterhole and chased all the other animals away, proclaiming that God had put him in charge in order that all animals should benefit from his leadership. He set up camp right next to the water and built a big fire which he kept burning day and night so that no animal might slip past him and take a drink unobserved in the dark. All day long baboon strutted about engaged in the self-appointed task of deciding who could and who could not drink at the waterhole, based primarily on who was prepared to flatter baboon or offer him favours. After five days or so of this and when almost all animals in the bush had somehow or other cajoled a drink out of baboon, zebra came down to the waterhole (zebra only need to drink once every five days) and stopped in front of baboon's big fire. 'You shall not drink!' proclaimed baboon. 'Says who, sunshine?' (or San words to that effect) replied zebra. 'I do, the mighty, the wise, the unstoppable baboon.' Upon hearing this the zebra drew himself up and delivered a huge kick which caught the baboon square on, lifting him high up into the air to come crashing down on top of a nearby hill of jagged rocks. So hard did baboon land that all the hair was knocked off his buttocks and he got such a fright that he was too scared to come down from the rocks and just stayed up there screaming abuse at everybody, which accounts for the appearance and behaviour of baboons to this day. For his part, so much effort did zebra put into his kick that he inadvertently scattered baboon's big fire, causing the burning logs to fly up into the air and then land on his back, burning dark stripes into his skin. These dark stripes were such a badge of honour amongst the animals that zebra's descendants continued to wear them for ever after.

This just goes to show that if you mislead the people you might end up bare-arsed and screaming from a rock, something politicians should note, but if you genuinely and selflessly serve the greater good, admiration for your character will never fade.